WOMEN NOVELISTS IN SPAIN AND SPANISH AMERICA

LUCIA FOX-LOCKERT

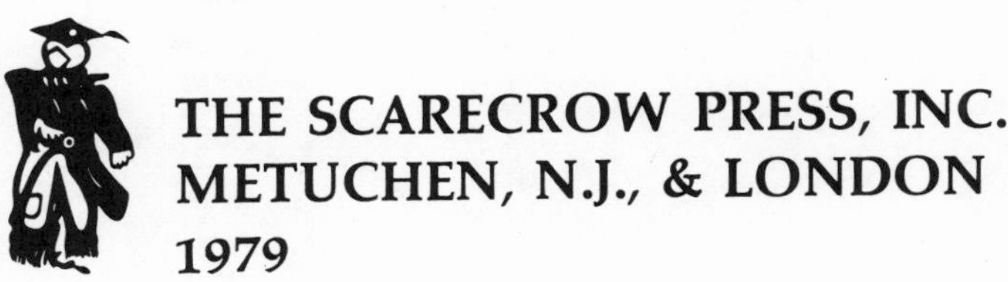
THE SCARECROW PRESS, INC.
METUCHEN, N.J., & LONDON
1979

Library of Congress Cataloging in Publication Data

Fox-Lockert, Lucía, 1928-
Women novelists in Spain and Spanish America.

Bibliography: p.
Includes index.
1. Spanish fiction--Women authors--History and criticism. 2. Spanish American fiction--Women authors--History and criticism. 3. Women in literature. 4. Women and literature. I. Title.
PQ6055. F6 863'. 03 79-23727
ISBN 0-8108-1270-3

ACKNOWLEDGMENTS

I wish to express my appreciation to my husband, Clint, for his continual encouragement and patience. Also, I wish to extend my thanks to Walter Burinski, head of the Inter-Library Loan at Michigan State University, for his continuous assistance. I would like to thank Danielle Ranes and Jean Baker, secretaries in my department, who have been very cooperative with my work at all times. I want to thank, especially, Arthur Olds and Debby West for their assistance in the translation and editing of the manuscript. Finally, I want to show my recognition to Michigan State University for the All-University Research Grants that helped pay some of the clerical expenses.

TABLE OF CONTENTS

Acknowledgments iii

Foreword (Bobby J. Chamberlain) vii

INTRODUCTION 1

I SPANISH NOVELISTS

María de Zayas : Novelas amorosas (1637) and Desengaños amorosos (1647) 25

Fernán Caballero (Cecilia Bohl de Faber) : Clemencia (1852) 36

Emilia Pardo Bazán : Los pazos de Ulloa (1886) 49

Concha Espina : La esfinge maragata (1913) 66

Carmen Laforet : Nada (1944) 73

Elena Quiroga : Viento del norte (1951) 85

Elena Soriano : Trilogía (1955) 94

Dolores Medio : Diario de una Maestra maestra (1961) 107

Concha Alós : Las hogueras (1964) 114

II SPANISH AMERICAN NOVELISTS

Gertrudiz Gómez de Avellaneda : Sab (1841) 127

Clorinda Matto de Turner : Aves sin nido (1889) 137

Mercedes Cabello de Carbonera : Blanca Sol (1889) 147

Teresa de la Parra (Ana Teresa Parra Sanojo) : Ifigenia (1924) 156

María Luisa Bombal : The Shrouded Woman (1948) [La amortajada, 1938] 166

Silvina Bullrich : Bodas de cristal (1941) 175

Clara Silva : La sobreviviente (1951) 185

Marta Brunet : María Nadie (1957) 195

Rosario Castellanos : Balún Canán (1957) 202

Beatriz Guido : Fín de fiesta (1958) 216

Elena Garro : Los recuerdos del porvenir (1963) 228

Luisa Josefina Hernández : La cólera secreta (1964) 241

Elena Poniatowska : Hasta no verte, Jesús mío (1969) 260

CONCLUSIONS 281

Chapter Notes 293

Bibliography 312

Index 343

FOREWORD

Bobby J. Chamberlain
Michigan State University

Those who have at one time or another had occasion to do research on the role of women in Hispanic societies must have experienced some degree of shock and frustration at the dearth of published materials. Only recently has the topic acquired enough "respectability" to attract the attention of a smaller number of serious scholars.

Much of the fiction produced by Hispanic female writers over the last three centuries has fared no better. When not dismissed out of hand as "subliterature" possessing no significant esthetic value, it has often been appraised on the basis of esthetics alone, to the exclusion of ideological and sociological content. Such neglect has been particularly apparent with respect to the feminist message.

The present study, *Women Novelists in Spain and Spanish America*, is a response to this neglect. It is the first work of such scope and depth to examine the fiction of Hispanic women novelists over time from a sociological and feminist viewpoint. In it, Lucía Fox-Lockert not only evaluates each writer's treatment of such topics as family, social class and sexuality as they relate to female characters, but out of her evaluation also constructs a composite portrait of Hispanic woman, free of the clichés and stereotypes that have often characterized this sort of study. In so doing, she has made a fundamental contribution, filling a conspicuous void long apparent in the study of Iberian and Ibero-American literatures.

Lucía Fox-Lockert is associate professor of Spanish at Michigan State University. She has distinguished herself over the years as a poet, playwright, novelist, historian and critic, having authored numerous books and articles on such diverse topics as Spanish American colonial literature, the New Narrative, the history of the Spanish American independence movement, Peruvian literature and magical realism. In recent years, she has come to be recognized as one of the foremost experts in the field of Hispanic women's literature. In addition to the present volume, she is the editor of a bilingual anthology of female poets of Latin America.

INTRODUCTION

There have been very few studies treating women novelists of Spain and Latin America and the few that do exist have concentrated on the literary aspects of a few of the outstanding women.[1]* For the most part, however, the human message these women writers try to communicate through their novels has been ignored. Thus, in making my selection of novelists and their novels I have chosen those that in my opinion best represent awareness of feminist ideals. In my study I shall deal with family relationships, society, and interaction between the sexes from the woman's point of view. Since these writers use their feminine protagonists as mouthpieces for their own hopes and frustrations, I have concentrated my study on these characters. In general, each protagonist finds herself in a new and uncertain situation. She is forced to confront a rupture in her normal life pattern and is thereby forced to examine her own individuality in the light of her circumstances. This identity crisis allows her to separate her own personality from the social indoctrination she has received. When she makes a choice, she is then forced to live with the consequences of that choice. At times she finds herself free and at other times she feels impotent and oppressed by an inflexible system. As we shall see, the dyamics of liberation may be observed in operation at the same time as the mechanics of Hispanic repression.

I have selected 22 women novelists and have grouped them into two sections which correspond to Spain and Latin America. While they represent three hundred years of individual exploration, when seen as a whole we can observe a sense of unity and continuity. In general I have discussed one novel by each novelist, one exception being María de Zayas because she has included several short novels

*Notes to all chapters will be found beginning on page 293.

within a larger work. (Another exception is Emilia Pardo Bazán whose two works covered form one continuous story). With each author I present a brief biography and an analysis of the novel I have chosen to discuss. Then I concentrate on three areas: family, social class and sexuality. As a conclusion to each analysis I have interpreted the message of the author from the point of view of her feminine consciousness.

It is hoped that this book will aid students to better understand not only the feminine novelists but also Hispanic women in general, especially in their struggles to achieve equality and justice. I also believe that this book will encourage other scholars to recognize the great literary and documentary importance of these women, especially concerning the history and evolution of feminine viewpoints. Finally, I believe that both men and women of Hispanic descent will be able, as they identify with the protagonists of these novels, to help the feminine cause. Today, more than ever, we need the close cooperation of people from many fields if we are to achieve significant social change.

SPANISH NOVELISTS

María de Zayas was the first woman to write novels in Spain.[2] Although much of her life is still a mystery, she is generally thought to have been a noblewoman, born in Madrid in 1590, and the author of *Novelas amorosas y ejemplares* in 1637 and *Desengaños amorosos* in 1647.

There is a peculiar disharmony between the attitudes of the antifeminist critics and the priest-censor who authorized the publication of her works. Pfandl, one of her critics, considered her novels "licentious stories that at times degenerate into the terrible and perverse and at other times into lewdness and nothing more than a libertine enumeration of amorous adventures." Ticknor also affirmed that her stories, although written by a lady, were lewd and immodest. Father Pío Vives, however, in giving his permission for the publication of *Desengaños amorosos,* said: "I see here a refuge where feminine weakness can take solace from coaxing wiles. It is a reflection of that which man needs most in order to give the proper direction to his deeds. And thus, by my stamp of approval I judge this book to be of great worth and deserving publication."[3]

María de Zayas was a pioneer in every sense of the word: in her ideas about equality of education, about the abolition of the double standard, and about the need for women to take pride in their own sex; in her denunciation of the common social pitfalls for women, and finally in her rebellion against the system of matrimony. This last is sharply dramatized at the end of *Desengaños amorosos,* in which a group of women enter a convent so as not to submit themselves to masculine injustice in marriage. María de Zayas occupies a special place in feminine protest literature because she can with great precision unmask those men who accuse women of inferiority. The agility of her free expression and her willingness to protest injustice make María de Zayas the Mary Wollstonecraft[4] of Spanish literature.

Since this Spanish author predates that English pioneer of women's rights we can say with all justice that María de Zayas deserves to be recognized among the first proponents of feminism.

After a silence of more than a century, Cecilia Bohl de Faber makes her appearance in 1796. She adopted the masculine name of Fernán Caballero in order to publish her novels. She gives the reason for her actions in a letter to her friend Juan Eugenio Hartzenbusch: "No one knows me in Madrid and it is just as well that no one does, because as I have said repeatedly, if a woman is known to be the author, a book loses not only merit and prestige but also the moral force of its good religious ideas."[5] In reality, however, there is no doubt that the author hid her true identity because her father, in spite of being a cultured individual, had created a sense of guilt within her about writing. This is evident from what he states, according to one biographer, in the following: "I have never chanced to read anything she has written while she was single since woman's things were not of my liking."[6] He thought all a young woman had to do was to get married and become a mother. Since Cecilia was never a mother, and she enjoyed a position of independence, she began to write instead of limiting herself to the care of the house as her father would have wished. It is revealing that her novels show women who are obedient to the point of marrying a man they do not know, as Cecilia did. Later, however, the same woman may affirm her individuality. Fernán Caballero found recognition as the creator of the "new realism" in the Spanish novel, and we must recognize that in her novels she achieved a balance between traditional values and a new sense of independence. Clemencia, one of her protagonists, obtains with maturity a clear vision of what is needed to realize her self worth and marital happiness.

There is again a lapse of time until a new important figure appears: Emilia Pardo Bazán, born in 1852. She denounces the decadent aristocratic customs of the nineteenth century and especially the manner in which women were treated. In *Los pazos de Ulloa* she illustrates the results of the double standard. When women who have been raised as strict Catholics marry licentious men, the problems of lack of communication are accentuated. Pardo Bazán portrays the fatal results of the pressures men place on women. She also took up the cause of Naturalism and endorsed the new means of social analysis, determinism, in her collection of articles, *La cuestión palpitante*. Her husband forbade the publishing of the work, and, though she complied, he later abandoned her nevertheless because of this work.[7] Her two classic novels, *Los pazos de Ulloa* and *La madre naturaleza*, present women trapped by rigid feminine role models. The protagonists uselessly sacrifice themselves. Emilia Pardo Bazán was an ardent feminist and thanks to her character she took over many positions men had previously reserved for themselves. Although the men made great fun of the evils of women—"the wicked womb, motherhood, breast feeding," [8] they could not keep her from becoming one of the most important persons of her day in Spain. During her entire life she elaborated, in her novels, her ideas concerning the traditional role of woman and especially the future evolution of womankind into "the new woman." While in her lectures and articles she promoted the cause of feminism, she herself realized that in her time women could not yet break their chains because they were not prepared. She blames the bourgeois society for teaching young girls to depend on marriage and for keeping women in a state of permanent infancy. In breaking out of this state of dependency "the new woman" could be fighting prejudices so deeply impressed upon her that a sense of guilt would accompany her for the rest of her life.

Concha Espina was born in 1879. She was a woman with a great feeling for the literary profession. In spite of the great difficulties she encountered when her husband abandoned her, she took her three children and went to Madrid to earn a living from her novels. This was almost an impossible task in her day. Her perseverance and fighting spirit were rewarded by the success of her novels. In her works we find people who, much like the author, undergo great trials in a hostile environment. In *La esfinge maragata* and *El metal de los muertos* we can perceive the stoic character of the novelist. In *La esfinge maragata* she presents an environment so desolate and poor that the women have no choice but to accept their roles with dignity; they bitterly realize that the men, together with their sons, will abandon them in an effort to find work. The author herself said of her novels:

> With a more rustic instrument I have woven in this book the humble lives of women, obscure, tormented lives, filled with sorrow and abnegation, which aroused deep echoes in my heart. Perhaps you would prefer happier stories, and joyous inventions, sunny romances of some fortunate land where flowers never cease to bloom. But I have already told you that I am recounting the lives of women. If the little tales seem too sad, if they stir your heart to suffering, pretend as you close the book, that they are not true—that you dreamed them.[9]

She received many literary prizes—including a nomination for the Nobel Prize—and many invitations to travel and to give lectures. She was at one time a visiting professor in the United States. The most notable aspect of her novels is the depth of her explorations into the relationship between the settings of her books and the men and women who live in those places. Her women, although held down by the responsibilities of caring for their families, acquire an awareness of their strengths, strengths that destiny continually tests. While her best novels describe an atmosphere of apathy, she has also left us a diary of her experiences during the Spanish Civil War which shows a deep commitment based on her Christian faith.[10]

Carmen Laforet was born in 1921. She published her first novel, *Nada,* while she was still a law student at the University of Madrid. The novel achieved great success and brought her many awards, among them the Fastenrath Prize from the Royal Academy of Language. She was then 23 and she can easily be identified with

Andrea, a girl who at the end of the Spanish Civil War finds herself in a world of contradictions and chaos. The situation was very much like the one described by Ortega y Gasset in *La rebelión de las masas:*

> But the party is short-lived. Without rules which oblige us to live in certain ways, our lives are without focus. This is a horrible, intimate situation in which the best youth of today find themselves. They feel empty, since they are completely free, without impediments. A life without purpose is a greater negation of self than even death. Because to live is to be forced to do something tangible—to fulfill a purpose—and to the extent which we avoid fulfilling our existence, we void our lives.

The author, still in her youth, captures this desire for freedom and lack of obligation which Ortega y Gasset denounces. Toward the end of *Nada,* however, we begin to see that this crisis has passed for these girls and that now they will dedicate themselves to a life of marriage and motherhood—much as happens with the author who twenty years later finds herself married and with five children. In one interview she was asked: "Which comes first for you, your family life or your life as a writer?" and she answered: "Every woman artist, if she has a family, has a double life which is at times impossible to separate." The very fact that she does not renounce one of the two shows that both are of equal importance.[12] The impact of *Nada* on the Spanish novel is notable, especially among women writers. It gave them great confidence to see a woman capable of escaping her conservatism. Carmen LaForet was capable of unmasking masculine hypocrisy. She emphasized masculine neurosis and showed that it is the Spanish woman who maintains the family structure at the price of her own sacrifice.

Elena Quiroga, although she was born in 1919, did not start publishing novels until 1948. She has become important both for the quality and the quantity of her work. Even a misogynous critic like Juan Luis Alborg said of her:

> There are innumerable observations in the pages of Elena Quiroga which denounce the role of women but, on the other hand, her entire work reveals, in both theme and

> word, a valiant sincerity that lacks the hypocritical, the petulant and the artificial boldness which many women writers show.[13]

One of her most important novels is *Viento del norte,* which won the Nadal Prize in 1950 and went through three editions in one year. The surroundings and the atmosphere portrayed overshadow mere description of quaint customs in her novels. She penetrates deeply into social and sexual differences. Women are shown to have no alternatives in a narrow environment. She also emphasizes the unchanging state of social customs and the vital conflicts that have their origins in the uncomfortable proximity of the different generations. Coming from Galicia, the author is in a position to point out the values of that region which seem anachronistic. The feudal "lord"is still venerated by the local farmers even though the economic system has changed. The women live in a traditional world that traps them and makes them victims of a collective malevolence. In another novel, *La sangre,* the author has captured family relationships across four generations. In *Viento del norte* we find two beings who could have changed their lives, but because of hundreds of years of traditional separation of the sexes, they remain strangers even in marriage. Marcelina, young and of humble circumstances, cannot avoid the envy and suspicion of those around her. Don Alvaro, an intelligent man, is also trapped by his almost feudal role as lord of his domain. The lack of communication between them is exacerbated not only by the distance between lord and servant, but also between their respective roles as a father and a mother. The author wonders how womankind can change, given these centuries-old customs. She understands that the collective mentality which imprisons women must be changed.

Elena Soriano was born in 1917. She is a novelist who, with great authenticity, develops crucial themes about the torments that women have suffered since man imposed his selective criteria upon them: they are to be young, beautiful and virgins. Her *Trilogía* (trilogy) presents a sketch of this threefold problem: *La playa de los locos,* virginity; *Espejismos,* beauty; *Medea 55,* youth. Of her novels, those of the *Trilogía* seem to best analyze the subtle threads in the relationship between husband and wife. Those problems are subjectively examined, for example, in *Medea 55,* where a beautiful and fairly young (in her thirties) woman is so insecure that she feels her world is at an end when her husband leaves her for a younger girl. The author presents her female protagonists as people trapped by a masculine will that manipulates and uses them like mere objects. These women cannot satisfy their emotional needs with their husbands and cannot do so outside of marriage due to a deep feeling of fidelity, purity or modesty. Although they do not want to, they begin to dissolve emotionally in the first serious crisis with their lovers. In *Espejismos* the protagonist says:

> But, really, if marriage is a divine institution, why hasn't God made it perfect or, at least, more intelligible? Why does he permit such darkness? What is the reason for it? Can it all be a great error, an evil historic and social organization? There are countries with divorce, polygamy, even free love. But, an interesting thing is that in all of them marriage is the foundation—is then, marriage more simple, more satisfactory there? No, it is not possible. Out of necessity, by its very nature, marriage is the same everywhere—more profound and unassailable; every freedom cannot bring harmony to the couple. . . . People speak, I am not sure if jokingly or in seriousness, of the cross of marriage. Perhaps they are right. Yes, that is it: the cross of our species, a cross that saves us from private sins. . . .[14]

But there is a need to contrast her philosophical explanation of matrimonial problems as dealing with two opposite beings, with the practical, analytical observation which the author, as director of the literary magazine *Urogallo,* made concerning woman's liberation in Spain:

> Aside from the emphatic use of the great words—equality, development, peace, happiness, etc.—the truth is that such a program establishes many important questions, it proposes activity, study, legislative reform. . . . Nevertheless, it avoids—and this seems to me to be the essential fault—precise reference to the problems of woman's liberation that are highlighted by modern feminist movements like divorce, birth control, abortion. . . .[15]

Elena Soriano shows the frustrations of every woman, both the ordinary, normal women from the middle class as well as the rebellious, non-conformist and independent. Self-image, dignity and pride are cruelly subjugated in their day-to-day confrontation with men who decide what should occur in their marriage. The frank style of the author captures the horrible struggle of women trying to reconcile their feminism with the bitter realities of life.

Dolores Medio was born in 1920. She won the Nadal Prize for her novel *Nosotros, los Rivero.* This novel, like others of hers, show the rebellion of women against social stereotypes. The desire to be like men is natural when women begin to see the differences in treatment between men and women:

> When Maria asked 'Why doesn't Ger help us with our work?' Her sister answered 'Ah, no, Ger is a man; he must study; he is the only son in the family and mother has all her dreams riding on him.' If you were to ask Aunt Mag, 'Why are you taking out the garbage? Ask Ger. . .' she would answer, 'Ger, Nita? Are you crazy, he might get his clothes dirty. Besides, he is a man. Leave him alone with his books. He has enough to do with his studies. . . .' 'Your brother is always right,' Mrs. Rivero would always say, 'Besides, since he is a man. . . .'[16]

Years later, this same girl, now a popular writer, returns to the home she had abandoned. She has been able to rise above her environment and has triumphed. This same type of personal success, perhaps in a more modest way, can be observed in *Diario de una maestra,* published in 1961. This novel develops, point by point, the search for identity and purpose in life by a girl of humble means who is, at the beginning, bound by romantic ideas about love. Like Lena Rivero, the protagonist of *Nosotros, los Rivero,* Irene is a girl who becomes independent when she goes to study at the University of Oviedo. There she meets her "great love," one of her teachers. He becomes her lover for a while until work and the Spanish Civil War separate them. Her greatest criticism is directed toward men who speak of great ideals but who at the moment of self-sacrifice turn coward. On the other hand, women are capable of giving themselves completely to a great love affair or to some other cause in spite of great difficulties. Our protagonist is such a woman, loyal to her lover and to her ideals. Her lover, on the other hand, would give up his ideals for a more comfortable existence.

She waits for twenty years for him to return home, then, when they meet, she realizes that he has changed and that she will have to face the future without her old illusions. Dolores Medio, in her post-war novels, shows the revival of interest in human beings:

> The Spanish Civil War, in its spiritual upheaval, a profound, vital experience, brought about a new literary awareness and, logically taught the artists a renewed interest in man, both his pained conscious and his torn and disjointed life, a result of the war of father against son. Thus the novel, after the war, undergoes a 'rehumanization,' a renewed interest in man and his problems and conflicts.[17]

Concha Alós was born in 1929. She represents what would be called in the Spanish narrative *tremendismo existencialista,* which emphasizes boredom, sickness, anguish, cruelty, suffering and death. In her novel *Las hogueras* she presents two extreme cases of women who are to some extent victims of a sexist society: a parasite and a worker. One is a slave to her beauty, the other renounces her femininity in order to become independent and in the end is a woman who lives only to work. Since Sibila is on display as a precious object, the highest bidder soon appears. Although her husband tries to educate her, she is too socially indoctrinated to see what an opportunity she has. Asunción, the spinster, renounces the company of the common men around her in order to wait for her ideal companion, someone who will appreciate her for herself and not for her beauty. Asunción remains single and society does not value the lone woman. In the small towns marriage is the only aspiration for the girls and for many, like Asunción's sister, it is preferable to be married to a vagabond than to earn an honest living. Concha Alós uninhibitedly presents the sexual lives of her protagonists, especially in her collection of short stories. In "La coraza" which forms part of *Rey de gatos* she presents the self analysis of one of the protagonists as she observes her lover:

> He caresses me and reflects: 'A body of a girl with the soul of a woman.' He is ecstatic: Would you like to be mine? Give yourself to me? But inside of me a powerful voice, the voice of a giant breaks loose, 'No I won't give myself to anyone. I belong to myself. Don't you see, stupid, that I am only experimenting, that the only thing I pretend to know is

> where I am headed? What am I trying to do if the men are right? What am I trying to prove, that I am a foolish dreamer?'[18]

The protagonists in Concha Alós' stories hesitate between insecurity and daring because even though they rebel, they still feel hampered by the rules men have made.

LATIN AMERICAN NOVELISTS

Gertrudiz Gómez de Avellaneda is the first female Latin American novelist. Born in 1814, she is found in both Cuban and Spanish anthologies because she resided in Spain after 1838. As she confesses in her autobiography, she was misunderstood from her earlier years:

> The reading of novels, poetry and plays became our controlling passion. Mother would scold us even after we were older for being more like savages than other girls of our society and for being so careless with our clothing. Our greatest delight was to lock ourselves in our room with our books and to read our favorite novels and cry over the follies of those heroes we loved so much.[19]

Her imagination and temperament frequently caused her to live in a fantasy world and this led to conflicts with the vulgar world around her. In spite of her great talent and creative ability, she felt insecure. When men failed to understand her passionate spirit she tended to blame herself. Like her contemporary George Sand she was able to describe the attitude of women faced with an oppressive, prejudiced system. In 1841 she wrote *Sab*, a novel which portrays a noble and passionate being—a male slave—who analyzes men's laws and finds that he is being exploited in order to benefit others. In my opinion, Sab is a woman who poses as a slave in order to rebel against the masculine social system. It is a well-known fact that, like Sab, the author in her personal life paid the consequences for her untamed spirit. She was incapable of freeing herself from the personal bonds that tied her for so many years to the poet Ignacio de Cepeda. He married another woman and in the last letter she sent to him she stated "I feel the need for a great change, something to free my life from the state of corruption in which it has fallen." Nevertheless Sab, like Gertrudiz, shows his spiritual superiority in the midst of extreme suffering and despair.

Clorinda Matto de Turner was born in 1852. She was "the first Peruvian woman to earn a living through her writings."[20] She is also the first woman to openly denounce the economic, social and political systems of her country. Among the victims of this system are Indians and women who, as González Prada pointed out, are in the same category as the youth, the slaves and the handicapped.[21] While she appears in the histories of literature as a precursor of *indigenismo,* little emphasis has been placed on her role as a true leader in politics and on her fight for freedom of religion and for women's independence.

The women of her novels are generally women of action like herself. In her famous novel *Aves sin nido* both Lucía, the white woman, and Marcela, the Indian woman, strive to resolve the struggles of the Indians who are ignored by whites. Clorinda often challenged the double standard and was a severe critic of the politicians and religious leaders who abused their privileges. In her novel *Herencia* some women who have been observing the men comment:

> Are we living in times when the men are honest? What kind of an example do they set for us? What help do they offer to others. . . . Don't they all have a mistress around the corner? Don't they all chase after velvet and silks, not even bothering to wonder if these silks and velvet are impregnated with the odor of others?. . . That is how it is, for the girlfriend is all the kindness and indulgence while the wife gets the housework, the responsibility for the family name and all of the gossip associated with that position.[22]

Clorinda Matto de Turner married an English doctor at a very early age. She was widowed a few years later, after which she earned her living as the editor of her own newspaper and proprietor of her own printing press. She always supported the liberal cause, which brought her under attack from the Church and the Conservative party. With the publication of her novels, hostility mounted to the point where she could not return to her birthplace in Cuzco, was faced with excommunication, an attack on her press, and finally, exile. She was a champion of civil rights at a time when women were seldom seen in public. She visited prisoners in jail and translated the Bible into Quechuan. Her activities were of such worth that she occupies a special place in Peruvian history. In *Aves sin nido* we can appreciate the message from the point of view of the woman who observes the family, social and sexual lives of her characters. She died in exile in Argentina. She willed the proceeds of her last book to the Cuna de Huérfanos (foundling hospital) in Cuzco. This is perhaps her last commentary on the situation of lost women that abandon children fathered by irresponsible men.

Mercedes Cabello de Carbonera is to Peru what Pardo Bazán is to Spain because each introduced Naturalism, with all its social implications, into their respective countries, and each wrote a treatise on modern novelistic trends. Carbonera's *La novela moderna* expounds on various literary trends and their purposes. In her several novels she has tried to deal in depth with the problems of Peru that arise from the loss of a war with Chile. *Blanca Sol, Las consecuencias* and *El conspirador* deal with the social decomposition of the period, much as Zola does when he analyzes the cause of the disasters of the Franco-Prussian War. But she also adds a synthesis:

> The novel of the future will be formed, without a doubt, from the moral precepts of Romanticism, taking the useful and wholesome attitudes fostered by the new school of Naturalism and having as its only ideal the plain and unvarnished truth. This will give new life to our realistic art; this is at once humanistic, philosophic, analytic, democratic and progressive.[23]

Blanca Sol can be studied on several levels. It is evident that the novelist uses Blanca, the protagonist, to teach a moral lesson. The social climate of Peru at the end of the last century is magnificently captured: political corruption, social mobility, economic problems caused by foreign investments, educational values.

Teresa de la Parra was one of the first of the Latin American women writers to deal with the problem of a career versus marriage, and the conflict between personal choice and social convention. In clarifying her position concerning her novel *Ifigenia,* which had appeared a few years before, she said:

> The diary of María Eugenia Alonso is not a book of revolutionary propaganda, as some have tried to say; no, on the contrary, it is an exposition of a current contemporary sickness. . . . In order that the woman be strong, whole, and truly free from hypocrisy, she should not bow before other's rules but, on the contrary, she needs to be free with herself, aware of dangers and responsibilities of her lifestyle, useful to society even if she is not a mother, and monetarily independent—not an owner, enemy or exploitable person, but a companion and friend to man. The true enemies of feminine virtue are not the dangers which wholesome activities may bring, not books, universities, laboratories, offices, nor hospitals—it is frivolity, the empty fluttering of butterflies with which the young married woman, or the lady with a poor marriage, educated in the old way and sick with scepticism, tries to distract herself, an activity which had it been channeled towards study and work would have had a much more noble and holy end.[24]

In her own life she was able to evaluate marriage with a balanced attitude, and turned down many proposals, preferring to remain single. On the other hand, María Eugenia, the heroine of *Ifigenia* is driven to marry a man she detests by her fear of becoming a spinster. María Eugenia is forced for years to stifle her spirit, an artistic spirit, free and vital. She has become obsessed with escaping the tragic destiny that had befallen her spinster aunt, a shadow of her former self. Teresa de la Parra took her inspiration for *Ifigenia* and *Las memorias de Mamá Blanca* from respectively, two of her intimate friends and her grandmother. They died before the books were published, upon which Teresa reflected, "Situated at the extreme ends of a lifetime, they stayed with me for a while, they told me of their desires for life, the sadness at having lived and when they had finished their confidential stories they discreetly went away when it came time to edit the books."[25]

María Luisa Bombal was born in Chile but educated in Paris. She had a brilliant literary career that lasted only until she was 40. Like the protagonists of her novels she became lost in a mist for the rest of the world. She is interested in looking beneath the surface rather than seeing only the outward appearance and she captures the frustrations of women with great clarity. Her women torture themselves with "unrequited" love.[26] Helga, the protagonist of *La última niebla* is unable to find happiness in her husband. She has recourse to her imagination, creating a being she believes is real, who loves her and who makes the rest of her existence tolerable. In *El arbol,* Brigida is married to an older man who ignores her. She remains isolated, projecting all her emotions to a tree near her room. She finds spiritual refuge in the tree, but when it is cut down she abandons her home in desperation. While Bombal's protagonists can escape from a husband they do not love, it is a worse situation when they passionately love a husband that does not love them. This is the case of Ana María, the protagonist of *The Shrouded Woman,* who cannot resign herself to being cheated by her husband who is the center of her life.

Silvina Bullrich is one of the most prolific of the Argentinian novelists. Her books are found throughout Argentina and the principal reason for her popularity is revealed in a statement by the publishers appearing on the cover of *Teléfono ocupado:*

> Silvina Bullrich has the gift of touching on transcendental themes in an unforgettable way, she has the courage to treat social classes in an ironic manner and has the audacity to make fun of herself. In this story she offers us a completely correct picture of people who live their own lives, of a woman who is the epitome of the way of life and beliefs of many women.[27]

Her spontaneous presentation of the situations allow the reader to participate in the more common life situations of the educated upper middle class of Argentina. She presents almost photographic observations of life, and her protagonists show much of her own personality. In *Mañana digo basta* a woman alone on the beach explains:

> I did not come here with a girl friend, a boy friend, a lover or a relative. I came alone because I hate solitude. I fear solitude, I can feel it around me all the time, like a deadly frog quietly waiting in some corner; I know my life is in its power, that it can kill me whenever it so wishes. But in the

> midst of the emptyness that forty-nine years can bring to a Latin woman, I suddenly found indispensable to study—solitude because life is leading each of us, with a kind but firm hand, to a period in which we will be unwanted on earth. It must be something like our birth: 'A girl!' exclaims the doctor, nurse and father, all with resignation. 'Well, the next one will be a boy.' Why didn't anyone say, "Perhaps this girl will become another Madame Curie, or do something for humanity like Florence Nightingale, or perhaps a great artist. . ."?[28]

In her novel *Bodas de cristal* she shows machismo in action. The "el macho sagrado," the wife, and the "other woman" are upper-class Argentinians. Although these women are on the borderline of emancipation, the author shows that they are still trapped by the economic realities of their social class.

Clara Silva, from Uruguay, was well known as a poet, novelist and essayist. She was the wife of one of the most important critics of Uruguay, Zum Felde. She died in 1976 and a friend of hers supplied the following biographical account:

> As for some of the information you ask me for, I can help you. For example, she did not travel before she was married because she met Zum Felde when she was still almost a child. Zum Felde was an eminent critic from our country, a national glory, that is, he was more than 'very intelligent' as you have stated, and the marriage between him and the extraordinary personality of Clara Silva had nothing to do with anything 'relatively ordinary.' As for the anguish revealed in her novels, Clara was an extremely sensitive woman and it is not at all strange that she felt the trials of other women in her own flesh. I think that the work of a great genius does not have to be autobiographical. I mean to say that she found in the man who accompanied her for fifty years 'the understanding and the inspiration for her spiritual growth' and the unconditional support for her artistic career. But this does not mean that she never suffered (in her whole life) because that would mean that she never lived.[29]

Clara Silva presents sexual problems and the lack of communication between man and woman. Her protagonists are disgusted by the sex act and are full of anguish because they are searching for something more, something transcendent that does not come to them with or because of men.

The title of her book, *El alma y los perros,* shows the distance that exists between the soul (*alma*), representing woman, and the dogs (*perros*), representing man, dogs with the dominant animal instinct. The protagonist of this novel feels sexually used by her husband, a man of great prestige as a university professor, a man much older than herself. She is an ignorant girl but is eager to learn. However, she only receives sarcastic remarks which cause her to lose what little confidence she does have in herself. It is not only her husband but her whole society that confirm that a woman alone is worth nothing. Once she overhears a conversation in the office where she works:

> They say that a girl needs a man in order to grow up, that a woman is nothing without a man, that to be a woman is a disgrace, unclean with that which happens to them every month, a burden, etc. . . . The man who is at her office, her desk companion, says 'a man and a woman take off their clothes. The woman is no longer an object, she becomes a person when she takes off her clothes,' and so forth.
>
> The amorous vocabulary escaped, it was as if they were talking in private. Yes. Only he thinks their relationship is thus. He is a person. He takes her for an object like a radio for example. He takes her brutally, with hunger. He is only interested in her submission, in her sexual capacity. A woman. They are at the point zero on the scale of affection. He is the absolute ruler of her destiny. And the more he rules her destiny, the less he knows her. He is almost a stranger at her side. And he directs her life without asking. A rising and ebbing tide. A wave comes bubbling along. A wave inside another wave. And they fall on her body. They flood her. A truce. And her tired body lies on the beach. Out of breath . . . broken, dirty. Heavy breathing covers her body. Voracious lips. Harsh legs like claws. His contagious animal heat. A convulsive, rapid contraction. A shout.[30]

Many of these women carry over attitudes from their strict upbringings. Under the stress of the prejudices retained from early family life, communication between husband and wife breaks down. The women begin to feel like strangers in their own marriage. The protagonist of *La sobreviviente* feels needs that cannot be satisfied by sex alone. Her desire to transcend herself causes her to look for something that will give meaning to her life and allow her to become a necessary and responsible part of humanity.

Marta Brunet began her career with short stories still within the "Criollista" tradition. Later on, however, she arrived at a novelistic style that belongs to psychological realism. The principal character of *María Nadie* has much in common with the author, especially in the scope of her ideas and imagination. A biographical detail helps to better understand her novel:

> Marta Brunet received instruction at home since there were no schools for girls in her town. She always played with boys and dominated and ruled their games. She never liked dolls. She was very much taken by fantasy and by the imaginary world. At age twelve, her family took her to Europe where they stayed for two years. There, Marta, at a very impressionable age, went through the shock of seeing the reality of many things she had imagined quite differently.[31]

The novelist also explores the theme of homosexuality in *Humo hacia el Sur* and *Amasijo;* in both cases she shows sensitive people who have to confront their own homosexuality in a hostile world of heterosexuals. In her work in general, the author shows that solitude and tragedy await anyone who departs from the social norm.

Rosario Castellanos presents conflicts between the races and between the sexes. In rural Mexico, there is something in common between women and Indians—both are subordinate to masculine power. This masculine power has its own hierarchy in the workplace, the community and the family. Customs make the woman a slave to appearances. The novelist graphically captures the process by which women are excluded from the social organization. When the author was very young, she abandoned Chiapas, her hometown, in order to continue her education:

> I thought that my abandonment of Chiapas at seventeen and going to live in Mexico, separated from these people and

> their problems, would force me to write about very intellectual matters. It was not to be. The people of my writings who struggled for freedom were from Chiapas. In three books I don't think I have exhausted this theme—it is rich, complex reality that remains practically intact. I am greatly interested in the mechanism of human relations in this land. In order to understand these relations better, when I worked in the Instituto Nacional Indigenista I read Simone Weil. She offers, within a social context, a series of constants that determine the attitudes of the subjected to those who dominate them, the treatment of the powerful towards the weak, the whole picture of those in subjugation, the evil that flows from the strong to the weak and returns again to the strong. This type of contagion seemed both painful and fascinating.[32]

In Castellanos' novels, those who submit are the women. They may be chosen, bought, violated or used. In marriage they must always follow the dictates of the double standard. Marriage implies the obligation of procreation and of producing a male heir. Millan noted that in the protagonist of *Oficio de tinieblas* we can see the peculiarities of family life among cultured white or mestizo classes. The strong man seeks and obtains power, an easy life and pleasure, but women are often trapped in the traditional roles of virgin, wife, girlfriend, mother and daughter. Very few women can assert themselves without failing to follow the normal pattern of family and male domination and in that case they are severely punished or repudiated. These women must then go far away because the system is all-powerful and will not tolerate transgression.

The author expressed her ideas about the mutilating effects of social hypocrisy on the honesty and individuality of women. She believed that her mission as a writer was to denounce the artificial dreams women have about their roles. The author tried to counteract the effect of "romantic love" with a more realistic view of love.

> The only function of love is this: expose us to harm and then disappear. It is not something that can be completed and obtained in its fullness. Its mission is to break the circle of selfishness in which each of us dwells and by so doing, it

> puts us into communication with others. Since our basic essence is one of selfishness, this breaking action brings great pain and never goes beyond the making of scars, closing the circle once again.[33]

Thus, only during that "brief bolt of lightning" are men and women aware of each other and of the meaning of their lives.

Beatriz Guido belongs to the "angry generation" of Argentina during the years of 1950-1965. She depicts, from the point of view of the oligarchy, the disintegration of the upper classes and the social changes that take place with the advent of Perón.

The author uncovers the special world of women during this historical period. In *La casa del ángel,* Ana, the daughter of an important politician, is raped in her own house by one of her father's good friends. In *Fín de fiesta* women appear living out decisions made for them by men. The author shows clearly the great influence that the education of the sexes will have in their future activities: aggressive or passive roles in society are enforced by men to the extent that women are always treated as weak people incapable of making important decisions.

Elena Garro is another of the Mexican writers with a marked individuality. Her name became well-known with the appearance of her novel *Los recuerdos del porvenir.* She is obsessed with the passage of time and this obsession can be seen in her characters who seem to change clothing but not roles in the magic cycle of time. The women of her works live in their own worlds and invade reality by means of their imagination. Thus, Laura, the protagonist of "La culpa es de los tlaxcaltecas, " says:

> I fell in love with Pablo in a flash, during one minute in which he reminded me of someone I knew, someone I had forgotten. Later, at times it seemed as though he was going to become this other person. But it wasn't true. Immediately it became absurd, without the memory of my beloved, he became only another man who repeated the same gestures of all the men in Mexico.[34]

Very often her characters fall in love in a moment of passion, as if only in this momentary action can they escape their solitude. Garro's feminine protagonists give themselves completely to love. They very often appear imprisoned by society, so for them to love is to choose and to escape. Men seem to have a right to imprison women in order to possess them against their will; when this situation occurs women can escape in order to reunite with their beloved ones by means of their imagination.

Luisa Josefina Hernández is one of the most important figures of contemporary Mexican theater. She has received grants, honors and prizes and has traveled a great deal. Recently her novels have begun to attract the attention of the critics. She analyzes the frustrations of the individual who has to confront the truth. When asked why she wrote *La primera battalla,* a book that brought sorrow to many, she answered "because I did not wish to continue hiding—as do many Mexicans—the defects of my country."[35]

In her novels women are the ones who try to break the tenuous net of hypocrisy. In *Los frutos caídos* and in *Agonía* the protagonists are divorced women that must face up to their families and friends. Hernández' novels show a desire to unmask hypocritical patterns of behavior. One critic has said:

> Her ire is especially aroused when it deals with the human propensity for protective cover, when that cover becomes a license and justification for deceit or just plain weakness. When her characters demonstrate those traits or are simply naive, she is uncompromisingly rough on them. And she makes them work back towards the essence of their being—its limits, its energies, its general nature—they are made to feel that each day, each parting, each encounter is but a hint of things to come. This knowledge is searing and personal; it is also unavoidable and we share it with them.[36]

For the author, the pessimism of a rupture with the past may also bring hopes for the future. Love is the moving force that can bring hope to frustrated lives. Love appears also as a destructive force. As a result, there are several levels on which love can induce people to act: the redeeming love in *La cólera secreta* and *La plaza de Puerto Santo,* the unattainable love of *El lugar donde crece la hierba,* the vengeful love of *Los palacios desiertos,* the evasive love of *Arpas blancas, conejos dorados* and *Los sordomudos;* altruistic love in *La primera batalla,* the sick love of *La noche exquisita* and *El valle que elegimos,* and rejecting love in *La memoria de Amadís.*[37]

Elena Poniatowska is one of those frequent cases of a woman forced to postpone her true creative functions in order to make a living. Fortunately, her work on the important newspapers of Mexico has placed her in direct contact with the realities of that country.

We can see the effects of this in an interview with María Luisa Mendoza:

> Look, you have to venture forth . . . fight for great things, not the little ones . . . life is very short . . . you must travel . . . you have to write a novel . . . you have to defend someone . . . newspaper work has always been a terrible struggle for me. . . . I have always felt great nostalgia because I have not made any serious studies, I also feel this nostalgia for literature. . . . Instead of spending my energies in literature, I spend them in newspaper work . . . it pains me . . . and for this reason I always write my own material along with my newspaper articles. . . . Right now I am writing about the humble, yet mysterious life of a laundress, Jesusa . . . titled: *Hasto no verte, Jesús mío.*[38]

This novel has made Poniatowska famous. It is a documentary account of the life of a woman that comes from the lowest ranks of society. A confessional tone pervades the whole work and we can see Jesusa, the protagonist, as a remarkable woman who overcomes all barriers of ignorance and poverty in her search for her development as a human being.

Part I

Spanish Novelists

MARIA DE ZAYAS

One of the most important figures among feminine writers, and the first woman novelist, is a Spanish woman of whom relatively little is known. Her identity remains somewhat a mystery, although the critics[1] have chosen from several women one who best fits the chronology of her two novels. María de Zayas was born in Madrid in 1590, belonged to the upper class socially and participated in the literary life of the court. Lope de Vega alludes to her as a "clear, lively mind" and a distinguished poet.[2] We have no data on her personal life; we do not even know if she was single, married or a widow. Her two works are: *Novelas amorosas y ejemplares*[3] (1637) and *Desengaños amorosos*[4] (1647). If we take Lisis, the protagonist of *Desengaños,* as the mouthpiece of the author, we might assume that María de Zayas entered a convent after the publication of the novel because nothing else was ever heard of her afterwards. Although the two novels were published in numerous editions for two centuries, no one bothered to document the biography of the author or to verify several points concerning her existence.

The two novels have a similar structure: ladies and gentlemen get together to tell stories, and separating these love stories we find exchanges and interactions among the storytellers. Thus there is both unity and diversity in the narration. The lady of the house, Lisis, gives the themes to those present and these themes become the titles of the two novels: *amores* (love) for the first and *desengaños* (disillusion) for the second. There is also continuity among the tales in both novels in that they all have a beginning, suspenseful development, and a resolution to the love affairs. The same characters appear in both novels with the exception of a few which are added to the second one. Both novels take place over a limited number of days, since these people have gathered together in their literary groups at significant dates on the Catholic calendar: during the Christmas season and in the days before Carnival.

In *Novelas amorosas* the action takes place in Lisis' house on five nights. Men and women alike take their turns in telling a story of love. Lisarda tells "Adventurarse perdiendo," Matilde "La burlada Aminta y venganza de honor," Lisis "El desengaño amado y premio de la virtud," Miguel "Al fín se paga todo, " Lope "El imposible vencido," Juan "El juez de su causa," Laura (the mother of Lisis) "El jardín engañoso." Lisis, the protagonist, is being courted by Don Juan. After a while, he is attracted to Lisarda, one of the ladies present in the group. Lisis, out of spite, accepts the advances of Don Diego. The novel ends when the two protagonists, Lisis and Diego, announce their engagement. Two months later the group returns to the same house. On this occasion Lisis and Diego announce that their wedding will take place on the last day of Carnival. Two new people have joined the group: Estefanía, a nun who is recuperating from an illness, and Isabel. Lisis states that this time only the women will speak on the theme of *desengaño* and with the express purpose of defending and warning other women of the dangers that await them in various circumstances. The first night Isabel tells the tale "La más infame venganza," Laura "La inocencia castigada," Nise "El verdugo por su esposa," Filis "Tarde llega el desengaño," Matilde "Amar solo por vencer," Isabel "Mal presagio casar lejos," Doña Francisca "El traidor contra su sangre," Doña Estefanía "La perseguida triunfante," and on the last night Lisis tells "Engaños que causa el vicio."

I shall only examine the novel *Desengaños* by analyzing the position of the author as regards her feminism and I shall put special emphasis on the basic relationships of family, social class and sexuality. The story "La esclava de su amante" presents social conflict. The protagonist, Isabel, is from the upper class and is violated by Manuel, a boy from the lower class. Manuel does so because this is the only way he could have anything to do with her. Isabel is only 14 years old and describes thusly her reaction: "I do not know what has happened to me because the fright caused me to faint. Oh! Weak womankind, intimidated from childhood and weakened because we were taught to make hem-stitches rather than to play at war games" (p. 29). When Manuel abandons her, she follows him to seek vengeance dressed as a man and accompanied by a gentleman friend. When they find Manuel, he insults her because of her bad reputation—of course he admits no responsibility for her dishonor! Nevertheless, they become reconciled and carry on together in several adventures. She is carried off by the Moors and is sold as a slave. Meanwhile, Manuel decides to marry a rich lady and Isabel arranges for her gentleman friend to kill him out of vengeance. She then flees, continues her life as a maid, and thus arrives at the house of Lisis. There she is known as Zelima. Isabel makes known her true identity and begs Lisis to allow her to enter a convent because "in the company of such a Husband . . . I will no longer feel shame and now that I have had a sad youth, at least I may rest in my old age" (p. 65).

In "La más infame venganza" social and economic differences play an important role in the seduction of a poor girl (Octavia) by a rich man (Carlos). Juan, the brother of Octavia decides to avenge Octavia's dishonor through Camila, Carlos' wife. Armed with a knife, he threatens and then violates her. Camila takes refuge in a convent but her husband makes her come out with promises of pardon. When she returns home, her husband poisons her, but instead of dying she is horribly disfigured. The two men flee, leaving the women to fend for themselves.

In "La inocencia castigada" there are no family or social barriers between Doña Inés and Don Alonso, who are both rich and of the nobility and who are married with the approval of all. A lazy, rich, young man, Don Diego, brings disgrace to the couple. When he finds it impossible to seduce Doña Inés, he obtains the services of a sorcerer who bewitches her. While sleepwalking, she keeps several rendezvous with Don Diego. Her brother finds her and takes her home and he and her husband plot to take vengeance on her and bury her alive. Years later a neighbor hears her cries and with the help of the authorities the crime is uncovered and the guilty punished. Doña Inés enters a convent, having now acquired a reputation of holiness. The narrator concludes that "as far as cruelty is concerned, unfortunate women should trust neither brother nor husband, for all are men" (p. 138).

"El verdugo de su esposa" shows us Pedro and Rosaleta, a married couple, who suffer because Juan, a friend of Pedro, falls in love with Rosaleta. Juan constantly harasses her and she threatens to denounce him to her husband. Juan persists and Pedro plots vengeance, but Juan miraculously escapes. Pedro now becomes enamored of Juan's lover and punishes Rosaleta by bleeding her to death. The narrator puts special emphasis on the fact that whether the wife speaks or remains silent, the husband will take revenge on her whether or not she is innocent. The husband is more interested in the loss of his reputation, and would rather see his wife disappear than to suffer public dishonor.

"Tarde llega el desengaño" has a magnificent introductory discourse in which the narrator expounds on the fact that the fear and envy of men deprive women of education in the arts and in weapons. She concludes that "it would be better for women to use swords than to allow a man to aggravate her at anytime" (p. 177). The protagonist of the story is a rich and noble gentleman who allows his black slave girl to take the place of his wife at the table. He forces his wife to go about on all fours, like a dog, picking up the crumbs that fall from the table. He explains that the reason for his action is that the slave girl has confided to him that his wife has been having an affair with the chaplain of the castle. In the end he discovers that it was only a plot on the part of the slave to gain his favor. The narrator concludes that "women have such a bad reputation these days that neither with suffering can they conquer the hearts of their husbands nor can their innocence be esteemed" (p. 208).

"Amar solo por vencer" offers an interesting case of a man who passes himself off as a woman in order to seduce a woman he is interested in. The author feels that education plays an important role in the making of "effeminate" women: "Men make us more effeminate than Nature, if Nature gives us kind hearts and weakness, at least Nature gave us a soul that can encompass all, just like men" (p. 211). Differences in social class cause Esteban to dress as a maid in the house, for in no other way could he even consider courting Laurela. The other maids notice something wrong and make jokes about "the woman in love with another." The author takes the opportunity here to digress on the spiritual identity of her characters whose souls "are neither of men nor of women." Laurela's father arranges a wedding for her with a nobleman. Esteban hurries to uncover his identity, declare his love and seduce her. After he has possessed Laurela, he abandons her, taking all of her jewels. Ashamed, Laurela seeks refuge in her uncle's house. Once again, the men of the family, in this case the father and the uncle, plan to avenge her dishonor: they cause a wall to fall on her which buries her. A maid, witnessing the event, tells Laurela's mother and sisters what has happened. Disillusioned and frightened, the women seek protection together in a convent. The author tries to understand how a lover, after so many professions of his love, could do this thing simply because he has obtained his goal. She believes that Laurela, like any woman, would have believed him and asks: "How can you expect a woman to be good, if you have made her bad and even have taught her to so be?" (p. 254). This is the same argument that Sor Juana Inés de la Cruz, a Mexican nun, was to use many years later in her *Redondilla,* " Foolish men, who accuse. . . ."[5]

"Mal presagio casar lejos" presents an interesting use of male homosexuality. This is the woeful tale of four daughters of a noble Spaniard. The oldest was killed when her husband laid a trap for her in which she appeared to be unfaithful. The second was hanged by her own hair because she praised a gentleman who was passing by. The third daughter, who was a witness, jumped from the window so her brother-in-law would not kill her also and was crippled for the rest of her life. The youngest daughter, Blanca, after seeing what happened to her sisters, does not want to take any chances and places the condition that any man who wants to marry her must be well-known to her for at least one year. A prince from Flanders has asked for her hand and accepts Blanca's condition: "To love through familiarity and to know through dealings the condition and graces of the husband" (p. 262). Blanca realizes that interest, convenience and fear play an "important role in matrimony" and prefers to go to a convent if the boyfriend does not satisfy her requirements. Since the boyfriend accepts the betrothal condition, after a year they are married and they travel to Flanders. She takes with her a court of ladies and gentlemen because she is a lady of high social standing. A political element now enters the story since the Spaniards are hated in Flanders. Her husband takes leave of her once they arrive at his palace. His only company there is a 15-year-old page. One day Blanca surprises them together in bed "in such twisted and abominable pleasures that are lowly, not only to say but even to think of" (p. 286). Since she has been a witness, she knows that both of the men will kill her and she prepares to die. First she confesses, then she says goodbye to her ladies, giving them her jewels and telling them what has happened. The husband, page and father-in-law open her veins and she dies. The hatred of the father-in-law toward Spain is well evident when he comments: "How I wish I could have all of her nation as I have her" (p. 290). The narrator comments that beauty, virtue, wisdom, royal blood, and innocence were of no good to the four sisters; all were sacrificed on the "altar of disgrace." Their wretched star was to "be born women."

"El traidor contra su sangre" shows the great conflict that exists between the various social classes and the role that money plays in the marriage of both sons and daughters. A rich gentleman has a daughter, Mencia, and a son, Alonso. A rich farmer, Don Enrique, is in love with Mencia, but he is from a lower social class. Alonso, following the desires of his father, kills Mencia because she has been having secret meetings with Don Enrique. In another city, Alonso falls in love with a very beautiful but poor girl, Ana. When his father finds out about Ana, Alonso's father disinherits him. Alonso begins to hate her, "at each step insults her with her poverty" (p. 322) and starves her. Even though they have a son, he kills Ana and demands his father support him as when he killed his sister. The father simply comments: "I would rather have a hanged son than one poorly married" and allows him to be executed.

"La perseguida triunfante" the tale of the nun Estefanía who, due to her little worldly experience ("from a child she consecrated herself to the Bridegroom"), tells the only story that deals with the life of a saint. Ladislao of Hungary marries Beatrice, daughter of the king of England. Federico, brother of Ladislao, is charged with bringing her to Hungary; on the way he falls in love with her. Since Ladislao is away at war, Federico continues to pursue her. She has him put in a lion's cage to stop his advances and then rules the country, "the vassels so content that they do not even miss the king" (p. 356). When Ladislao returns, Federico accuses Beatrice of having "lacivious and impure desires" toward him. Ladislao publicly slaps Beatrice, has her eyes put out and then abandons her in the forest for the wild beasts to eat. A miracle occurs and she is saved. Meanwhile, Federico hires a sorcerer who makes known to him that she is still alive. He goes to the forest to once again try to violate her but she is again miraculously saved. After many years she returns to the court of Hungary, her innocence is proved, and she discovers that her protector was the Virgin Mary. When Ladislao tries to assert his rights as a husband, Beatrice tells him that she already belongs to the Celestial Bridegroom. She asks permission to found a convent and retire along with those ladies who wish to follow her.

The narrator reflects that even a woman so virtuous as this has to suffer "the treachery and cruelty of man" (p. 409).

"Engaños que causa el vicio" is the story of two girls raised as sisters. When the parents die, the girls go to live with their aunt and uncle. Although they love the girls, the aunt and uncle will not allow them to marry in order that they might keep the girls' dowries for themselves. In spite of this, Magdalena marries Dionis and takes Florentina to live with them. Unfortunately, the sister falls in love with Dionis and they have an affair for four years. She incites Dionis to kill his wife, but the husband goes crazy and kills all the women in the house, including the maids. Only Florentina escapes, badly wounded, and she enters a convent to expiate her deeds. The author here shows us the situation of a sister who turns on her own sister and the message is obvious: women should not become divided and should at all costs remain united. As it is Lisis who is telling this story, she remembers the fickleness of Lisarda, but she also reminds the men that when it comes to satisfying their desires, they never pass up an opportunity. Lisis wants "to defend all women and correct all men," but since men are the natural enemies of women, there is no alternative but "war." At the end of her story, Lisis reveals her intention not to marry Don Diego as she had announced at the beginning, she does not wish to take part in that battle which so many women have lost. She affirms that "we need to take arms and defend ourselves from their evil intentions and from our enemies" (p. 460).

In all of the narrations the man is the executioner and the woman his victim. From the story told by Lisis we can observe that a man, such as Dionis, may be educated and seem to be noble and honorable, yet he kills women. There is the constant threat of war between the sexes. Lisis insists that the women tell the stories in order to reflect their point of view, because "since men are those who preside, they never tell the evil they do, but rather speak of the evil done to them, and if you look closely, the men are at fault and the women follow the men's opinion since they believe the men are right; the most obvious thing is that there are no bad women, only evil men" (p. 10).

Within the social framework of this period, women occupied a place superior only to that of animals and crazy people. Even if she belonged to the higher classes, this only imposed certain dress standards and added more limitations. Within the family, the woman was a possession that could be given, exchanged or done away with according to the circumstances. Honor was so fundamental in the Spanish system that it could be besmirched by simple indiscretion and as Lope de Vega put it, "Honor is that which comes from another. No man gains honor by himself." Especially with respect to the woman, the social system was organized to strictly watch over feminine conduct. The father, brother and husband were those impowered to carry out retribution. One aspect of the work of Zayas that is new and different is that she denounces many of the situations that masculine writers tried to hide: crimes and hatred toward women. Even when the man found out that the woman was innocent, he saw to it that she disappeared because she was a witness to his dishonor and humiliation. The husband could easily find ways of doing away with his wife without interference from the authorities and it seems that family conspiracies were common, with the men as accomplices and the women as victims. Another aspect of her work is the latent homosexuality exhibited by the men. Men also seem to transfer their repressed sexual desires into action against the wives of their friends or against their own sisters.

Education, according to the author, is one of the principal forms of repression. This masculine system kept the woman ignorant and apart. The author mentions various examples of what women learn and which in no way prepares them for the dangers they face nor allows them to realize the full potential of their intelligence. She insists many times that the soul is neither masculine nor feminine and thus places emphasis on the equality of men and women. Several of her protagonists show themselves to be fearless as they follow those men who abandoned them. In other cases, women make the decision to retreat from the world, for many this is the immediate alternative of escape from the slavery of men. There are many other women, however, who prefer the convent because it signifies "Holy Sanctuary," from which no one could remove them because of the religious laws. Education does not prepare women to earn a living and they must depend on their families unless they marry. In the convent they at least find a number of tasks that allow them to justify their existence. Zayas also notices that girls who are raised in the great houses—she is speaking of the higher social classes—by their relatives or maids are ignorant of what goes on outside the four walls of their home and thus are easy prey of the tricks of men. There is a definite purpose to Zayas' novel: to warn all women of the things that happen in the relationship between the sexes. She offers many examples of women who have been queens or wise governors when they had the opportunity. She definitely believes that women must stop thinking of themselves as weak and evil, as taught by masculine indoctrination. She tries to induce women to analyze the simple examples she presents and to begin to see the causes and effects of the actions of both sexes. She believes that it is possible for women to begin to reason for themselves without recourse to masculine teachings, which only create a poor and defective vision of themselves.

The sexuality Zayas discusses is principally that of the youth of the higher classes, which she knows very well. The male children are sent to religious schools and the girls remain at home where, following Arabic customs, they are given room to roam about in without being seen by strangers—thus there is little filial affection between the two. The girls generally find out that some gentleman is in love with them through the maids. And the gentlemen, using the menservants who in turn use the maids, then establish contact. Women thus receive a false idea of love. Courtly love predominates and the men, who are well-versed in this art, go through the rituals in order to convince the victim of their devotion. Laziness, wealth and great freedom in the young men help them convert this art of love into a favorite pastime. The man wants to make as many conquests as possible and he has no interest in remaining with any woman who has given herself to him. In Spain, predominantly, the Arab has reinforced the double standard: the man may have many wives but the woman must remain absolutely faithful. Once the man becomes infatuated with a woman, he throws himself into the conquest like the soldier who lays seige to a city, but after satisfying his sexual desires, he loses interest; "after sex all animals are sad." The women, on the other hand, live in their gardens dreaming of love and of being loved. When a gentleman presents himself, they reject him if they are virtuous. Many times they are convinced that this gentleman truly loves them and they take the risk, knowing that they may sacrifice their honor and expose themselves to the scorn and vengeance of their families. This risk freely taken reveals, ac-

cording to the author, the superiority of women in that their desires are not sensual but spiritual and thus can remain strong even after men have defrauded them.

Marriage appears to be something arranged out of convenience by the families. The women must have a dowry in order to attract candidates from the same social class. She never really knows her future husband until after the wedding, when she begins to discover a world much different from that of courtly love. Now she is a recluse in the house, allowed only to go to Church or to go visiting with her husband. Danger is ever present, especially if she is young and beautiful, for other men will try and court her, placing her reputation in danger. We must assume that while she must be prudent, she is never free from the chance that some man might take advantage of her. Zayas reveals another aspect of feminine sexuality that male writers of this period never discuss: the terror of the woman when faced by masculine violence, a crime which is viewed by the author without mercy. But the woman also suffers when her boyfriend or husband is unfaithful; this pain is exceptionally well captured by the author. The woman needs to believe that her lover will not fool her and when all fails, she has no other recourse but Jesus. Many women enter the convent "seeking perfect love from the Bridegroom who never fails." But even here we find masculine indoctrination concerning honor. Santa Teresa, in her *Relaciones espirituales,*[6] says that when Christ appeared to her in visions he told her: "See this nail, it is a sign that you will be my bride from this day forth; until today you did not merit it; from now on you will watch out for me as Creator, King, God, and you will also guard my honor."

Lisis, the voice of the author, is the most militant of the group. She sees the situation as a "cold war" between the sexes, which are in continual battle. Men have their own code and work together against women. Historically, the thesis that woman is superior to man in the telling of lies, working of intrigues and the playing of tricks has been perpetuated. Thus man always has had little confidence in his wife, even if she is virtuous. The author does not believe that a single woman like Lisis can fight the whole system by herself. Her mission is to proceed to gather the women together so that, united for a common cause, they may protect their virtue and individual integrity. Following the system, Lisis and those that follow her retire to a convent. Many years later, Sor Juana Inés de la Cruz, the Mexican nun, explained her decision to enter the convent: "It was the least abnormal and most decent way I could assure myself of the salvation my soul longed for." Ascetic retreat in the Catholic Church represents a decisive move for the woman—she either thus rejects society or has herself been rejected. It is difficult to imagine the convent as the last stronghold of feminine nonconformity; paradoxically it is also their means of spiritual vindication. While men writers have never bothered to consider why women enter convents, Zayas has given us a full spectrum of cases which allow us to visualize all the social abuses heaped upon women. We often believe that fathers force their daughters to go to the convent in order to hide their shame and disobedience.

Zayas shows us that the fathers and brothers in no way understand either their wives or those women in their custody; they act according to specific conventions which cause them to lose sight of feminine sensitivity. Perhaps victims and executioners are a product of society motivated by honor and love. If the man kills for honor, the woman dies for love. He spends his life looking for conquests while she imagines a place of pure love. He believes himself free and is a slave to his own mistrust. She believes herself to be a slave and yet within her spirit she has found the path that not only will make her free but that will also bring her eternal love.

FERNAN CABALLERO
(Cecilia Bohl de Faber)

Cecilia was born in Switzerland in 1796. Her mother was Spanish and her father German. Her parents were en route to Germany when she was born and when they returned to Spain they took up residence in Cadiz. As a child, her mother encouraged her many literary interests. Although her father was an intellectual, he thought that his daughter's interests were foolish and that they took away time that Cecilia could use in sewing and other pursuits.[1] This was a typical attitude for her day and is perhaps one reason why Cecilia hesitated to publish her works and why, when she finally did, she chose a masculine pseudonym: Fernán Caballero.

Cecilia's marriages are important to us here, especially as the first served as a model for her novel *Clemencia*[2] which we will study. When she was 20, a man who had come to Cadiz and had known her only eight days asked for her hand in marriage. Surprisingly, her parents consented and she was married.[3] She obediently followed her husband to Puerto Rico and shortly thereafter found out what kind of a man he was; dissipated and jealous to the point of brutality, he treated his recent bride abusively. Fortunately, he died within the year, thanks to the riotous life he lived, and she was able to return home to her parents. Once again she renewed her acquaintanceship with the Marqués of Arco Hermoso who had been in love with her before her marriage. They were married and were relatively happy until he died 14 years later. Her third marriage was to a man 18 years her junior and who suffered from tuberculosis. For many years they lived apart, since he worked in Australia. In 1859 he committed suicide over financial troubles and for a while she considered entering a convent. Her work began to appear in the newspaper *El Heraldo*. Her favorite novel, *La Gaviota*, gained a great deal of success. In 1852, in serial form, *Clemencia* appeared and was widely acclaimed. No one knew that the author was a woman.[4] Cecilia was the creator of the *costumbrista* novel in Spain.[5] After some study into the customs and habits of both Germany and France, she decided to highlight the traditional values of Spain. She also wrote in French and German. She died in 1877.

She said: "A novel is not invented, it is observed." She remained loyal to this maxim and her novels are a combination of the customs, ideas and habits of the Spanish people. Her major novels are: *La gaviota*, *La familia de Alvareda*, and *Clemencia*.[6] We shall examine *Clemencia* because it contains biographical elements and because we can follow the psychological development of the protagonist with great fidelity. The views and morals of our novelist are reflected in her favorite characters. She also chooses to illustrate that which ought not to be done and thus gives us an idea of the changes that were occurring even in the strict conservative society of her day. Fernán Caballero is not a feminist, but as a faithful observer of her society she does capture several rebellious and combative women.

The action of *Clemencia* takes place in Seville. The Marquesa of Cortejana is a widow who lives with her two daughters, Constancia and Alegría. A 16-year-old cousin, an orphan who has been raised in a convent, comes to live with them. Her name is Clemencia and she is poor, timid and very religious. The Marquesa is determined to find good marriages for her daughters and this beautiful orphan is a threat, thus the Marquesa marries her to the first man who asks for her hand, a young captain named Fernando de Guevara. This man, who has only known her for seven days, takes her to his family home in the town of Villa María after the wedding. He is corrupt, jealous and vulgar and treats her so badly that she becomes ill and cannot follow him when his regiment leaves. He dies a little while later and she returns to her aunt's house. There her cousins are involved in intrigues and boyfriend problems. Constancia's secret boyfriend dies while she and Clemencia are in a seaside town where the Marquesa has sent Constancia to recuperate. Alegría, the other sister, marries a nobleman whom her sister had rejected. Her husband, the Marqués of Valdemar, then takes her to live at the court in Madrid. When Clemencia returns to Seville she receives a letter from her late spouse's parents, who invite her to come and live with them. She travels back to Villa María where they live and there she meets her husband's uncle the priest, his cousin Pablo and her other in-laws, who are the most important landowners of the region.

Pablo is a simple man of the provinces and although he falls in love with Clemencia, he feels inferior to her. The priest instructs both in the basic principles of the Church. Her father-in-law Don Martín is ready to see them married but Pablo is afraid Clemencia will accept out of duty. Meanwhile, the father-in-law dies without leaving Clemencia anything. Pablo offers to allow her to remain with him and the priest. When the priest dies, he leaves his fortune to Clemencia who then returns to Seville. Pablo had confessed his love, but she decided to leave in order to begin a new, independent life. In Seville she opens the doors of her house to a distinguished group of friends. An English aristocrat, Sir George Percy, and a French nobleman in exile, Carlos de Brian, court her.[7] She observes both of her suitors carefully and although she falls in love with Sir Percy, she rejects him following several arguments. She finally has Pablo come to see her and she proposes matrimony; in her evaluation, he is the only one who offers her authentic values. After the wedding they go to live in Villa María. The novel ends idyllically as they await their first child.

Family

With a great deal of detail, the novelist describes the relationship between a rich egocentric, widowed mother and her two rebellious, intelligent and independent daughters. Another feminine character is Doña Eufrasia, the widow of a colonel Matamoros. She is much like a sister to the Marquesa; she advises her, informs her of what is going on and has tremendous influence on her decisions. Constancia is absorbed in the fiery passion of her cousin Bruno. This young officer without a future is not the match the mother had hoped for and thus the two young people must secretly love each other without hope of marriage. Alegría cares little for the wishes of her mother and does as she pleases. The Marquesa is a woman more interested in the opinions of her neighbors and friends than in the happiness of those that surround her. She has been a very spoiled woman, "first by her parents and then by her husband," and does not seem to be aware of what is happening in her children's hearts. In inviting Clemencia into her house, her motives are also in compliance with social demands. The whole family treats Clemencia as a poor relative and her aunt marries her off without consultation. Clemencia's cousins only accept her as an equal many years later when she is rich and a widow.

If the aunt is representative of an aristocratic family of the city, Clemencia's in-laws are representative of the rural aristocracy. Don Martín, her father-in-law, is the prototype of the rural patriarch who treats Clemencia with affection because she is under his protection, but there is a great deal of egotism in this protection. It pleases him to have a young, beautiful, gentle girl in the house, but he treats her as if she had no feelings of her own and he makes decisions for her without consulting her at all. He leaves her without the inheritance destined for his son and instead gives it to his nephew because he is the only "man" in the family. Clemencia's mother-in-law is a strict, stoic woman who is only waiting for her husband to die in order to enter a convent. She treats Clemencia without affection and as if she were a foolish, emotional child. The priest is the only one who becomes a friend to Clemencia. He treats her with respect and educates her as befits a woman of the period:

> As a woman, you must consider knowledge, not as an object, a necessity or the base for a career but rather as a means of refinement, perfection, that is, something that makes you more agreeable, not something useful. . . . [T]he great wisdom of the woman is to conceal wisdom with benevolence . . . and as regards morality: it is not enough to be good, one must also appear good [p. 122].

Nevertheless, the priest is the only one who is concerned with Clemencia's future, and together with the inheritance he leaves her this advice:

> The life of a woman, especially when she is young, brings some demands and necessities beyond those of the heart, in order to live peacefully. She needs either to retire from the world or, if she remains in it, be of some help; in any other way, dearest Clemencia, alone, independent, useless, her sterile life is exceptional and apart from the simple conformity in which human society lives. Celibacy, my daughter, is holy, or it can be a vicious and egotistical tendency

> which tends to break down social and religious laws: do not depart from the holy mission of wife and mother; I charge you, I beg you [p. 58].

Social Class

Don Silvestre and Don Galo, gentlemen from good but impoverished families, come to the parties given by the Marquesa in Seville. Doña Eufrasia is a woman from the middle class. There are several young students, among them Paco Guzmán, who come from the higher levels of the middle class. The Marqués of Valdemar is both the only foreigner and the only nobleman. The Marquesa is interested in him as a husband for Constancia and thus she is strongly opposed to the love of Constancia for her cousin Bruno, who is poor. Constancia is to receive an inheritance from an aunt if she marries in accordance with the wishes of her mother, but as she rebels, the inheritance goes to Alegría who marries the nobleman. It is subtle economic intrigues that force the daughters to obey when words fail. As Constancia says to her maid Andrea:

> What a fine thing my aunt proposes with her 'inheritance!' An inheritance with conditions . . . well let her keep it. What would I want that money for? To gild my shame? No, no; I want to be happy and to feel on my own terms and I will, without an inheritance, without positions, without titles . . . [L]et whoever appreciates and desires those things have them . . . [p. 38].

In Villa María the social stratification between rich and poor is well marked. The patriarchal system rules and Don Martín acts out his role with "the despotism of the head of a large house." He is true to the image of the Andalusian gentleman who personally takes charge of the affairs of his subordinates. It is interesting to note that the members of the high levels of city life are fearful of life in the country: Alegría tells Clemencia that she will not live in a little town because to do so is to become degenerate. Clemencia responds that those who have land ought to live on that land. The foreigners, like Sir George, also criticize this provincial attitude of the Spaniards. Clemencia defends the Spaniards: "You will never understand that the moral independence of the Spaniard respects holy authority and will not tolerate boyish pranks" (p. 87). Thus Clemencia defends the traditions and sentiments of the rich class who live in rural areas.

Doña Eufrasia is a widow who lives on a small pension. There is much truth in the joke Paco Guzmán plays on her:

> Oh! Widowhood . . . widows, what a curse; there is no country on earth with more widows than Spain. They are innumerable, immortal, they double, they swarm, they multiply: each soldier leaves a hundred, each worker a dozen widows behind. There is no budget that can accommodate widowhood. . . . [T]here ought to be some wise and frugal Herod who would be willing to cut off the heads of some innocent widows [p. 108].

Paco calls them "monstrous leechers" and he extends the insult to include those women who depend solely on a small pension which is barely enough to live on decently. Thus another aspect of the woman who is advanced in years is presented by the author and the indomitable spirit of Matamoros is thus rendered all the more admirable.

There is a great deal of change that takes place in the three feminine protagonists. Constancia begins as a passionate romantic and changes into a religious fanatic. Clemencia loses her timidity and becomes a woman sure of herself. Alegría loses her carefree, burlesque view of life and becomes rebellious and resentful of the social double standard.

Constancia, who is ready to sacrifice marriage as long as she may continue with Bruno, is a witness to the shipwreck in which he dies. She passes through a spiritual crisis and finds God. She wishes to enter a convent but her mother is very ill and needs her care. Thus she punishes herself for her early years of rebellion:

> Religion gave her more than acceptance; it gave her consolation and virtue, banishing from her soul, after a period of desperation, pride, sharpness, rebellion, and self-centeredness, which had for so long a time held sway in her life. These were replaced with meekness, benevolence, charity, patience . . . [p. 64].

Constancia, who at the beginning of the novel is ready to marry no one unless they will allow her to continue to see Bruno, interprets his death as a warning from God. The presence of eternity opens her eyes to a new reality. Her mother is only a means by which she may accomplish her penitence. She renounces all: marriage, clothing, elegance, comfort, even her independence.

Following her marriage to the Marqués de Valdemar, Alegría lives for several years at the court in Madrid. We know nothing of her first years of marriage nor if her husband is faithful. We next meet her while on vacation in Seville with her husband and three children. There she meets Paco Guzmán, her first love, once again, and their affair begins anew. Even though the author presents her as living an agitated, eventful life, we learn that she is disillusioned and has a sad idea of marriage. She tells Clemencia: "Since you're getting married, I hope the yoke will be light; may you have many blessings, let the burden of children be light; since you are burying yourself while alive, let your life be easy" (p. 178). From her own words we learn that Alegría's mother forced her to marry the Marqués so as not to lose the inheritance from her aunt. Alegría is a victim of a "ridiculously jealous and foolishly mistrusting" husband (p. 176). The letter her husband writes to her as he is about to abandon her is interesting:

> A man cannot take back a woman who has belonged to another man; the tie that was defiled ceases to exist, authorizing him, defended by human and divine law, and forced by his heart and his honor, to act [p. 112].

Alegría is abandoned by her lover, Paco, at the same time, "out of human respect" and searches throughout Seville for "someone to console her emptiness" (p. 113). While the author deals harshly with Alegría, we must realize that we are never given the true story behind her marriage.

Sexuality

In the beginning Clemencia acts with great passivity; her first marriage is the direct result of her obedience to her aunt. She does not love her husband and her modesty is offended by this soldier who is accustomed to easy conquests; her illness is a result of her shame. He also strikes and insults her. To a woman who has spent her entire life with other women—in a convent and with her aunt—this man is the incarnation of Lucifer. With Pablo, she has more time to know him personally and feels more comfortable, without tension or expectations. Perhaps because he has never been attractive to her explains her lack of interest. Her father-in-law and those who know him well agree that he is a plain, ugly man, without any gallant refinements, but he does have a valiant heart and is an unconditional lover of Clemencia. When she comes face to face with Sir Percy, she realizes that there are those men of great intelligence who are full of cynicism and irony. Sir Percy falls in love with her because she is so different from those women he has known in London. For the first time she feels attracted to a brilliant man but she soon discovers that this man has neither compassion nor kindness for those who surround him. She clings desperately to what the priest has taught her in order not to succumb to this man who makes fun of all she considers sacred. When she finally realizes that it is only her body in which he is interested and not in her "spiritual attributes" she decides to break off the friendship:

> 'Do you believe that the happiness of love is ephemeral? Do you think that love ends?'
>
> 'Clemencia,' answered Sir George with a jovial sincerity, 'only a recently graduated student would argue. Love is the most transitory of things, and is precisely that which has most pretensions of immortality; common lovers are those who are romantically candid enough to swear this "eternal love," this utopia, this myth, this phoenix, this fantastic creation.'
>
> 'If love is so ephemeral, if it is a castle of cards that falls with a breath of wind, what will become of this happiness that comes from our love?'
>
> 'Before I loved you,' responded Sir George in a light manner, 'you amused me; I was enchanted with your grace, talent, uniqueness, wit, gaiety, all of which are yours alone and which give you the enchanting privilege of interesting me, surprising me, entertaining me and making me happy.'

> 'Have you not noticed any of my virtues, that is, if you think I have some?'
>
> 'Virtues! . . . That is another matter,' answered Sir George, 'that I greatly respect, but I think you are changing my compliment because there are some virtues that are ridiculous, Clemencia, in high society and which cause a certain ridicule and then there are others more severe, which are intolerable, and tolerance is the great virtue of this age; therefore, my dear Lady Percy, let's make some economies in the accountbooks of virtue.'
>
> 'I suppose, then, that the first of these "economies" will be fidelity' [p. 144].

Clemencia fears losing the affection of this man. She is desperately seeking eternal values, security, absolute guarantees without which she does not dare to accept this kind of love, however long it may last, or this lover, however long he may love her. In a desperate and defensive action, she sends for her cousin Pablo, and when he cannot believe that Clemencia loves him, she affirms:

> I love you with all the conviction with which one loves virtue, with the fidelity with which one loves happiness, with all the kindness and abandonment with which one loves who is free to voluntarily choose a companion pleasing to both God and man [p. 161].

She herself needs to be sure that Pablo loves her as she wishes to be loved and so she asks:

> Do you like my figure? Do you find my sentiments attractive? Or do my thoughts seduce you?

And he responds:

> Nothing like that, Clemencia. Your body, your capacity for feeling and thinking are pleasing and attractive and are seductive because they *are yours*. If you lost your beauty, your talent, your lively poetic feeling for life, I would love you just the same, passionately, without any thought of re-

> compense, even if you were dead I would love you . . . even as I have loved you for so long without hope! [p. 162]

Perhaps this too is a myth like that of the "romantic candor" of Sir George, but Clemencia has a need to believe, to be convinced, that there is someone who loves her totally, without any shadow of doubt or indecision whatsoever.

Message

All of the names of the protagonists are symbolic. Constancia (Constance), in her love for Bruno as well as in her love for God, manifests a temperamental obstinacy which causes her to act in extremes. In the fulfillment of her family duties there is a certain masochism; she wants to be punished, she wants to pay for the sense of guilt she still has for hating her mother: "Blinded by love and pride, I did not love the mother who gave me life" (p. 71). She goes from one type of renunciation (marriage with Bruno) to another type of renunciation (life). Her temperament causes her to act as if her reality was the only one and she ignores all that goes on around her. Alegría (Joy) is the extreme example of the search for egotistical pleasure. In comparison with Constancia she is frivolous, excitable and practical. It does not bother her to lie to her mother about her husband's urgent call to Madrid nor does she mind scandalizing society. Alegría is detested by the author because she represents the type of woman who breaks the traditional molds for the behavior of the good Spanish woman. Clemencia is the golden mean. Her name (Mercy) indicates a virtue: the moderation of justice. But more than the representation of a virtue, she becomes for the author the epitome of the Spanish Ideal.

Clemencia, in her several stages, represents the various alternatives for the women of this period. In her first years, she manifests a sense of obedience and submission. When her mother dies at her birth, her father sends her to a convent to be educated by nuns. When she leaves the convent, the contrast is great. The Marquesa Cortegana, whose name is appropriate (*corte* means "court" and *gaña* means "win") for a woman who wins in all she does, provides a mundane and superficial atmosphere consisting of letters, gossip, and friends who, in order not to be bored, get together every night with other young people in order to flirt. The widow of Matamoros is loyal to her name (killer of Moors) as a dynamic, manipulative woman who never fails to take advantage of every opportunity to impose her will on the Marquesa. The two cousins who constantly make fun of Clemencia are, in a certain aspect, trials for her humility and her perseverance in her nunnish beliefs. Her first marriage is the greatest test of her obedience. But what else could a girl in her position do? She had no place to go if she disobeyed her aunt and besides, without a dowry, how could she refuse the proposal of a rich young man from a distinguished family? Clemencia is the typical girl who has only one path in life and who follows it. In her second period she is a widow living with her in-laws. Now her greatest virtue is conformity. She takes easily to the house's system and to the teachings of the priest, which are very similar to those of the convent. With one exception, she can there use her own judgment because she has already had some experience with human wretchedness. The moment of her true test, unencumbered by family or social pressures, comes in her third period, when she has her own house, friends and lands. There she may choose her own spouse.

There are two different currents of influence at work in Spain at this time. One comes from France, for social upheaval and political chaos followed the Revolution. The other comes from England, a current much more open, free, flexible, thoughtful and protestant—both in terms of sexuality and of morals. Clemencia must use all of her religious, moral and spiritual preparation to counteract the constant attacks of Sir George. In her change from innocence to maturity she has to re-evaluate all that she has learned before of love, marriage, sexuality, kindness and mercy. The last test, corresponding to her name, comes with Sir George and the poor. Sir George is incapable of feeling compassion even though he is capable of giving money to charity. What he needs, in Clemencia's opinion, is a human feeling for Christian charity. She also has to re-examine the true values she looks for in matrimony. Her two cousins give two opposite views: a religious life or a profane life. She has confidence that, with a solid marriage, adherence to the teachings of the Church, and living near to the land, a married woman with children is the hope of Spain. But how can she accomplish this goal with men for whom love is an appearance and who have no concern for her most vital and profound desires? Her only recourse is the memory of those idyllic moments spent with Pablo when the priest taught them the fundamental doctrines of the Church. She sincerely believes that Pablo will make her happy. The author is very much convinced that this is the correct solution, and since she has molded Clemencia somewhat according to her own biography, this is also probably what Cecilia Bohl de Faber needed in order to be happy. Clemencia is the model of virtue in the following dialogue with Alegría:

> 'Yes, yes,' added Alegría, 'now that you are getting married, be careful and teach your husband from the beginning to not be ridiculously jealous and foolishly mistrust you.'
>
> 'In Villa María there are few occasions which could give rise to such tendencies, even if Pablo had them.'
>
> 'Do you have to live in Villa María . . . ?'
>
> 'The heads of the Guevara household have always lived here,' answered Clemencia. 'Why should I change, especially since I don't want to, since I love the land so and since it would not please my husband?'
>
> 'But that is to bury yourself alive,' exclaimed Alegría, horrified.
>
> 'If the woman who proposes to live in the house of her elders, beside a husband she loves, and dedicates herself to raise such sons that God may give her, must bury herself alive, I believe then, Alegría, that every good wife should gladly put on the shroud of that burial. Why not? Do you think perhaps, that the woman, when she marries, follows the natural and correct path if instead of self-sacrifice and dedication to the holy and sweet duties of wife and mother, she were to turn her back on them and give herself over to diversion, parties, the exterior world of distraction? Would you thus devalue the holy mission of womankind?'
>
> 'Moral novelettes,' responded Alegría, 'with an income of twenty-five thousand "duros," to live in a dingy village is not only vulgar, it's stupid . . . ' [p.177]

Clemencia is a completely traditional woman who has two qualities that are very much a part of today's world: she needs to be loved for herself and not as a doll, as something pleasing to the eye or as an amusing clown; and she wants to base her selection of a husband on thought and not on an emotional impulse. She comes to a knowledge of her own worth and of her mission in life. After having lived in the country and in the city, she can choose the country based on her own experience. After having a brilliant but cold man like Sir George and a mediocre but devoted man like Pablo, she chooses the latter. Ater having been loved only for her body by her first husband, she chooses from among those men who surround her the man who best seems to recognize her virtues.

Alegría is the anti-heroine of the novel and thus adds a different dimension to it. She rejects motherhood as the principal reason for marriage and she wants her freedom at any cost. She warns Clemencia not to remarry, since as a wife she will not be able to do the things she wishes. Clearly, Alegría is speaking of her own condition following her husband's abandonment. I am also sure that her friends rejected her and made her life miserable. Alegría is an admirable character for the courage she shows in throwing society's hypocrisy back in its face, especially with regards to men: her husband and her lover are both cowards who cannot face up to their obligations, both men rally around the system of honor and leave her to fend for herself. Perhaps Alegría is a premature version of the modern woman. Her warning to Clemencia is that all she may expect is many children and many years with the same man, who keeps a mistress somewhere. It is to be hoped that her fears may never come to pass, but they nevertheless serve as a warning to the young of the flaws of married life.

EMILIA PARDO BAZAN

Emilia Pardo Bazán was born in La Coruña, Spain, in 1852. She belonged to an aristocratic family and her father encouraged her education.[1] She married José Quiroga at age 16. With him she traveled to Madrid and frequently to Paris. Greatly interested in science and philosophy, she studied Kant, Hegel and Schelling, among others. She also studied French literature and therefore adopted the technique of Naturalism, which caused much scandal in Spain. In a series of articles which appeared in the newspaper *La Epoca* and with the title "La cuestión palpitante" (which appeared as a book in 1883), she studied the naturalistic movement as Zola had done in France under the title *The Experimental Novel*.

The great resistance of the Spanish to Naturalism stems from the fact that Zola had an anti-religious spirit and found the church a house in which God is absent. Pardo Bazán, however, was a devout Catholic and synthesized her conception of Naturalism thus:

> Beneath the question is an admirable idea about which I have dreamed for a long time: the union of scientific method and art. And here it is! This arbitrary division has disappeared and experimentation and observation can be equally applied to the novel and to anatomical studies. The problems are still many, but when they are unraveled, the twentieth century will be beautiful indeed.[2]

Even though she admits to agreeing with some of Zola's pessimism as far as human wretchedness is concerned, she does not blame Christian doctrine but rather the men who have twisted the message and misapplied it. The great debate and the rumors of excommunication that circulated as a result of *La cuestión palpitante* created much tension between her and her husband, who came from a very religious family. He asked her not to publish the book and she refused. He then threatened to leave her and a separation took place. They remained married in name, but each one had his own life. She lived either in La Coruña, Meiras or Madrid, while he stayed at their estates at Orense or in his castle.[3] She traveled to Rome, where they found nothing heretical in her works and absolved her of the charges.

Pardo Bazán is a pioneer in the feminist movement.[4] In her novels she begins to search for those barriers in each social class that keep women from advancing. She methodically experiments with different typical and atypical cases, trying to extract from Spanish society those things which do not allow a woman to become spiritually or materially independent. In 1883 Pardo Bazán wrote *La Tribuna,* a social novel about a young girl working in a cigar factory who fights for social reform, becomes a leader of the workers and ends up seduced, pregnant and abandoned by a rich young aristocrat. The myth of romantic love had made her believe that the social problems of Spain may be overcome with promises of love. *La dama joven,* published in 1885, deals with Concha, a girl of great artistic ability who prefers to marry a carpenter rather than risk a career that she fears will bring her dishonor because men might try to seduce her. More realistic than the girl in *La Tribuna,* she prefers the certain to the doubtful; her life might be full of poverty and sacrifice but at least it will be honorable. Matrimony is still the usual means of man's trickery. In *Morrina,* published in 1889, the author wonders if women are destined to fall. For them love is but an ephemeral escape from the disgrace that follows them from birth, from life with their parents and from their living conditions. They are extremely vulnerable, especially if they are young, beautiful and without an education. Esclavitud, the protagonist, who is an illegitimate child, says of herself: "You came to it [the world] against the will of Our Lord. . . . God looked down on you . . . you were born in the power of the evil one. . . . No matter how hard you try to be an angel, you will always live in mortal sin."[5] The novel, of course, is more complicated than this. Morrina, the illegitimate daughter of a priest, wants to overcome the stigma of her birth. She is a sad woman and really believes that any man who falls in love with her will save her. What actually happens is that her lover abandons her and she commits suicide. Once again, he is an aristocrat and she is a maid, illustrating the author's awareness of the

Spanish sense of class distinction. In *Una cristiana—la prueba*, published in 1890, she shows us several women who are the products of different types of education. The daughters of Barrientos represent the middle class, and the author is horrified at what is taught to these "legions of future wives and mothers" and the conditioning they receive from society:

> Dolls that laugh when their string is pulled... [and who] all walk like puppets.... [T]o look innocent, they put on stupid faces in the Zarzuela where all has a double meaning.... [T]hey go to Mass routinely but only to see a boyfriend or to make a girlfriend jealous of her new clothes.... Dolls who have been taught that it is honorable not to know too much and to marry the first husband they find and afterwards....[6]

There are two other alternatives: Carmen, the traditional Spanish woman, and Maud, the beautiful and cultured daughter of an Englishman. The latter is liberated, has her own profession, and perhaps follows the letter of the conventions but not the spirit. Salustio Portal, the male protagonist, prefers Carmen, the young wife of his uncle, who is an old and tyrannical husband. Carmen passes the test (*la prueba*) by practicing the strict doctrines of the Church. Fortunately her husband dies and she marries Portal. Why did he not choose Maud? The reason is that she is a Protestant, "of a faith which is abominable to the immense majority of Spaniards and which even we unbelieving rationalists do not find acceptable."[7] But *la prueba* has not completely solved the problem of the ideal woman, the "new" woman. In *Memorias de un solterón*, published in 1891, the author presents Feita, who, unlike her sisters, does not live only to catch a husband or a rich man to help her out. She, like her brother Froilan, wants to graduate and get her diploma, "in order to exercise a profession... whatever it might be... [and thereby to] earn a living... and fame... and live from my knowledge and work.... I don't want to depend on a man.... I will earn my own money and will laugh at them all."[8] This dynamic hardworking girl, without any prejudices, still has one obstacle: "Society is completely against the ideas that inspire your actions. The woman who wishes to become emancipated, as you do, will only find thorns in her path...."[9] The author realizes that "Feita was a 'new' woman, the dawn of a society different from that which *now* exists."

In 1889 Pardo Bazán denounced the situation of the Spanish woman in *La España de ayer y de hoy*, in which she discusses the illiteracy of millions of Spanish women and the difficulties they have in obtaining an education. The only alternatives open to them are marriage, a religious vocation, prostitution or abject poverty. She founded a library for women. In 1890 she published a series of articles, "The Modern Spanish Woman,"[10] in which she compares women from the various social classes: "Today there exists between the middle-class woman and the lower classes a deep abyss; the lower classes realize they must work to earn a living, the bourgeois thinks she may be supported entirely by her husband's work. Thus the bourgeois has a greater dependency and less originality and spontaneity."[11] The author believes that the key to the regeneration of womankind lies in her instruction, in her personality, within her own consciousness.[12] It is noteworthy that even the author, with stellar importance in Spanish letters, encounters great resistence from men who would not allow her to become a member of the Royal Spanish Academy of Language. Even such eminent writers as Juan Valera spoke of pregnancy and lactation as obstacles to her "literary" rights. With this, she wrote a letter to Gertrudiz Gómez de Avellaneda, who had previously been denied a similar position in the Academy for the same reasons: "First of all, illustrious friend, there is no more noble feeling than the conviction of one's own worth when it is based on true merit."[13] She did not give up her fight and finally entered the Academy and also held many government positions that until that time had never been held by women. Years later she stated:

> I am a radical feminist. I believe that every privilege a man has should also be for the woman. . . . It is in underdeveloped countries that the woman is considered a beast of burden and a sex object. Spanish men make a great pretense of always being preoccupied with the love of women and there can be no greater obstacle than this for the advancement of women. It perpetuates the battle between the sexes which has existed since primitive times. For the woman to advance here, it is first necessary that she have the desire to do so, and second, that she find the field ready and some help from the man. . . .[14]

Her work continued until 1911 and is enormous in volume. She died in 1921.

In this study I will present two of her novels, *Los pazos de Ulloa,*[15] published in 1886, and *La madre naturaleza,*[16] published in 1887. In these two works she analyzes the problems of adultery and of illegitimate children within the social and ecclesiastical framework of Spain in that period.

Los pazos de Ulloa shows us the conflicts between rural and urban life through the character of Don Pedro Moscoso, the heir to some property known as a *pazo*. This man, who belongs to the upper class, has a concubine, Sabel, who is the daughter of his overseer, Primitivo. The overseer is an opportunistic man and forces his daughter to obey Don Pedro. Meanwhile Don Julian, the chaplain, arrives, and when he finds out about Sabel, he advises Moscoso to look for a wife from his own social level. Moscoso goes to his uncle's house in the city where there are four eligible girls. He chooses Nucha, the least attractive, because she is a religious woman. After the marriage, he takes her to live with him at Ulloa. Shortly thereafter Nucha becomes pregnant and when a daughter is born instead of a son, her husband no longer bothers to keep up appearances and lives with Sabel in the same house. Nucha and the chaplain make plans for her to escape and return home to her parents. Moscoso surprises them, and accusing them of adultery, he dismisses the priest and humiliates his wife. She dies shortly thereafter and her daughter Manola remains with the servants. Moscoso has a son, Perucho, by Sabel and because he is a son, he is Don Pedro's favorite. Perucho is the only one who takes care of the little girl and a love relationship develops between the two.

La madre naturaleza presents Perucho and Manola as adolescents. Nucha's brother, Gabriel, a bachelor, goes to Ulloa to rescue his niece. He wants to marry her in order to remove her from the ambience in which she lives. His visit brings out Perucho's jealousy and precipitates the sexual act between Perucho and Manola, who loves him. Only when the two find out they are half brother and sister do they feel shame, guilt or terror. Perucho flees and the girl decides to become a nun. Julian, the chaplain, once again plays an important part in her decision, even though Gabriel still wishes to marry her and help her to forget what has happened.

Family

We can see from *Los pazos de Ulloa* that in any social class the daughters are the means by which the father may satisfy his own interests. On the lower level of the farmer, Primitivo forces Sabel to submit herself to Moscoso in order to have more control over him and the estate. On a higher level, Don Manuel Pardo de la Lage, the uncle, wants his daughters to marry in order to provide tradition and an inheritance for the family. We can also see that the daughters have no choice but to obey. Sabel is threatened with a gun and is beaten. Nucha's father uses the kind of fatherly influence that is no less authoritative and effective than physical force. It would do Nucha no good to resist, since her father will not allow his nephew to leave without a wife.

Another element is the absolute power of the "feudal lord" to have a wife *and* a concubine. The adultery greatly offends Nucha because she is puritanical and the act takes place in her house, but this situation is by no means as rare as it might seem. The double standard allows the men, especially if they are powerful, to have amorous adventures with women from lower classes.

A third element of interest is the situation of the illegitimate male versus the legitimate daughter in a family where there are no other male children. Nucha's husband only tolerates her pregnancy because he may gain an heir, a son to carry his name. Thus he says:

> It must be a little boy; if not, I'll wring the neck of whatever else it might be. I have already ordered Nucha not to bring me anything else but a son. I am capable of breaking her ribs if she disobeys. God would forgive me. In my family there has always been masculine succession, Moscosos raise Moscosos, it is already proverbial [p. 218].

Nor does he hide his preference for Perucho, Sabel's son. The villagers comment:

> And thus when the lady of the house died, everyone believed that the Marqués would marry Sabel . . . after all, she had given him a son and the Marqués had a terrible fondness for him. . . . [A]s for the legitimate daughter, the one he had with the lady of the house, he had no use. . . . We all knew that Sabel was pregnant again and was having an affair with Angel, a musician from Naya, a good-looking fellow and she swore and swore that the child (Perucho) belonged to the pauper. . . . There was no way of dissuading her—it was all, 'I'm getting married, I'm getting married and I'm leaving with my husband.' The Marqués, for fear of losing the child, had them remain servants in the house [p. 303].

It was common in this period, when a mother died in childbirth, for the child to be raised by one of the maids, an older sister, an aunt or a grandmother. Many times the maternal instincts of the women were satisfied in this manner and at the same time it created a permanent bond between the child and the substitute mother (this can also be seen in *La dama joven*). Nucha and her brother Gabriel have always been close. He was sent away to college, and when he learned of his sister's wedding he almost suffered a nervous breakdown. In *La madre naturaleza* this same brother will look for the sister he loved so much in her daughter Manola. Thus while incestuous marriages between cousins or paternal uncles and nieces were permitted and accepted by society, there was great scandal attached to the same situation between half-brother and half-sister. Indirectly the author is critical here of the rigidity of society and of those families that intermarry for personal gain.

The men of the family understand each other. The uncle says the following about his nephew, "you will find my nephew rather common . . . the country, when one is raised there and never leaves, makes one vile, poor and brutal" (p. 174), and yet, in spite of their differences, there exists a tacit agreement between the two as to their common interests. Likewise in *La madre naturaleza* there are great differences between Manola's father and her uncle Gabriel, Nucha's brother. We already know the former, while the latter is a civilized man, compassionate and free from any prejudices. Between them they understand that if one wants the daughter of the other, there she is; after all, they are all from the same family.

On the other hand, the author points out the enormous rivalry that exists between sisters when it is a question of a future husband. Rita, Nucha's sister, detests her because she blames Nucha for stealing her boyfriend. Even though Nucha tries to explain the situation to her father, he doesn't listen:

> When father told me of my cousin's intentions, I told him that I did not want to take my sister's boyfriend from her and then father kissed me many times on the cheeks like he used to do when I was a child and . . . I can still hear him . . . he responded thus: 'Rita is foolish . . . be quiet.' But in spite of what father says, Rita still likes our cousin [p. 272].

Their father does not care if the sisters hate each other as long as the "male" of the family is happy. This masculine bond is also present at the end of *La madre naturaleza* when Perucho says he is leaving Don Pedro's house and will never return, Don Pedro wallows in sorrow yet he never thinks of visiting Manola who desperately needs his help in those difficult times. It is not strange then that the women find in the father confessor the substitute father they long for, having no communication with their real father, they need to talk to a man who understands them. Both Nucha and Manola seek out the same chaplain, Don Julian, in moments of crisis. Of course, the other men do not like this and being jealous, they have little trust in these "confessors," who know their wives and daughters better than does any member of the family.

Social Class

Throughout the novel there is a great conflict between liberals and conservatives. The liberals blame the decadent situation on two items: feudalism and theocracy. In the rural areas, the villages and small towns, the lord of the manor (*pazo*) is still a feudal lord with all the attendant power of that "office." This lord psychologically needs the Church to back him up. Thus the chaplain, who attended to the spiritual needs of the lords, is a common figure in the period. Don Julian comes from rural stock, his mother being the head housekeeper for the Lage family, and thus he was raised very near the children—Nucha, Rita, Carmen, Manolita and Gabriel. Was he in love with Nucha or is this only speculation? The only thing we know for certain is that Don Julian was educated and protected by the family and that they paid the costs of his attendance at the seminary and got him a scholarship. Don Julian's loyalty is with the higher class and not with the poor people of which he is a part. He is very influential in the marriage between Don Pedro and Nucha, and when she arrives at the manor they renew their spiritual relationship. The alliance between the Church and the upper-class women is traditional. Don Julian detests Sabel and the woman with whom she associates—maids and ignorant farmers. Although he is unjustly accused of adultery by Don Pedro and is therefore sent by his superiors to work with the poor, when he returns he is still loyal to the memory of Nucha, who represents to him the good side of the upper class:

> [she was] the holy one, the victim, the little virgin, always innocent and celestial. There she was, alone, abandoned, subdued, abused, slandered, with wrists bruised by a brutal hand and her face blanched by sickness, terror and pain . . . [p. 283].

The middle class is represented by the businessmen and they take the side of the poor in their political struggles. Maximo, the doctor, refers to the farmwife as a "human cow" because she must nourish the lord of the manor's child while hers goes hungry (p. 228). Similarly, the author shows with graphic detail that moment of Spanish history in which a continuous struggle is taking place between the liberal and conservative factions.

The lower farmer class is perfectly captured in Primitivo and his daughter Sabel. Since the feudal lord and the servant girl are having an affair, the caretaker (Primitivo) takes advantage of his master's lack of care and his disorganization, lasciviousness and impulsiveness in order to rob him and to dominate the other farmers. Gallo, the future husband of Sabel, is not much different. Both of these men are types produced by the rural milieu. Even Perucho—although we never see him as an adult—has the farmer's astuteness and will to survive and is thus blessed by both classes. Sabel, unfortunately, has the whole system against her, but she nevertheless is strong and manages to have her own way and later leaves with a man who pleases her. Both Don Pedro and Don Julian treat her with disrespect, especially Don Julian, who refers to her as "a thing, a vile little girl, a servant, a dishwasher, shameless" (p. 238).

Another aspect of the class situation is the obligation of the upper class to follow the rules of their class. Don Pedro must inevitably marry a girl from his own station in life. Sabel likewise marries Gallo. The only ones to alter this pre-established order are Manola and Perucho, who although she is a lady and he is a farmer, still think of marriage. With them, the situation at the manor has changed; it is in such decadence that the youths are uncontrolled, as if no one cared what might happen. It is the uncle, Nucha's brother, who will bring civilization to the manor when he comes to take care of the orphaned child. He views Don Pedro as representative of the deterioration and degenerate state of the feudal lord:

> I feel sorry for you, you shadow of a man! You could not even raise up the pitchfork to thrash the wheat this morning. Don't raise your fist at me, I won't pay any attention and besides, I won't argue with you since we are father- and son-in-law, really more like father and son as they say . . . and since you no longer care for my future bride as you ought, I am going to look out for her, do you understand? And by my oath as Gabriel Pardo de la Lage, I swear she will never again wander in the hills nor will you know what has become of her [p. 378].

Sexuality

There is a dichotomy between body and soul that dominates the work and has become mixed in with the customs and the habits of the people. Don Pedro is the best example of this kind of moral schizophrenia. He is strong, a magnificent example of a race well suited for war and life in the hills in feudal times, and one who was being consumed in the miserable lifelessness of the village where nothing is produced, taught, learned, nor anything happens. He must use his masculine power to dominate Sabel: "Each day I have to hurt her as I would a rabbit" (p. 192). Sabel, a robust and healthy farmgirl, is the feminine counterpart of Don Pedro; it is a pity she does not love him. Wanting to marry he thus goes to the city, since there are no girls of his standing in the village. When he arrives at his uncle's house, he is sexually attracted to Rita, the only one of his cousins who in his opinion "shows promise of being a fertile mother and an inexhaustible suckler" (p. 200). But he also wants a girl who is "as clean as a mirror" (p. 205). It is not a question of Rita's being impure, but her voluptuousness and frankness disturb him. He observes: "It is not the same to have a good time with a girl and to take her for a wife." Of the other cousins, one already has a boyfriend and one is about to enter a convent, and thus only Nucha, the saint, is left. Her father and the priest both recommend her since she is the least attractive to him; thus out of caprice he marries her. Their marriage begins with her fear of her husband and of sex when he acts out of duty and the obligation to keep his honor clean and to maintain his race. "Don Pedro understood conjugal love in the Spanish Calderonean style, indulgence on the part of the man, total abstinence for the wife" (p. 205). Nucha's sexuality is determined by the image others have of her as regards marriage:

> They call me ugly and cross-eyed and assured me I would never find a husband. . . . I laughed at them: Why did I need to get married? I could live with father and Gabriel forever. If they died, I could go to a convent: to the Carmelite one, where Aunt Dolores is; I like it there . . . [p. 272].

Since Nucha has thought of herself from childhood as ugly, she sublimates her sexual instincts by being a mother to her brother and later by taking care of her father. The wedding between Nucha and Don Pedro is sad, almost like a funeral. Even more terrible is the wedding night when she passes through 'the little death': "I trembled like the leaves on a tree and a shiver constantly set my nerves on end, not out of anything tangible but from a certain undefinable and holy terror" (p. 210). She had resisted the marriage but had finally given in to her father's insistence, promising "to be good, love him, obey him, take care of my children" (p. 272). But is it enough to promise this? Both Nucha and Don Pedro make a mistake in believing that people can be forced to love those displeasing to them. He begins to criticize the "ladies from the city" who are prudish and weak, and compares them to the frank and robust farmgirls. Little by little he begins to appreciate their lack of communication, takes part in the local orgies, and goes hunting for the pure pleasure of killing. When a baby girl is born instead of the hoped-for boy, he abandons Nucha completely. She then takes refuge in her motherhood with an hysterical obsession. The author describes her this way:

> She hardly left her room, she lived there enslaved by her child, tied to her day and night. At the table, while she ate very little and with even less desire, she kept silent and at times Julian, who never took his eyes off of her, could see her move her lips, a frequent occurrence among those possessed by an idea which they utter without a sound. Don Pedro, intractable, did not even bother to open the conversation. He chewed and swallowed and had his eyes on his plate or on the ceiling beams, never on those at the table [p. 269].

At first Nucha tries to have the chaplain throw Sabel out, but it is impossible. When she finds out later that Perucho is her husband's son, she is horrified and has an attack of nerves. She begins to imagine all kinds of crimes that will happen to her and her daughter. Father Julian also becomes nervous and believes that Sabel and Maria, the local witch, are going to poison Nucha and the infant. More pathetic still is the thought of death that occurs to Nucha after Don Pedro has sent Julian away and has refused to allow her to go back to her parents. She repeats: "My interests are not important. . . . [P]atience, it is all a matter of patience, of suffering, of allowing oneself to die. . ." (p. 273). After the horrible accusation of adultery, she realizes that patience is of no value. Her subconscious decision, "my will first," takes the form of her own destruction—suicide—which is masked by the symptoms of a nervous breakdown.

Sabel, too, is a victim. She has been forced to become Don Pedro's mistress. She is despised by the upper classes. Nevertheless, in the beginning she believes Julian will help her marry Gallo. Julian throws her out, believing she wishes to seduce him, and he later treats her as a woman bewitched. Sabel now knows that she may only count on help from the women of her own social level, one of whom is Maria, who reads fortune cards and gives advice. Her escape with Gallo is made possible when Don Pedro loses interest in her. It is interesting to note that toward the end of *La madre naturaleza* Sabel is once again presented to us. She is now an old woman; her beauty disappeared at 30; her marriage to Gallo brought "a submission in the flesh that was near brutality and an all-encompassing feeling for homely beings making this the most 'happy' of all marriages" (p. 333).

The first novel shows us the treachery men do to themselves when they try to obey or comply with man-made rules, be they taught or understood. The thesis of *La madre naturaleza* is that if two beings, free and in love, follow nature's course, they too will pay the price society imposes. Here the children pay for the guilt of their parents. Manola and Perucho are like Adam and Eve in the Garden of Eden before original sin. Their sexuality is based on kindness, friendship, love and absolute confidence in each other. The sin lies in ignorance, which is followed by curiosity, and this leads to the sexual act. When the two find out later that they are half brother and sister, the author comments:

> Here two different essences have become morally entwined; the lives of two people in the flower of life have been ruined. Each produce horror in the other; both believe themselves to be guilty of so frightful a crime . . . and both of them, as I see it, will continue to love each other for a long time yet. Are they really bad? Well, they did not know and so. . . . No, according to natural law . . . this is not nor never has been a crime. If in early times, from a single couple the entire human race was formed, how in the devil was it done if not with 'that'? [p. 402].

At first the two react with incredulity. After Perucho is convinced, the first thing he asks for is that no one say anything to Manola. She, while going through an attack of nerves, is afraid for him. Her uncle Gabriel insists that Julian make known that he is there to marry her:

> Make her understand that she has lost nothing; she is not defamed nor damned and her uncle, a completely decent person, asks to marry her with all his heart and is ready to be for her all that luck has denied her until today: father, mother, brother, protector, beloved husband . . . with each of these different aspects of love I know how to love her [p. 406].

But if we understand Manola, we know that because of the way she has been raised, these concepts of honor have no meaning for her, since her love for Perucho is her only motivation. Now that he has left she can only make her uncle promise that he will go look for him and keep him from doing something rash. The uncle, always a gentleman, promises to do it. Until the very end Gabriel mistrusts Julian because he is sure that Julian will try to convince Manola to enter a convent where the "Grace of God" will correct and redeem her from the error caused by the instincts of human nature. Julian indeed repeats: "How I wish that the mother too had entered a convent! God is calling the daughter. . . . Let her go! Let her go! Most Holy Virgin, protect her, receive her, sustain her, retire her from the world" (p. 409). In this final struggle between the priest and Gabriel, Manola decides to become a nun and calmly announces it. The last words of Gabriel show forcefully who is the winner in this dilemna: "Priest of Ulloa, neither you nor I. . . . [Y]ou were deceived and I was foolish. He who has won is . . . the king. . . . No! The tyrant of this world!" (p. 410) If we read between the lines we find that he is speaking of love, and love in two youths such as these is more than instinct or spirituality; it is a fusion, a unity of body and soul, the ultimate union of two sexes which emanate from the same vital beginning.

Message

In the prologue to *Viaje de novios*, published in 1881, Pardo Bazán states: "From the struggle came some fertile ideas and I believe the most important of these is that the novel is no longer merely for entertainment, a way of wasting several hours, and has become a social, psychological, historical study—at least, a *study*."[17] Given this attitude, we can separate the two novels onto various levels and see them on each level as a first and second part of the same saga.

On the social level, *Los pazos de Ulloa* shows clearly the decadence of the upper classes in the rural areas. This decadence is due to laziness, lust and ignorance and has two basic sources: social pressure to maintain a privileged class and religious pressure to perpetuate the idea of a *pure* woman for a wife. The following passage by Thomas Wilson Page which describes the woman's situation in the literature of the Southern United States also describes the perfect Spanish lady:

> What she was only her husband divined, and even he stood before her in dumb, half-amazed admiration, as he might before the inscrutable vision of a superior being. What she really was was known only to God. Her life was one long act of devotion to her husband, devotion to her children, devotion to her servants, to the poor, to humanity. Nothing happened within the range of her knowledge that her sympathy did not reach and her charity and wisdom did not ameliorate.[18]

Nevertheless, for the Spaniard this is not sufficient, since "religiosity" on the woman's part is necessary for her *to be good.* Within the Catholic Ethic it is easy to fulfill all these prerequisites, especially if one puts emphasis on "obedience and resignation," both of which are very typical of the firmly believing Spanish woman. Another similarity with the American South is the sexual power of the master over his servants (slaves in the United States) as favored by the rural economy. Two differences are that there are no slaves in Spain and that we are not speaking of different races. But in actual practice the servant is bound by family pressure, which does not allow her any freedom unless the master permits or does not interfere in her actions. Primitivo is the most opportunistic of the "honorable" fathers, but the author also shows us other fathers who through diverse methods force their daughters to act according to their own interests.

The psychological aspects of the novel are important. Don Pedro is not a beast, in the strict naturalist sense of the word; he is a product of his world and if he is brutal and violent, he can also be kind and open. What destroys him as a human being is his incapacity to accept the fact that a wife is not something one buys at a fair and then ignores. It would be very difficult to change his opinion that women must have many children and must be strong. There is another side to the story which the author also shows us. Nucha is a delicate and vulnerable woman. Not only is she scandalized by what is going on between Pedro and Sabel, but she also becomes ill. Her only outlets are her child and Father Julian, both of whom give her company and meaning in her marriage. When she decides to return home, Don Pedro could have permitted it, but the possessive, jealous and violent temper of the "offended husband, Calderonean style" will not permit it:

> Nor will Julian ever forget the day such unexpected events occurred. It was the most dramatic of his life, one in which he could never have imagined the events that transpired: to be accused by a husband of having an affair with his wife; by a husband who complained of mortal affronts, who threatened him, who ignominiously threw him out of the house forever; and to see the unhappy wife, she who was truly offended, powerless to deny the ridiculous and horrible slander [p. 280].

After showing the conflicts within the first generation, the author passes to the second: Manola and Perucho are neither degenerate beings nor are they socially destroyed. The author perhaps has in mind a symbolic plane on which they represent an historical moment. Perucho, the bastard son of an aristocrat and a farmgirl, is a combination of the education of the city and the strength of the countryside. Likewise, Manola is not a weak and nervous girl from the city, like her mother, but is more like the farmgirls—strong and without repressed sexual desires. In the moment of sexual consummation, it is Perucho who is a bit shy:

> Two or three times the boy turned back, his conscience bothering him, like some unseen warning. It was not for nothing that he was a few years older than his companion and in some ways more experienced. She, on the other hand, approached him confidently and loving [p. 368].

In order to understand the role of Father Julian in both novels, we must look to *La cuestión palpitante:*

> In matters of religion and society, the naturalists proceed as did their brothers the positivists in regards to metaphysical problems—they leave them alone, waiting for science to solve them, if it is possible. Abstention is one thousand times more dangerous than the socialist and heretical propaganda of the novelists that went before. . . . In regard to passion, especially amorous passion, beyond the barriers of

> duty, far from glorifying it, the realists have sought to awaken humanity by showing its risks and depravities, making it less attractive. From Madame Bovary to Pot Bouillé the movement has repeated with ever increasing zeal that only in duty may one find tranquility and happiness.[19]

The author does not back away from the religious question of matrimony, a matter of much importance in Spain. For her it is impossible to separate the social domain from that of religion, family customs and the value judgement system for choosing a mate. If, however, we look at Father Julian, we can see a young idealist who was raised in a city atmosphere surrounded by fanatics and guarded girls. He is powerless to escape his strict role of chaplain, servant to the "great house." He is not a priest interested only in the souls of the poor, the ignorant, the sinner. He feels comfortable only beside devoted women and innocent children. Julian lacks compassion and hates Sabel and the rest of the farm girls because he is protecting Nucha. After being thrown out of the house, his superior sends him to work among the shepherds, far away from upper-class society. When he returns to Ulloa he seems to have lost all reason, acts strangely, communicates with no one, and is a man obsessed. It is true that he has suffered, but he has not learned his lesson of love and he condemns the two youths. He can see only the sin and is incapable of helping Manola return to society. Manola, the free and primitive girl, is not the oppressed and civilized Nucha, but Julian believes he must fulfill his duty. When Gabriel calls him a deceived and foolish man, he is really pointing out the basic problem of this type of priest. Times are changing, even the social classes are being renovated, but the priest can see nothing but sin and penance.

For the author, the children's love is not sin but simply the natural result of two human beings' loving each other, needing each other, capable of social change but victims of an unfortunate past.

CONCHA ESPINA

Born in Santander, Spain in 1879, Concha Espina was educated by nuns. When her father went bankrupt, the city of Luzmela became the permanent residence of the family. At a very young age she married Ramón de la Serna and almost immediately they went to Chile to work out the details of an inheritance. The trip was of little success; they did not obtain the inheritance, and they suffered through an earthquake. Even with two young children she still found time to collaborate on a small journal, *El Porteño*, and later won a prize for her short story "La riada." They returned to Spain and in 1908 she was separated from her husband and went with her three children to Madrid to seek a career in letters.[1] In 1909 she published *La niña de Luzmela*, in 1910 *Despertar para morir*, in 1912 *Agua de nieve*, in 1914 *La esfinge maragata*, and in 1920 *El metal de los muertos*. These are her most famous novels. She published other items and became quite well known.[2] In 1927 she was nominated for the Nobel Prize but did not win.[3] She traveled to Germany and to the United States,[4] but remained in Spain during the Civil War; in 1938 she published *Esclavitud y libertad*,[5] her diary of the war. She died in 1955.

La esfinge maragata[6] is the result of a visit by the author to her sister in the province of León, on the plateau of Astorga. There were only 36 villages of the Maragatos people left early in this century and this novel captures the customs of these primitive Celtic people. The novel begins with Mariflor and her old grandmother as they leave the city of La Coruña and travel to the village of the grandmother, for Mariflor's mother has just passed away. Her father is a Maragato and has emigrated to America to look for his brother Isidoro and to try and make enough money to sustain the family. On the trip by train, Mariflor meets Rogelio Terán who is on his way to a nearby village, and they fall in love. She is not yet willing to accept the marriage her family has arranged between her and her cousin—a person whom she has never met. When she arrives in her grandmother's hometown, she cannot adapt to the life style and cannot comprehend the terrible poverty of the family. They all are counting on her marriage to Antonio (her cousin) who is rich and who will pay the mortgage on the land. She, however, is taken aback by the proposal. Antonio is willing to marry her even though she has no dowry. Meanwhile, she renews her acquaintanceship with Rogelio Terán when he comes to visit the village priest, Don Miguel. Rogelio does not wish to marry her and leaves without a word. The family pressures become even stronger while she waits for Rogelio. In a letter to the priest from Rogelio she learns of his situation. Disillusioned by love, she decides to "comply" with her "duty" and accepts an immediate marriage with Antonio.

Family

It is interesting to note that Mariflor's father married outside the clan in the port city of La Coruña. Thus, Mariflor has received an education very different from other Maragato children. Her father himself does not return to the village with her but travels to America. According to the priest Don Julian, the grandmother has always had a "blind passion" for her son Isidoro, the husband of Ramona, to whom she gave the family's money. Isidoro and Mariflor's father do not make their fortune in America and live in poverty; thus there is no hope for the family. Mariflor's Aunt Ramona and her cousins all assume that she will take care of them because that is the way things are done in the extended family group of the Maragatos. Among her cousins she comes to feel some affection for Marianela, who dies of tuberculosis, and for Olalla, who is her confidante and who wants to enter a convent but has no money for the conventual dowry. The other children in her family—like the others in the village—will leave for other cities as soon as they are able, in an attempt to find work. Mariflor feels nothing for her Aunt Ramona who is a harsh woman, dried up by the excessive work of the fields. As she says:

> Could we wander through the world with our household and our children? Who would work the fields? The young girl dared not answer because in her heart and on her lips she was struggling with rebellion: right there, before her

> eyes, oxen and women sighed with resignation, confounded by the cruel land [p. 274].

Her family is composed of single women with young children and old people who cannot move. The power of her absent father is curious, since his influence has more weight for Mariflor than does that of her relatives. Her father, in a letter, advises her to marry Antonio as soon as possible: "The reward of God will make you happy." She, on the other hand, feels like a stranger:

> I am not an egotist. I would like to have a lot of money in order to give it openly to my relatives, strangers, to all those who suffer, to all those who live in abject poverty. . . . But to marry that man simply because he is rich . . . a man I don't know, whom I don't love . . . [p. 297].

On the other hand, if one examines the family of Rogelio, one realizes that he is the victim of another set of circumstances. His father abandoned his mother when he was young and he has thus lived obsessed with being a "victim of love and poverty." He, therefore, is not ready to begin another life like that out of "love." It is these "humble realities of life" that frighten him and cause him to leave Mariflor and her troubles.

Social Class

We must distinguish between the social values held by Mariflor and those of the Maragatos. The dress of the Maragatos that she wears on the train is only a costume her father had had made for her portrait. She is a young girl who has had a bit of comfort and luxury in her life. She is not lazy, she has even learned to read and write. She disdains some types of work and is slightly influenced by romantic novels. When Terán asks her about her intended's interests, she responds: "A businessman is not my ideal" (p. 245). It is the priest Julian who warns, "You dream too much." And she responds: "Is not dreaming living through the spirit?" (p. 297). It is very difficult for her to accept women, like her Aunt Ramona, who at 40 are all used up: "If she was once pretty, she did not retain any evidence of it; her breasts were fallen, her features weathered, she was dry and harsh in appearance, tall and quiet. Ramona inspired fear" (p. 262). Mariflor discovers from her cousins that for a Maragato, to survive is all-important. Her cousin, speaking of a couple, says "How are they to love each other, foolish one, since they own nothing" (p. 287). She comes to feel guilty for thinking love justifies marriage when all those around her are hungry. Julian, the priest, who is also a Maragato, is the only one to understand her conflicts and finds a solution which would not call for her self-sacrifice: "We'll declare your grandmother to be destitute, we'll send Pedro out to work, Olalla and Ramona can work in the fields to earn a living for the old lady and the children, and we'll get a dowry for Marianela so she can become a nun" (p. 300).

Among these farmers who have no notion of social class, it is the possession of land that determines the differences between them—that is, whether they work their own or another's land. In this case, Mariflor's family has suffered a set-back and they are now living on a lower-class level. They are losing their lands to the loan sharks whose interest rates are eating them alive. Curiously, one of these loan sharks is an uncle, but since all the Maragatos are related, this does not mean much. Antonio has, besides his land, a business in town, and all consider him to be rich and a good marital catch. He, out of vanity, wants to marry a well-cared-for and educated girl like Mariflor, and insists that the wedding take place even though he sees that she, unlike the other girls, has no interest in him.

Sexuality

There are two types of women contrasted by our author: one is romantic, full of poetic emotion; the other lives in the harsh realities of life, for whom cruelty makes even the existence of God doubtful. Mariflor, when she meets Terán on the train, hears only what she wants to hear. He speaks of a book, *El señor de Bembibre,* in which the woman dies for love's sake. Afterwards, she sees her cousin who is dying of hunger and tuberculosis and the contrast between the "Rose" novel and this life of misery makes her hang on tighter to her "escape": Terán. Even if she were to marry a rich man he would treat her as all the other girls are treated. Julian, the priest, says:

> They think they are a caste apart and are so set in their ways that they will not adopt anything from outside. They make excellent fathers, citizens, workers; they are thrifty,

> loyal and peaceful. If they don't know how to smile or compliment their wives, at least they don't know how to cheat on them nor pervert them; they treat them neither well nor badly, they hardly deal with them at all. They take them to create a family and support them, blindly complying with inalterable laws, and forcing themselves brusquely upon the passive condition of the woman; not with hatred or perversity, but with the fateful power of the strong (p. 312).

The author does not want to indicate that the Maragato women are insensitive. Motherhood is one of the principal outlets for their warmth and humanity, expecially since their own husbands are beyond the expression of these feelings. The girls in the family are in charge of the pigeons; when a feather sticks to the apron of Olalla, the author asks: "Is there no other mark of a caress on the breasts of womankind . . . no other?" (p. 259). Julian is much more of a realist, and in discussion with Rogelio he notes that in a marriage without love the woman—although in these cases she is a victim—at least can conform and enjoy her motherhood. He also observes that in the nonconformity of Mariflor there is sadness, because if she does not marry Antonio, she is destined to the life of a spinster, without even the consolation of a son: "Of the Holy Flame, of the Divine Breath, we have an unconscious witness in the extreme love of mothers" (p. 311).

Another aspect of the novel is the sexuality associated with the imagination. Mariflor is a romantic girl and has so much influence on her cousin Marianela that Marianela falls secretly in love with Terán, the poet, even to the point of becoming ill. Her illness is diagnosed by the local witch as "the work of the devil." Her mother would rather believe in this, since otherwise she would lose her faith in God: "I do not desire this, God is just and would not allow some to enjoy life while others suffer all the pestilence of life" (p. 339). Marianela escapes in her delirium into a world of beauty: "Look at that flame shot out by that star. Let's see if the sky lights up! Now all is covered with snow" (p. 361). Even death is escape for the Maragatos and they call those who die "the blessed ones."

The differences that exist between the Maragato men and those of the outside world can be clearly seen in the relationship between Antonio and Rogelio Terán. Antonio swears "on the honor of his blood" that no one will trick the bride and affirms: "I am not begging for a bride—I put conditions on the protection that I am asked to give" (p. 327). Rogelio, however, is neither frank nor decided. He weighs the good and bad side of a marriage to Mariflor, but does not dare speak to her directly and must have Julian, the priest, speak for him. Mariflor does not like Antonio and feels that with such a marriage she is selling herself. She hopes for a "miracle," she suspends her will in the hope that God will manifest himself and stop the wedding—perhaps she expects a letter from her father in America saying he has made a fortune. But Julian knows very well that she cannot expect a miracle, she herself must decide. What is ironic is that no one in the village can understand why she would refuse such a catch as Antonio and they attribute her hesitation to a magic spell of the witch.

The witch, as a foil for God, lends meaning to the work through several of the characters. While Ramona and Marianela go to the witch, Mariflor never loses her faith in God. When she learns that Rogelio has through cowardice abandoned her, she takes a stoic attitude. She cannot value sacrifice which has not been freely chosen. She does accept the fact that she is a "slave," since her destiny is well evident and her wedding is the culmination of a life without love. We are not dealing with a choice between love and duty, ego or virtue, but with the simple fatality of not being able to change one's direction in life.

Message

There is a constant image in the novel which allows us to draw some conclusions: the region is like the frozen steppes and the women that live there have frozen emotions. The men may escape but the women must remain.[7] The land and their children tie them down in voluntary slavery—fate and responsibility have marked their lives. In Mariflor we have a woman whose own mother "lived free, happy and pampered." She for a long time, believes that she has a right to love and be loved and to choose her own husband. Her romantic dreams turn Rogelio into a hero, her savior, her ideal poet. Julian, who knows them all well, does not want to influence her one way or another, but he is convinced that Rogelio will not marry her and that Antonio will not make her happy because he will not give her what she needs. He feels that since she is between two evils, she should take the least—for the sake of the majority of the household.

The author places much emphasis on the transformation that changes the mari-flor (butterfly and flower) into a Maragato sphinx. The cold image of the grandmother who seems lifeless is an example of those women who live resigned to dream only when they sleep. In order to dream, it is necessary to live, and to live, it is necessary to eat. Thus, a succession of miseries occurs in which there are no miracles. Julian feels that if there were a miracle, it should happen not only for the girl but for all of those beings in misery. The only miracle within her reach is motherhood. A typical example is the grandmother who ruins the entire family in order to protect the son who is her "great love." When the parents grow old, the children can at least brighten their lives with a "smile on the hard face of the steppes" (p. 363). But perhaps this is a projection of the Catholic attitudes of the author. Her vision of the farmers as beasts of burden whose children leave home at age 14 is harsh and cruel, but very true-to-life for the Maragatos.

The author also wants to make clear the distinction between sacrifice and duty. Mariflor does not want to sacrifice herself for the family because she does not believe her sacrifice would be of value if she made it out of force or necessity. For her, the only sacrifice of value is one made for love. Unfortunately, Rogelio does not wish to sacrifice himself for her, nor does he ask her to sacrifice herself for him. There is a great lack of communication between the two. With Antonio there is also no sacrifice. Following a letter of Rogelio which shatters her hopes and illusions she marries Antonio. It is as if she were saying, "I surrender."

CARMEN LAFORET

Carmen Laforet was born in 1921.[1] She studied letters and law first in Barcelona and then in Madrid.[2] In 1944 she published *Nada*, which won the "Premio Nadal" and which made her famous.[3] *Nada* is considered a very inportant novel in Spain and has been translated into several languages.[4] Other novels of Carmen Laforet are: *La isla y los demonios* (1952),[5] *La llamada* (1954),[6] *La mujer nueva* (1956),[7] and *La insolación* (1963).[8]

Andrea, a young girl who was educated with her cousin Isabel, is the protagonist of *Nada.*[9] She goes to Barcelona to begin her studies at the university, living meanwhile at her maternal grandmother's house. Also living there are her uncle Román, who is single, her uncle Juan, who is married to Gloria, and Angustias, her unmarried aunt. Antonia is their maid and lives there with her dog. The atmosphere in the house weighs heavily on Andrea. She meets and makes friends with Ena at the university and later there is an amorous adventure between Ena and Román. Andrea searches among her friends at the university for the understanding she lacks at home. The novel ends with the suicide of Román, and Andrea goes to Madrid under the protection of Ena's family.

Family

Andrea's family has lived on Aribau street since the grandparents moved there as newlyweds. Since that time, even though the house has passed through several changes in doormen and owners, the first floor has remained as "an immutable institution" (p. 32). The grandmother outlived her husband. The girls have married the first men they met and have all moved away except the eldest, Angustias. She has not married and is having a clandestine affair with Jerónimo, an office manager, who was her first love but who is already married. The daughters accuse their mother of having preferred the boys and at Román's funeral they say: "Mother, you owe God much for that soul you have sent to hell. There you have a man, the one you pampered." And she responds: "Children, I have loved all of you . . . some were more unfortunate than others and needed me more" (p. 250). Andrea never mentions her father and seems to live only in the present. The only thing we know about her father is that when he died he left a modest pension which Andrea used for her personal expenses.

The family relationships are morbid. Juan, a poor painter, and his young and beautiful wife Gloria have one child. An undefined homosexual relationship between Juan and Román fills the atmosphere of the house with tension and hysteria. Román, morever, sadistically tortures Gloria. This is the result of his having seduced her some time in the past and of having then laughed at her. Angustias is also a victim of her brother, who spies on her and insults her. Angustias is the one who takes charge of Andrea because she is a daughter of her sister. Since Angustias is also a domineering woman, Andrea withdraws from what she considers her "vigilance" and is pleased when Augustias enters a convent. Another morbid figure, almost one of the family, is the cook Antonia. She is Román's woman: she adores him and he treats the dog Trueno as if it were their child. The inhabitants of the house are manipulated in their most intimate emotions by Román. In the beginning, he tries to seduce Andrea but she refuses and this causes him to act sadistically toward the rest of the family. Andrea feels like a spectator in the family, something of which she feels ashamed and comments on it to her friend Ena. She feels compassion and sympathy for her grandmother because she is the only one who tries to help her, but says she prefers the memories of her grandmother that she had as a child. Andrea does not speak of Juan. Only Gloria seeks her out in conversation; Andrea listens to her confidences but never responds. When Andrea abandons the house, she does so without saying good-bye to her grandmother:

> I did not dare to enter grandmother's room. I did not want to wake her. I went downstairs slowly. I was filled with emotion. I remembered the terrible hope, the desire for life which I had when I first went up there. I was leaving now finding *nothing* which I had so confidently hoped for: the

> fullness of life, happiness, compassion, love. I was taking nothing with me from the house on Aribau street. At least that is what I thought at the time [p. 260].

Ena's family, however, is ideal of Andrea. The mother was the only girl among several boys and her millionaire father catered to her every whim; she—after a whirlwind affair with Román—has married a good and gentle man. They have several beautiful, well-behaved children, but Ena is her favorite. When she discovers the affair between Ena and Román she tries to save her child at all cost from the "monster" and seeks out Andrea. Ena also feels very attached to her mother, but she is at an age when she wants to experiment and does not hesitate to avoid those she loves in order to accomplish her goals. Ena, however, does not feel at ease with her other relatives. She confides to Andrea:

> I can't help it. All of my life I have been running from my gentle and respectable relatives. . . . Simple yet intelligent, in their own class—well, that is what frustrates me. . . . I like those crazy people for whom life is not monotonous, even if they are disgraceful people and off in the clouds like you. . . . People who, according to my family, are undesirables [p. 150].

Social Class

The novel presents the great contrast that exists between the rich bourgeoisie (Ena) and upper-class provincial people who have descended to a lower status in the great city. Ena and Andrea both desire that which they do not have and in a certain sense they both feel deeply the effects of having been born on a specific socio-economic level. The family of Andrea came to the city from the provinces because of "something related to the loss of a fortune" (p. 31). Nevertheless their social prejudices remain. The proof of this is that the grandfather will not allow Angustias to marry Jerónimo, her first boyfriend, because he is the son of a shopkeeper. Ironically, after Jerónimo goes to America and returns rich, he hires the daughter of the very man who had held such disregard for him. The grandparents, even though they no longer have money, educate their children with aristocratic airs. Juan thinks of himself as a great painter and Román was an acceptable violinist when he was younger, but is now a smuggler. Angustias is the only one who supports the family with her work and with the help of her ex-boyfriend Jerónimo. She also tries to save money for her conventual dowry, where she hopes to redeem herself from her sense of guilt and adultery. Gloria, on the other hand, belongs to the city. Juan met her during the war and when she got pregnant, he married her. Both brothers treat her as an inferior person and even try to prevent her from visiting her family. Gloria confides to Andrea: "What do you think of that, not even allowing me to see my own sister? A sister who has been like a mother to me. . . . All because I have humble beginnings and not as much money" (p. 122). Gloria concludes that it would have been better to have married a worker who "at least eats well" and who lives better than they do. Gloria "escapes" from time to time and plays cards at her sister's house. When she wins, she pretends that the money is from selling Juan's paintings. Once again, the author shows the great hypocrisy of those social classes that cover and even excuse their own weaknesses. The flirtation between Ena and Román is also indicative of the fascination she still feels for that perverted and decadent type of man, a man who has aristocratic airs, but traffics in contraband.

Andrea also suffers because of her limited resources and to the appearances which she must maintain. When she sees some beggars she thinks that these people no longer try to hide their poverty: "Oh, you wretched people. You who fill your bellies at the Social Service lines, you who never have an empty stomach." She also suffers when she comes in contact with the bourgeoisie to which her school companions belong, because her shoes are worn and she cannot dress as well as the other girls. Andrea receives a monthly pension, which she also must use for eating expenses. The grandmother insists that Juan not charge her for her room. Nevertheless, her pride causes her to sacrifice some meals in order to give some flowers to Ena as a gift for her invitations to her house. She does not believe, as does Gloria, that "the workers live better than the masters, Andrea, they wear sandals but they eat well and earn a good living. If only Juan had the work of a factory worker!" (p. 123). Andrea can better identify with the children of the lower middle class who, like Gerardo exclaim: "Barcelona, so haughty and rich and yet how hard life is there" (p. 133). Nevertheless, Andrea feels a friendship for Ena that goes beyond class and money. Neither does she feel out of place with the bohemian students who, even though she is a woman, accept her because she "uses no make-up." Andrea realizes her own human dignity and is realistic enough to know that these same boys—like her boyfriend Pons—even though they are critical of the bourgeois women, sooner or later will marry one from their own socioeconomic group. She reflects in a very traditional Spanish way on the various levels and roles of man in society:

> It seemed to me that if one has to always follow the very same enclosed pathway of our personality it is worth nothing. Some are born to live, others to work, others to observe life. Mine is the small and worthless role of spectator. There is no way out. Liberation is impossible. The only reality in those moments was a tremendous anguish [p. 201].

Sexuality

Andrea, who was educated in the provinces by nuns, arrives in Barcelona relatively innocent; her greatest sin had been to smoke a cigarette, which caused a great scandal. In Barcelona her tormented family presents an inferno of passions. The sexuality of Angustias is rather twisted; Román, who reads all of her letters, daily calls her a masochist—but the truth is that she has broken the sexual taboo of having sexual relations without being married and is therefore tormented by her guilt. Jerónimo's wife is in an insane asylum and we do not know whether or not Jerónimo and Angustias have put her there by force. Angustias has never been religious nor has she ever visited a church. When she puts some money aside to enter a convent, Jerónimo follows her everywhere trying to make her change her mind. According to Gloria, Angustias is filled with hate. According to Román, she is overly proud and wants to play the martyr. Andrea senses a vague hypocrisy on the part of the woman. Angustias' last good-bye to Andrea is significant:

> Life will thrash you, it will mash you, it will flatten you, and then you will remember me. Oh how I wish I had killed you when you were young so that you would not grow up like this.... Don't look at me so surprised. I know that you have not yet done anything bad. But you will when I leave.... You will, you will, you will! You cannot dominate

> your body nor your soul. Not you . . . not you . . . you cannot dominate them . . . [p. 100].

In reality, this is a monologue. Angustias is talking to herself and here is the key to her intimate hell: her body has won. She has given up. Now, through great effort, she will make her soul triumph. Jerónimo suffers and it seems that he has always loved her, ever since he was her first boyfriend, but neither of them can see an alternative. Divorce and civil marriage are words which do not exist for them. Heaven or hell, body or soul—the dichotomy of Angustias is projected into Andrea and she feels like a condemned woman.

Gloria also suffers from a slightly twisted sexuality. Since she gave into Juan after only two days, he has no confidence in her and towards the end of the novel he follows and beats her cruely. During the war Juan asked Román to take Gloria back home. On the road, he seduced her and caused her terrible humiliation. She remembers:

> That day you had gotten me drunk and were kissing me . . . When I went to your room I loved you and you made fun of me in a most cruel way. You had hidden your friends there . . . you insulted me . . . I don't know what your motives are but you are a traitor like Judas. I do not know what you are doing with Ena, that blond girl you have bewitched. . . . You have made me cry a great deal, but I have been waiting for this moment. If you think I am still interested in you, you're wrong. I hate you, I have hated you since that night you tricked me, when I had forgotten all. . . . Do you want to know who put you in jail? I did. Do you know who will denounce you again if they could? I will. Now I am capable of spitting in your face and I spit on you! [p. 187].

Gloria torments herself trying to prove to everyone that she *is* good, because after the priest married her and Juan, she never again listened to the treats and entreaties of Román. Her desire for vengeance is obsessive and it dominates her life which revolves around Román, on whom she spies constantly. Her final refusal of sex is almost a manifestation of her destructive hatred. Gloria suffers terrible beating by Juan under the constant attacks of Román and his lies.

She lives obsessed by a painting, of her nude in a field of violets, that Román had made years ago. When she learns that he has hanged himself, she wonders if she can find that painting in his room. She also feels responsible for his death: "I denounced him to the police and he committed suicide. . . . That morning they were coming for him" (p. 248). Juan goes crazy at Román's death and although Gloria speaks vaguely of putting him in an asylum, Andrea knows that it will never happen. Vengeance and hatred tie Gloria to the ghost of Román or is it a sadomasochistic love that dominates her?

The most complex relationship is that between Román and his brother Juan. No literary critic has concerned himself with Román's suicide/murder. I am convinced, however, that it was a crime. Juan killed Román before he could flee from the police; Román was in a sense a victim of his "Frankenstein monster." When he speaks of his power over the house of Aribau he brags:

> All that troubles Gloria, the ridiculous stories of Angustias, all Juan suffers. . . . Haven't you realized that I control them all, their nerves, their thoughts. . . . At times I am about to drive Juan crazy . . . but you have seen for yourself. I work on him, twisting his understanding, his mind, until he almost breaks . . . at times when he shouts I almost cry from happiness. If you could only feel the thick, strange emotion you would understand: With only one word I can calm him, quiet him, make him mine, make him smile. . . . You know, don't you, just how much I own Juan, how he follows me about, how I mistreat him! Don't deny it. . . . I don't want him to be happy. I am leaving him thus, let him sink by himself [p. 89].

What effect does this confession have on Andrea's sexuality? How does she begin to look at men after such a spectacle? The majesty of the protagonist is that she does not stop to speculate, but like a sponge soaking up all of this human misery, she will years later discover the far-reaching dimensions of these confused, tragically miserable people.

In order to better understand Andrea, we need to focus on Ena, for she forms the emotional center of Andrea's life at this time.

When Ena's mother was 16 she was in love with Román. Both were studying music and this explains the attraction he held for her. Once he asked her to cut off a lock of hair as proof of her love, which she did, and then he insulted her: "I have the best part of you at home. I have stolen your charm. Why did you do this foolish thing? Why do you act like a dog for me?" (p. 209). Ena's mother at the time became ill but later reflects: "Seeing things at a distance, I wonder how we can reach such a level of humiliation, how we can get so sick, how we can take such pleasure in pain . . ." (p. 209). She recovered and her father paid Román to stay away from her forever. But twenty years later Ena searches for Román, using Andrea as a means of meeting him. She then avoids her mother, her boyfriend, and Andrea so that they cannot interfere in her affair. While her mother thinks that Ena is characterized by a "perfect and healthy human condition," she ignores the fact that Ena flirts with the boys in order to make them suffer (p. 130). She also does this with Andrea. When Ena takes Andrea on her walks with her boyfriend Jaime, she kisses him in front of her and she says, "How I love you" and adds, turning to Andrea, "I love you too, dear" (p. 128). Thus Andrea says later: "At times I want to cry, it's as if she had tricked and fooled me and not Jaime" (p. 177).

Ena herself once says, "You excite me and even make me laugh" (p. 149) which clearly indicates that a latent and sadistic lesbianism dominates Ena. Andrea, who wants to fall in love with someone, cannot do so. She is constantly at Ena's house and it is not because either Ena's mother or Jaime have asked for her help. She is always there for her help. She is always there, and once she is surprised and acts as if "she had been caught in the act of picking a stolen flower." The symbolism is clear. This prohibited passion is the only thing that makes life tolerable and she is ready to sacrifice even her own life for Ena. Thus she puts herself between Román and Ena when they break off their relationship and she fears that Román will shoot Ena. The ironic thing is that both Román and Ena make fun of her; Román calls her "foolish" and Ena says, "Why so tragic, darling?" Andrea runs away, with Ena following her:

> Do you know I love you very much, Andrea? I did not know I loved you so much. . . . I did not want to see you again, nothing to remind me of this cursed house of Aribau. But when you look at me like that, when you went away . . .

> but no . . . I don't know how to explain it. You looked at me with desperation, and I know you love me so, with such loyalty. Like I love you, believe me [p. 232].

To better understand Ena, we need to understand her relationship with Román. She herself admits that there is a constant duality in her personality: "When I have been too quiet for a time, I feel like scratching. To cause a little damage" (p. 234). Thus after the experience of a kind boyfriend like Jaime, she needs to confront the myth of Román, the evil one. She wants to know herself and she purposefully chooses the man who has been her mother's lover in order to reveal her need to tempt herself with that which is different, with the exotic, the perverted. She relates to Andrea her game with Román:

> When I saw his warm body, an unexplained fury came over me; it took great effort to hide it. Then, still laughing, I moved to the other side of the room. I drove him wild . . . this wasn't the only reason I wanted to humiliate Román. . . . How can I explain the passionate game this became for me? Each time it became more and more important. A fight to the death . . . this duel between the coldness and control of Román and my own assuredness and evil plans. . . . Andrea, the day I was finally able to laugh at him, the day I escaped and thought myself safe, was a splendid day [p. 236].

Andrea wants more facts and asks if Román made love to her but Ena responds evasively, "I don't know" (p. 235). If Andrea is bothered by the love of her schoolmate Pons, it is not a sign that her sexual drive towards men is negative. She is merely looking for something that they cannot give and thus explains to Gerardo, another boyfriend:

> He was another of those infinite number of men who are born to sentimental ideas and beside a woman, they don't understand any other attitude. Their heart and head never meet [p. 134].

On the other hand, with Ena she finds a spiritual bond and a physical kindness that do not threaten her, even though Ena's leaving does cause Andrea an almost emotional collapse "like the shadow of death at last" (p. 243). That same morning Román "kills himself" and she suffers terrible nightmares, as if the leaving of Ena and the collective terror of the house have broken down her emotional reserves. When she recovers, she still senses the phantasmal presence of Román in the house. Fortunately Ena—who had promised her that they would get together soon—fulfills her promise and has her come to Madrid with her father. This alleviates the tension Andrea has been under and she envisions a happy new life with Ena and her family and new friends at the university, far from the house at Aribau. But it is not so simple. Perhaps her life will take another route. Ena and Jaime have become reconciled and are to be married soon.

Message

Although this novel can be studied on many different levels, an important question from the point of view of the woman is, what causes such different women as Ena's mother, Gloria, Ena and Antonia to fall in love with Román? A second question concerns Juan and Angustias and their relationship with their brother Román. Although Andrea despises Román, she is still affected by what happens between him and Ena. Thus Román is the center of these divergent emotional tramas. Each of the characters passes through periods of indignation, passion, disillusion and vengeance or separation.

Ena's mother knew Román when he was a young violinist and his image as a "superior man," a "genius," an "artist," is important to her. Her sacrifice is her vanity, the lock of hair that signifies the loss of her beauty as a gesture of ultimate surrender. After recuperating from her illness, she marries Ena's father, who is quite normal. She learns to recognize the good and to separate it from evil. Ena, talking about her mother, confides once to Andrea:

> I noted from a very early age that she was different from the rest. . . . I spied on her. I thought she must have some dark secret. When I realized that she really loved my father and was happy I found myself somewhat deceived [p. 150].

Gloria has always been sensual. The painting of her naked in a field of violets is her psychological flagellation. She insists that she has been bad—or that she continues to be bad; we don't know for sure because there is some indication that she does more than play cards at her sister's house. Román has been her official scourge and thus her greatest desire is to see him executed. Kindness is Gloria's goal and is expressed through her sacrifice to put food on the table for the whole family. In spite of this sacrifice, Juan beats her unmercifully each time he learns from Román that she has gone to visit her sister.

Ena needs to confront a real man in order to learn that the legend built around Román, a vulgar and sick person, is only a myth. As she has a certain incipient sadism within her, she enters a struggle of wills with Román. As a result she leaves, disgusted, and wants to return to the safety of her home, boyfriend and her friend Andrea.

Antonia appears on a second level of the novel and becomes identified with Román's power. Her existence is one of constant sexual fantasy.

Angustias is the victim of her homosexual brothers. Román lives the hidden passions of a tormented man through the letters and diary of Angustias. This is why he constantly spies on her. Juan, for other motives, also insults and makes life miserable for her. Indirectly they serve as witnesses for the guilt Angustias cannot forget. Her decision to enter a convent is proof to them that in fact she can free herself from their slavery and from her own desires of the flesh. This woman, who has lived her entire life as the victim of her father's pride and of the snares of her brothers, makes a final decision that surprises everyone, including her lover. Her savings show that for many years she has been gathering money, as if she were paying for her freedom with her own blood. Suddenly Román's pleasure as a licentious voyeur is ended. As for Juan, he can no longer play the self-righteous moralist now that he no longer eats as a direct result of Angustias' working for the very man all accuse of adultery.

Román, who all the women claim to love, is only a projection of their erotic fantasies. In Ena's case, it is clear that as a child of the post-war years she does not conform to the romantic ideas of her mother's generation. She dares to explore prohibited territory and is saved by her good luck and perhaps by the fact that Román is homosexual. Since Juan and Gloria keep close watch, Román has not been able to treat her as he did Gloria, and perhaps because Ena belongs to the upper classes, Román has refrained from his evil ways. Nevertheless, Andrea believed that Román was going to kill Ena. We will never know for certain if the crime would have taken place. Ena, through her own desires, placed herself in the jaws of the wolf but managed to escape.

Juan is the only one who is really a sexual slave to his brother; he is incapable of escape. The fact that he took advantage of Gloria in the first months that he knew her creates a striking comparison to his brother Román. Although Gloria never realizes it, she has become the prey on which both brothers take out their cowardice and most bestial instincts. She always has bruises and, of course, cannot escape. The fact that she was married by the priest, has a small son, and is needed by her mother-in-law justifies her presence in the house, but Juan and Román despise her because she is not "of their class" and exploit her because they know Juan's paintings do not sell. This hypocritical attitude is a microcosm of the social classes in Spain. The bourgeoisie—Ena—can play cat-and-mouse with the lower class and get away with it, but it is the lower class that with its sweat and toil feeds the parasites from above. Andrea is not a parasite because she has a clear picture of herself as a spectator and not as an actor in this social game. Her shyness, her pathetic loyalty to Ena, her sense of sacrifice and generosity save her from being "decadent." She is the first of her family to have a clear understanding of the emptiness that exists in her class situation. The nothingness (*nada*) that she experiences is precisely the confrontation she has with the useless farce that all around her feel is indispensable. A year earlier we find her hoping for help and protection from her new family. A year later she departs, leaving behind a murdered man, an uncle driven mad, a senile old woman, and a much confused young lady. She leaves her family and goes to live with the bourgeois family of Ena, symbol of an escape to a golden, pleasant world from the ruined, phantasmal world of the house of Aribau.

ELENA QUIROGA

Although her family was from Galicia, Elena Quiroga was born in Santander in 1919.[1] Her novels include: *La soledad sonora* (1948),[2] *Viento del norte* (1951), *La sangre* (1952),[3] *Algo pasa en la calle* (1954),[4] *La careta* (1955), *La enferma* (1955),[5] *La última corrida* (1958), *Plácida, la joven* (1956), *Tristura* (1960) and *Escribo tu nombre* (1965).[6] She won the Nadal Prize for *Viento del norte*[7] and I shall concentrate on this novel because it is fundamental in showing the lack of communication that exists between men and women in spite of a great deal of love.

The protagonist of *Viento del norte* is Marcela, a girl abandoned by her poverty-stricken mother when she is born. The action of the novel takes place in the Pazo de la Sagreira which belongs to Don Alvaro. Ermitas, the maid who raised Don Alvaro, takes in the little girl and brings her to live in the master's house. Because of their superstitious natures, the farmers isolate the girl and Ermita is exceedingly protective of her. Don Alvaro is an old bachelor who has dedicated himself to medieval studies and who has never felt the desire to marry, but his Uncle Enrique wishes he would marry one of his five daughters who are all of marrying age. Lucía, Enrique's youngest daughter, takes Marcela home for a few years to be a companion for Tula, her sister, who is suffering from tuberculosis. When Marcela returns to Sagreira she is 18 and beautiful. Don Alvaro is secretly in love with her but in order to quiet his passion he goes to his uncle's house. He is now 50 and a very honest man. He decides to marry Marcela after she has been educated by the nuns for a couple of years. The marriage takes place. A little while later, Don Alvaro has an accident which leaves him paralyzed. Marcela has had a son but she is not happy; the intrigues of a young man who wishes to make advances add to her conflict. While Marcela is visiting Lucía one day, Don Alvaro dies and everyone blames Marcela for his death because she left him alone that afternoon.

Family

Both Don Alvaro and Marcela have been raised by the same servant, Ermitas. Don Enrique is like a second father to his nephew Alvaro. Don Enrique spends much of his time drinking, skirtchasing and hunting. On the other hand, Don Alvaro is introverted, studious and chaste. Marcela is raised apart from other girls of her class and she has only Lucía, her "Godmother," and the maid Ermitas as her friends. She has never had any contact with any man other than Don Alvaro, whom she respects as she does God.

Don Enrique's family is an important one in the region. He is authoritarian and not very understanding of his two sons, Jorge and Miguel. In fact, Miguel cannot marry the girl he loves because his father objects. The education of his daughters, as befits that of young ladies, is placed in the hands of their mother, who sends them to religious schools. Their mother also intercedes for them when their father tries to force his will upon the girls. Don Enrique believes that he is allowed to have other women and his wife is aware of her role in his life:

> She knew that he was right when he said, 'I love you more than all the rest. You are something different, now you understand.' She knew that along with the body that was growing cold, all of her youth likewise grew cold, so many memories shared only with him; the only thing that does not grow old is love, the modest, serene love that she always maintained while at his side, together with her childlike admiration for him, because he was strong, large and powerful [p. 252].

While this man is respected and even feared due to his social position, he himself maintains his image of being strong even in the moments before his death. He refuses to confess his sins and does so only because his wife insists that he should. As he had always done during their marriage, he stubbornly refuses to admit that she is right:

> He tried to sit up, trusting his own strength, but he fell flat on his back. Dona Lucia grabbed the hand that he waved

> pretending anger and held it, giving comfort. All looked on the tragedy contained in that manly hand, that hand which finally gave in to a stronger hand, the more serene hand of the person who had been his companion in life [p. 249].

Thus the author makes it clear that while he had held the physical power and authority, it was she who in the last moment was the true leader of the family.

In the family created by Don Alvaro and Marcela, we can see how important the son is for a man who, in his mature years, has few illusions concerning his descendants. The birth of his son brightens all that surrounds him: "Everything gained a meaning long hidden—work, the house, goods, fields and the forest; all shook and opened part of their inner being to view" (p. 229). For Marcela, who has never owned anything, her son is her only belonging and "she knew that the strong, lively child was hers" (p. 233). Marcela raised her son in her own way and when Don Alvaro berates her because the child is playing without shoes, she shouts: "I will not allow my son to become a milk-sop nor a book worm like his father, the only thing his father is good for. . . . He is mine also, the son, the one I gave birth to, remember?" (p. 265). He is forced to accept her words, since he realizes that everyone will "forget that he is the son of the master and will remember him as the son of Marcela" (p. 264).

Social Class

This novel presents a marriage between two extremes in social class—lord and servant—and it also presents the reaction of the farmers to that alliance. Don Alvaro is atypical, especially considering that his Uncle Enrique would have solved the problem by making Marcela his concubine and then protecting his son with his partiality. But Don Alvaro is older and knows what he wants and decides matters according to his respectful and discreet temperament. Nevertheless, he rules the life of the girl as if she were his servant and although he says "I know there are no social levels, save those we persist in saying we climb and descend" he still sends her to a convent so that she may be taught the manners of a proper lady of the upper class. Don Alvaro is ashamed when his wife dresses like a regional farmer when she attends the funeral of Enrique and people from his class observe her. However Don Alvaro does not really pay attention to the opinions of his uncle or cousins; he secretly looks down on them because they are not well educated. Since he is an intellectual, the only people to whom he pays attention are those with some education. His greatest treasures are his library and his manuscripts. For Marcela things are quite different, since she has been alienated from her own social class. She has always looked upon Don Alvaro as her master whom she must obey, to whom she is indebted for the bread she eats. She is obsessed with paying this debt and no longer being under his control. Ermitas has always repeated the same word to her—"gratitude." The local farmers, who had a poor opinion of Marcela's mother because she was a "free" woman, increase their prejudices against the girl because she has a mark on her body and they accuse her of being a witch. Ermitas keeps her completely separate from the servants because Ermitas herself is an alienated farm girl who is in absolute servitude to Don Alvaro, even to the point of choosing Don Alvaro over Marcela in some situations. She is very subservient and was already quite old when she took Marcela. The child therefore grew up without any friends, nor any dealings with other people. When the family of Don Enrique, that is Tula and Lucía, takes her away with them, they act as if it were their right to do so. Lucía, however, realizes that the girl no longer belongs to the world of the farmers because she has taught Marcela how to read and some more refined manners. The time Marcela spends in the convent serves only to confuse her. Even the nuns do not know what to do with her, since while she is a maid, she is also the "bride-to-be" of the master and thus they leave her alone, saying that they will make a "special place" for her. Marcela realizes that the male farmers desired her, while their wives envied her. Her marriage does not help, instead it isolates her completely because the farmers now treat her like a stranger who no longer participates in their affairs nor in diversions. It is only when Lucia invites Marcela to her house that she begins to know the society of people who chat, laugh and play cards. When Don Francisco tries to seduce her, she wants to believe that at last someone has accepted her for who she is and thus for the first time she learns to laugh and to express herself. Perhaps she has realized that Don Alvaro himself is not well suited to society, since he cannot speak to her nor communicate with her as an equal. He reflects:

> To each his own. . . . No I can see the results. It is not her fault; what has happened, has happened. But to have her to show off at mealtime and to sleep with is not the same as having her by my side through life, in that part of the social world destined for me and not for her [p. 261].

Social prejudices of this type are also evident in Enrique's family, since he will not allow his son Miguel to marry his girlfriend because she is the daughter of the local schoolteacher. Nor will he allow his daughter Dorila to marry a man from America, nor may Lucia marry her boyfriend who is a doctor. Perhaps this is a reaction to the amorous step Don Alvaro took by marrying a maid and not one of his cousins.

Sexuality

The novel begins when Matuxa tries to drown her daughter Marcela at the mill, but the dogs and the local women prevent it. Later Matuxa is found stabbed to death in an open field. Marcela has to live with this image of a beautiful mother who was destroyed by a jealous man. Perhaps she has sublimated these thoughts, but Marcela cannot hide the fact that she herself is beautiful and desired by all of the men. She even feels some anguish when Don Alvaro looks at her. Since she has not participated in the activities of other girls her age, even her bathing has become a solitary ritual. Don Alvaro anxiously spies on her and perhaps others do likewise. In Marcela we see two images of the same girl superimposed on each other: maid and young woman. Even after their marriage we observe:

> Next to her, he was astonished to find that her warm, healthy look faded as the light kept vigil over them, it was as if she had become a different woman from the calm, taciturn girl she was before and had become a quiet, meek yet opulent woman [p. 195].

That is, Marcela's repressed sexuality only appears in a hidden way—in her solitary baths or in the darkness of her bedroom. On many occasions both Don Alvaro and Marcela are about to confess their most intimate passions, but there is a block, a frustrating pride that keeps them apart. He who has lived isolated and alone for fifty years suffers because he cannot make a friend out of the woman whom he passionately loves. She, for her part, seems to guess at a certain superiority in him that she senses but does not express. He observes:

> Does her sullen appearance hide something? Is it only your imagination that perhaps behind that angry look she hides some pain? No, you are wrong; she is empty and foolish, like a good village girl and she only has that healthy look of youth. You despise yourself. There are those who live without preoccupations or ideas—Marcela is one of those and if she answers haughtily, it is because she doesn't know what to answer and her desperate silence is not due to a growing, but rather to an emptiness [p. 204].

They live side by side but there are no ties that bind them together sentimentally, even though he wishes to be everything for her—father, brother, husband—and ends up being only her "owner." Likewise, she feels that he has separated her from the others:

> Marcela was angry. If he hadn't been so defensive, if he hadn't married me, perhaps they would have accepted me. I hate him. Being a servant to him. My whole life serving him: of what value are titles? Maid? Wife? What difference was there? It was as if he was always doing you a favor and Ermitas always saying, 'Give thanks to God and the Saints for your good fortune.' Well let her give thanks because I can't see how he helped me! I was his maid and still am. The others were right in not wanting to help. Why should they? I never complained about the work, I never asked for help nor was I ever squeamish about doing this or that. It was like he was doing you a favor. A favor not to send you out into the cold or not to give you too much to do in such a large house. I almost never saw him and there was always enough to eat so that some could be spared for the poor. A favor by defending me. Didn't he already have this in mind when he defended me? Gentlemen don't do things because they are kind, if they give you something it is because they have too much. Did he ever know if we were sick or tired? He was always in his study with his books and we were

> below in the kitchen with our own cares. Marcela felt closer to the kitchen than she did to her master [p. 203].

Marcela suffers from being a misfit and her husband does not compensate for her loneliness and isolation. She is still the maid; although she has the title of "wife," she still does the same tasks. She is intelligent, and unlike Ermitas, she realizes no one has asked her opinion, nor have they wanted to know if she wanted to marry him or merely go to bed with him. Her human dignity overcomes her situation as maid and orphan.

There are two charges made by the country people against Marcela before her marriage which deserve mention—being a witch since childhood, and having used her black magic to cause her husband to marry her. But even more dangerous are the charges made against her after the marriage. When her husband falls from his horse following the discussion they had concerning the child and his shoes, Don Alvaro is paralyzed and everyone blames her. Of course, no one ever thinks that she is the first victim, especially since she is a lively young girl and is now left with an older husband who is incapable of fulfilling his conjugal functions. Then when she goes to visit Lucía and stays for the afternoon, Don Alvaro dies. Everyone now accuses her of being a poor wife for having left the incapacitated man, even though they all know very well that the house is full of servants as well as Ermitas.

Marcela never tries to defend herself. Perhaps the pain she suffers is very deep and on a plane that is hidden to the rest. She needs to communicate with Don Alvaro because her love is best expressed through communication and she wishes to express her love for him, but when the moment to do so comes, it is too late and he cannot hear her. In her own way Marcela has loved Don Alvaro because she has seen in him a father figure and, moreover, he is the only person who has shown any interest in her since she was born and came to serve in the big house.

Message

There is a classic similarity between Eve and Marcela and her mother Matuxa. In each of the three cases the women are accused by mankind for the loss of divine grace. Marcela is marked as a witch from her youth. She is not guilty of any of the charges leveled at her, but no one is interested in either excusing her or in understanding her. Like Eve, she is desirable and beautiful in the eyes of the men. Don Alvaro represents the "soul," while Marcela seems to represent the "body" or the "flesh." He dedicates his life to a religious pilgrimage to Compostela, as if it were symbolic of his search for divine grace. His good intentions towards Marcela lack substance because he is too preoccupied with his books to court and make love to her. He possesses her only in bed and even then she is passive and gives herself as a servant does to her master. This directly reflects their social position—he, the master, on top and she, the servant, on the bottom. There is nothing but gratitude between them; everyone expects her to be grateful to him for her food, clothing and name. It has never occurred to anyone that she gives more than she receives, for she is young and beautiful and gives him a son who is as healthy and vigorous as she. She works unceasingly to see that all is in order. She has no luxuries nor does she demand anything for herself. The only time she wishes to meet with a group of friends at Lucía's house—no one comes to visit her because of her sick husband—everyone accuses her of negligence. The author has clearly created in Marcela a feminine personality that, although she comes from the lowest social standing, is able to demand her rights, not as a wife but as a human being and by virtue of her own will. We can also see that for some women, marriage changes nothing, since they continue to do the same things as before the marriage. Don Alvaro represents the man of good intentions who nevertheless strongly feels that he is superior to women. He takes his stand and is very strict as to whom he will command and whom he will obey. The death of Don Alvaro only serves to aggravate Marcela's situation, for she is now a widow without the right to inherit because she does not belong to the same social class as her "master." Once again "Eve" is exposed to the anger of those around her who make her the victim of the circumstances.

A parallel can be made between *Los pazos de Ulloa* by Emilia Pardo Bazán and *Viento del norte.* In both we find the same social atmosphere and, in appearance, we also find a contrast—that between a dictatorial, patriarchal lord and a democratic, intellectual lord. Both, when they fall in love with a beautiful girl from a lower class, react according to their background. Noncommunication persists in both novels and both authors are trying to deal with an extremely powerful social situation which will allow instinct and love to triumph. Elena Quiroga is careful to point out that some women are more interested in maintaining their freedom than in having a relationship with an all-powerful lord who takes from them all possibility of being accepted as human beings.

ELENA SORIANO

Elena Soriano was born in Fuentidueña de Tajo, Spain, in 1917.[1] She studied to be a teacher at the College of Philosophy and Letters in Madrid. Her first novel, *Caza menor,*[2] appeared in 1952 and the trilogy *Mujer y hombre,*[3] which consists of *La playa de los locos,*[4] *Espejismos*[5] and *Medea 55,*[6] appeared in 1955. Today she directs the literary journal *Urogallo,*[7] which is published in Madrid.

La playa de los locos deals with a woman who in retrospect tries to explain why she was incapable of giving herself to her lover 19 years before. As she relives the past she simultaneously experiences the changes that occur in the present.

Family

The protagonist comes from the upper class, but as an orphan she has been raised by her aunt and uncle. Her uncle is a cold, pedantic scholar. Her aunt is a false, theosophical woman. She remembers: "I remember my stern infancy and horrible adolescence, everything in the past that has made me what I am today—imbued with the idea of perfection, pride and illusive aspirations" (p. 181). The family of the chief male character is never mentioned.

Social Class

Although only briefly, the narrator notes the social and economic changes that have taken place in her life after the Civil War. Originally of the aristocracy, she has now lost not only her lands but also the little inheritance of her aunt and uncle. Now she belongs to the middle class and lives modestly on her income as a professor. On the other hand, the owners of a local hotel, who were relatively poor and from humble circumstances, have now enlarged the hotel and belong to the rising middle class of businessmen. Our protagonist observes their bad taste and the "common decorations" of the hotel. The male protagonist is a doctor and therefore from the professional class, and most likely the two protagonists are from the same province.

Sexuality

In 1936 the female protagonist was young, beautiful and a virgin. Her first act of independence was to go on vacation to the seashore alone. When she meets her lover she hides her professional standing:

> I realized that as a young and beautiful girl I inspired a certain fear in men, that kind of fear men normally feel towards other women equally as intelligent as they are, a kind of superstitious belief that to love a beautiful and talented woman is a form of homosexuality, like a famous and sickly poet once said [p. 94].

She has never been kissed before and he is the first to do so. Her reaction is nevertheless "a horrible and unimagined analytical reaction which nullified her first moments of abandonment" (p. 110).

During their moments of bliss, which last only twenty days in July, she has a similar reaction:

> In vain I tried to hold on to those theories I had learned and to exault my rights to do as I please like you men do. It is all in vain. When I am away from you, I am more than ready to give myself to you, to give myself completely at our next meeting: but at the supreme moment, the contradictions between desire and upbringing arise, and I reject you cruelly and throw you out without pity, leaving me with only the dark and dirty regions of iniquity . . . [p. 134].

As we try to understand what she means by "upbringing" we note that she is not religious, that there is no social fear, and that it is not a plan for marriage that causes her to defend her virginity. What is it then? She herself tries to comprehend her actions and realizes that she has aspired to a perfect fusion of the body and spirit as an indispensable condition of surrender. Even though she knows that he desires and wishes to possess her, she realizes that the spiritual communication she requires has not been established. Even Miluca, the hotel keeper, knows that men act thusly: "That is the way they always are: business comes first, as always" (p. 168). She has had to pretend to be the same age and at the same cultural level as he in order not to increase the distance between them. She then begins to comprehend that he does not care for her as a person and he is only interested in her body. He attributes her reluctance to those causes normally cited by men of his class: (a) she is not a virgin and feels some shame, (b) she is married and has not told him, (c) she is a sadistic whore who delights in tormenting him, or (d) she wants to get married and is using sex as a lever. Twenty years later she says:

> Yes, now I too see that in those twenty days I found out as little about you as you did of me, Miluca was right. You even hid your real name and family from me, since every attempt to find you in the city by that name you gave me always was answered 'Unknown. . . . ' That is what you were, 'unknown.' This is what our love lacked in order to be complete: a mutual desire to have our souls know each other. Yes, dearest, my soul was ready but you had no interest in it and you jealously kept your soul for things you thought more worthy. But our entire trouble centers here—we both desperately and mechanically sought each other's souls. My great error was not to risk mine, knowing that a woman such as I prostitutes herself in little ways, useless, meaningless ways. I did not find out either that you can reach the soul through the body, which is also of divine origin, and that the body first makes us aware of other things, and that often love grows through twisted, evil paths to finally arrive at a clear and pure region [p. 196].

Message

Most interesting is the fact that she never married because she continued to search for this true spiritual communication which she never found. Her return is a late capitulation of her life-long principles, a frustrated epilogue.

The relationship between her and the young man began in casual circumstances. He protected her from some drunks and then assumes the role of the virile man who constantly demands sexual surrender. He is surprised at her attitude and comments:

> If you had said this in one of your furious moments, spurred by your unsatisfied desires, it would not have had the same meaning for me as indicated by your callous attitude, your firm and impartial manner, your careful, clinical study. I accepted it, closing my eyes and bowing my head, without protest or reproach [p. 144].

That which is certain is that it was not easy to accept the fact that the same night he tried to jump off a cliff and then the next day left without saying good-bye.

She returns to the beach twenty years later thinking that the hotel managers will recognize her, but they do not even notice her. At 43, she is a woman ignored by all. She tries to imagine what he must be like now: "A rich man about town, fat, frequenting the casinos and with a prolific and rotund wife" (p. 19). Her thoughts return to the present, to her last boyfriend, and to the expectations of all those who had known her of the possibilities of their marriage. After all, they were mature people and what more could they expect? In this novel, the protagonist faces the same problem as do many women that finally decide to marry anyone so as not to remain a spinster. The reader is left with uncertainty about her final solution.

In the second novel of the trilogy, *Espejismos,* the protagonists are Pedro María and his wife Adela. The action begins when she enters a clinic for treatment of a tumor. During the waiting, both relive their 12 or 14 years of marriage.

Family

Pedro comes from a family of women—his mother and three single sisters. Adela is an orphan and has no family nearby. She feels that the sisters exploit Pedro because he supports them. As a result, Pedro's family does not like her. Adela is very protective of her son Pedrito, even to the point of hiding the reason for her absence when she sends him to some friends while she goes to the hospital. Her husband thinks this is monstrous and absurd and comments: "With women you can't speak of death, nor of what lies beyond, nor of anything. . . . Immediately they become emotional, hysterical, and you can't reason with them for five minutes straight" (p. 108). Although Pedrito does not appear much in the work, the author makes clear that the boy suspects a separation or break between his parents, and thus through him the author indicates the hostile climate that has been in their home during the last few months.

Social Class

The hostility of Pedro's family towards Adela is very indicative of the attitudes of the middle class towards single women who work. Adela says:

> My mother-in-law considers me of lesser social standing than she because I was working when I met Pedro and she never has; my sisters-in-law are still single because they are vulgar and too proud. How happy they would be if I were to die! Thus they would recover him completely, they would triumph in their efforts against me, they would once again manipulate him, exploit him and order his life [p. 73].

Adela lost her parents during the war and has had to make her living by working, even at simple jobs. Pedro works in a store and while he is able to save some money, he realizes he will have no possibility of traveling or bettering his life unless he learns English. To do so, he registers for classes at an academy and there he meets Chiquita, who becomes his girlfriend.

Both Pedro and Adela have some of the typical middle-class prejudices, and upon discovery of the tumor go to the most expensive clinic, using up their savings of so many years. He wishes to prove to her that he is willing to sacrifice himself for her. When Adela arrives at the clinic she feels "defrauded, betrayed, forgotten, broken, misunderstood" (p. 61). This is a flashback to when as a child she "lost her smile when her parents died" (p. 52). Then she met Pedro, her only love, and she has never been unfaithful to him.

Nevertheless, as the years pass, she feels that the two of them follow parallel but distinct paths. Everything she does to try and attract him again is useless:

> To be a modern woman, dynamic, jovial; to make the home a sweet and comfortable place and to change its furnishings and decorations often; to learn culinary refinements that please the stomach; to polish my social customs in order to please and help him; to read a lot in order to acquire some culture and to impress him, to show understanding of his affairs and interest in his preoccupations; to express opinions about the important topics and to give him well thought-out advice concerning serious matters, in order to make him smile and say: 'Enough, enough, you women don't understand these things.' And many other things: to pretend indifference, to flirt and be frivolous, to excite him; to return home late and feign mysterious adventures to provoke his jealousy; to really leave him and look for vengeance; to adopt the position of a victim and withdraw into my own sorrows; to try and ignore the problems without solution and to become involved in absorbing activities; to be enmeshed in a frantic social life and acquire bad habits from my friends—dances, candy, canasta, to frequent the theatre, movies, tea houses; to amuse myself by learning languages, going to lectures, listening to good concerts; to elevate and calm the spirit by reading pious and philosophic books. . . . All useless! [p. 59].

Sexuality

Adela is going through a double crisis: the slow deterioration of her marriage, a process which has become more serious the past year (she does not know of the visits Pedro makes to Chiquita), and the rejection by her husband which she attributes to her age, her sickness and her loss of attractiveness. The possibility that her husband could deceive her has arisen, in which case she has several alternatives: make a scandal, separate, or forgive him. Since she has a child, the only solution *for her* is "to forgive," because after all, she says, "This is not humiliating nor dishonorable for the woman, it has been thus always: marriage is based on our loyalty and the infidelity of the men" (p. 42). Besides being a fatalist, she is puritanical, with the typical, ingrained modesty of the Spanish women. For example, she does not like the doctor to examine her, she does not like to undress in front of her husband because she feels ugly, and she will not keep dates with possible lovers because she fears she will disappoint them. Adela was very beautiful but she has no confidence in her feminine seductivity because her experiences with her husband have not been satisfactory; all of her passion is lost through his impatience:

> She realized, at first with wonderment and mistrust, that his caresses were mechanical, that the snatched moments of tenderness became more infrequent and more brief and the distractions, impatience, shrugging of the shoulders more frequent. . . . And to hold back passionate impulses out of dignity and out of fear of appearing imprudent or foolish, and to be ashamed of certain timid desires and to try uselessly to avoid going crazy from anxiety and grief and to put the ardor of the blood in the frozen waters of deception and to retrieve the soul from there tempered with resentment and a desire for revenge . . . [p. 56].

Pedro's sexual life began at 15 when he was "initiated" by an older cousin one summer at the beach. Between the ages of 18 and 23 he was insatiable. When he met Adela he calmed down and remained loyal until he met Chiquita. He has not yet consummated the relationship, but he hopes it will happen soon:

> Day by day his desire grows stronger and his conscience weaker and the impulse grows to trample those obstacles which more and more seem artificial and conventional. Yes, perhaps the truth, although hidden, of his conduct is this: a hidden purpose, a hidden, whispered labor, a sure hope for the fatal moment when neither he nor Chiquita will have sufficient moral resistance and then all will be consummated . . . [p. 188].

Until this moment Pedro has thought of his flirtations with Chiquita as a mere pastime which in no way compromises him. When the possibility of his wife's dying during the operation arises, he is filled with pride at the thought of having Chiquita, a young and beautiful woman, but he is also bothered by what will happen to his son. Nevertheless, his son will have to accept his father's decision. He dreams of telling Chiquita all about his former life and hearing her say: "I am now your wife. No, don't explain anything—I already know" (p. 202). Chiquita, however, is not as innocent as he thinks; some of her friends have seen him with his wife.

When Pedro sees his wife on the cart after the operation he thinks she is dead and feels guilty: "It was I. Punish me, I did it all" (p. 210). The doctors convince him that she is still living. Now he must face a life of duplicity, lies, and a continual tug of war between Chiquita who wants to marry him and his wife who will surely forgive him.

Message

These three lives are condemned to repeat these hypocritical acts which are but mirages—*espejismos*—of what the true relationship between a man and a woman ought to be. There is no bridge between the three and no possibility of communication. Women are "disposable" when they grow old and it is as hopeless for them as it is for the protagonist of *La playa de los locos* to be loved for themselves. Pedro, like the doctor in the preceding novel, could have found an easy solution by going to war and replacing both women, but he is destined for trouble and is left with the two.

The two protagonists of *Medea 55*, Miguel Darguelos and Daniela Valle, met at the battle of the Ebro during the Spanish Civil War in 1938. She followed him and they were married during a truce. First they escaped to France and later they came to the Americas, where they traveled through various Central American countries. Both managed to live by their wits, he as a politician, she as an artist. In 1955 we find Miguel at the height of his political career, which he wants to solidify by marrying the young daughter of an important minister. To Daniela's surprise, he divorces her and she promises vengeance. Two weeks later he remarries and the young bride receives a gift: a complete history in letters and photographs of the previous marriage!

Family

Daniela's father spoiled her. He always treated her like a child and when the woman within revealed herself it was too late; Daniela left home without his consent and took with her the jewels that had belonged to her mother. Other members of her family include an old aunt, an older married brother who runs the family business, and another girl, a schoolmate of Daniela's whom the family took in when she became an orphan. An interesting scene takes place between the father and his daughter:

> You are no longer a child? You are now a woman? Yes, you are a woman, a woman, with all of the responsibilities and tasks of that sex. My Dani, so small, vulnerable in your innocence, it is too soon for you to be an adult, impure, stronger than I, capable of desiring and accomplishing more than I ever dreamed of, capable of leaving, of attacking me, of mortally wounding me . . . [p. 186].

This scene continues, but the important thing is that Daniela does not vacillate when it comes to following Miguel: family, honor, country, friends—all become unimportant. It is only years later that she recalls her father.

With respect to Miguel's family, we only know that he ran away from home in Albania at 13 and joined the circus. Later, always the adventurer, he became involved in revolutions, wars and conspiracies. Misia Alva, much like an adopted mother for both, is a rich and well-educated woman who protects them when they arrive in Mexico and for 17 years she has been a confidante to Daniela. She and Daniela discuss Daniela's problem:

> They loved each other because they understood each other well. Beneath the unimportant superficial differences, they shared many of the same deep similarities of their sex. They arrived at the same conclusion: to get actively involved in the optimistic task of recovering the fleeing man. And they very much enjoyed the planning of an immediate solution [p. 83].

Social Class

Daniela is of aristocratic stock and her father is an Andalusian marquis. She has been educated in the arts and can dance, sing and paint. She does have several habits that cause a scandal: she smokes, drives fast cars and is free to do as she pleases. She has no social-class prejudices and says that "war, the reds, the blues" are of no importance to her. At first she does not wish to marry Miguel because marriage is a bourgeois idea, but at last she agrees. Miguel comes from a poor family. His father was a fisherman and little by little Miguel has managed to climb the political ladder until he is the conservative leader. Misia Alva is from the upper class and she is rich. She contributes much to the arts and to worthy social affairs. When she receives these political exiles from Spain she feels a special sympathy for Daniela whom she helps get started in her career as a movie actress.

Sexuality

At 18 Daniela is no longer a virgin and thus is the black sheep of the family. Even Miguel, an experienced "man of war," felt "terror in the midst of pleasure, felt her possessive violence, her unsuspecting, instinctive wisdom, greater than all the other women he had known" (p. 167). Daniela's temperament causes her to give herself fully, passionately—at first through driving fast cars and riding spirited horses, and then with Miguel. Daniela never hesitates to use her body to free Miguel from prision, concentration camps, death and starvation. For her, fidelity is not based on physical contact but rather on understanding and sincerity, and thus she has never lied to Miguel. He has been the one who insisted that she be sincere and when he uses her sincerity against her she rebels:

> I must be crazy, I can't understand you. While I was still but a child you killed my most noble instincts and turned me into a beast. You made me be always prompt and ready for your use and you paid me with a half hour of your attention. At last you confess your deepest desire and by so doing repudiate the son I offer you. Why? What do you really want from me? From womankind? You are a thousand

> times more egotistical and insatiable than I, both in the flesh and in the spirit. When I was about to give birth and you could no longer use my flesh, you hurried after another woman. When my body was once again ready, you got bored and my excessive love bothered you and you sought another lover. Miguel! Miguel! If I have been a monster, only you are to blame! [p. 218].

It is interesting to note that after the many abortions he forced her to have, at last they had a daughter that both loved dearly, yet she died very soon. Now, when Daniela is once again pregnant, he does not want a child by her but rather by the girl he is to marry, because that way the child will grow up in the conservative atmosphere of a decent family. Stubbornly, Daniela cannot understand either his logic or his reasons for the separation. She has not wanted to mention the child because she has not wanted to tie his love down that way, but at the last minute she uses all her resources to hold onto him. As a last resort she threatens vengeance.

As in the previous novels, the feminine protagonist passes through an identity crisis. Even though Daniela is only 34, she is at the end of her film career. This career has never been her only goal in life, since she has only held it to help out Miguel in his political career. Of course, he will continue to "protect" her, which a proud woman like Daniela cannot accept, nor does she like the implications of his promised "sexual visits." Daniela, who has always seen Miguel as her idol, is incapable of recognizing what Misia Alva sees so clearly in him: cunning, harshness, cynicism, cowardice, cold calculations and insensitivity. Daniela gives in to her desperation, forgetting her contracts and ruining her physical appearance by her emotional state. She has no other recourse but to avenge the abuse she has suffered, since he has already published the announcement of the divorce in the newspapers. She literally feels like a lemon completely drained of its juice. When he reproaches her for never having understood his aspirations, *his things*, she says:

> Your things, Men's things: organize and boss the men. . . . You have never shown me—nor any other woman that I know— that haughty expression, that enthusiasm that I have seen in your face when you talk with your male friends

> of *your* things: liberty, freedom, 'to the right,' 'to the left,' independence, compromise, unity, collaboration, triumph, ideals. What shallow words! And your interviews, reunions, partners, conferences, meetings, discourses. . . . I must confess that all this has always seemed absurd, incomprehensible, inhuman . . . [p. 219].

We must note that Miguel has never felt that Daniela is a part of his political life, he has used her but he has never included her. He even feels superior when he interprets the seductive attitudes of his wife as her "prodigious feminine wiles" (p. 177). Even though they have never been true partners, he thinks:

> It is true, even if it is painful to say so. At the moment of triumph, accomplices are in the way. Daniela and I have created too many scandals together, we have committed crimes that society cannot forget, nor forgive, as long as we are together. I think, sincerely, that we now cast shadows and that if we have fought for something superior all these years we cannot now destroy it for things that are somewhat frivolous [p. 121].

Message

Daniela represents a modern Medea who abandons family and social considerations to follow her lover. When she is betrayed by him she decides on a last act of vengeance and carries it out against the young bride of her former husband, a girl of 17. We must make clear that her crime—different from that in the Greek tragedy—is much more subtle: she kills the faith and hope of an innocent girl by showing her, through letters, photographs, and newspaper clippings, that her husband is capable of throwing the woman he "loves" into the waste heap when she no longer fits into his plans. Once again we have a man and a woman who disagree on what love is. For her it is something permanent, something that gives her reason to live. Miguel, on the other hand, sees her as a witness to his past and as a stumbling block to his future. He insists that he wants an "innocent" woman and he despises her for being a lusty female. As a practical man he cannot see why Daniela, at only 35, is at a loss as to how to remake her life and perhaps he is right. Love, for Miguel, is associated with a sense of respectability, and he has never had it. His second marriage is a dream of security; his new wife must respect him as a father and obey him as a God with absolute faith—and Daniela sets out to kill this image of perfection that he seeks, this last child of his male ambition.

DOLORES MEDIO

Dolores Medio was born in Oviedo, Spain, in 1920, and studied education and journalism.[1] She taught for ten years.[2] She won the Nadal prize for her novel *Nosotros, los Rivero* in 1952.[3] Her other novels include *Funcionario público* (1956),[4] *El pez sigue flotando* (1959),[5] *Diario de una maestra* (1961),[6] *Los que vamos de pie* (1963),[7] and *Bibiana* (1967).[8]

In *Diario de una maestra,* Dolores Medio presents Irene Gal, a senior in the University of Oviedo College of Education, who falls in love with her professor, Maximo Saenz, and spends a summer with him. She obtains work in a village, La Estrada, where she begins teaching elementary school and where she tries to bring about some changes. Meanwhile, Max insists that she return to continue graduate school in Oviedo, but the Civil War interrupts their plans. Max is imprisoned and she looks for him until she locates him in a jail in a distant village. There she comforts him from the outside. An official who is a friend of her family forces her to abandon this village and return to La Estrada where she learns she has lost her job. After some time, she is reinstated at the school and little by little the townspeople gain confidence in her and her new educational ideas. After 15 years she is still waiting for Max to leave prison even though Bernal Vegas, a good and well-to-do man, wants to marry her. At last Max is going to be set free and his only desire is to end his relationship with Irene. A few hours together is enough to demonstrate how much things have changed and Max departs, leaving her alone.

Family

At the beginning of the novel Irene is 19 years old, and having been an orphan since she was a small child, she lived for some time with her grandmother who died a few years before Irene went to Oviedo. The official who is a friend of the family comments: "And now I imagine that she will be set loose and free, like a dog without a master" (p. 102). When he forces her to return to her native town, she analyzes the situation; she doesn't want to go and see her relatives for she fears they will throw her problems in her face:

> And everything, of course, is a result of this pride. . . . If I could decide. . . . No, I can't! I prefer to die of hunger. . . . They know it and won't tell me anything. . . . If I went to them, they would poke fun. . . . They'd be giving me charity. . . . Maybe they would intercede for me with the Commission . . . for themselves, not me. I am the dishonored one in the family . . . they're all conservatives, people of order. . . . All moved by the Cause. . . . I, the black sheep. . . . Charity, recommendations and a hundred warnings. I told you so . . . that miserable. . . . No, no. . . . If they're proud, then so am I. It is the same family pride for both [p. 142].

Of Max's family we know absolutely nothing. It seems that Irene is the only person who worries about his well-being when he is in jail. He, as well as she, seems to be a person who wishes to break with the social conventions typical of their class. On the other hand, the lower class appears in the novel when Irene teaches in La Estrada. She confronts family situations in which the parents detest their children: the case of Timoteo, a 17-year-old boy who is hated by his grandfather because he is illegitimate; that of Bibiana, "doll-face," the little girl hated by her stepmother; that of Claudio, the son of a militant woman who abandoned him in order to fight in the war. In general, Irene identifies herself with them because as a child she felt alone and rebelled against her relatives who took care of her because of family obligations and not because of affection.

Social Class

The novel begins May 22, 1935, and ends May 4, 1950. Historically, it presents social changes and the evolution of the ideas of the intellectuals. Max, who represents the youths who came from other countries with radical ideas for social renewal, has followed the school of thought of Ortega y Gasset. However, in comparison with the official José Valles, the friend of Irene's family, Max appears to be an idealist but not a man of action:

> A revolutionary? No, worse than that. This isn't one of those who go out on the streets barechested . . . this is one who throws stones and then hides his hand . . . a philosopher of the narrow road. One of those of Ortega. They sow subversive ideas then wash their hands clean. . . . They are the true causes of what goes on. . . . One doesn't know how to treat them, how to undo them. . . . But they do harm [p. 101].

Irene has been a disciple of Max; she is also a girl anxious to bring about social reforms, but instead of limiting herself to talking, she wishes to apply her ideas to her humble village school. Two factions also exist in the village: the conservatives and the liberals. Trying to interpret each argument from the exponent's point of view, she finds herself being attacked by both sides. Only the children are on her side. Even during the war she did not want to take sides; she just followed her conscience. However, for being associated with Max, she is accused of being a "red" and cannot find work either as a teacher or as a factory worker. She realizes that the war has changed the system. Above all, the peasant women are beginning to work in factories, but even to do this they need some recommendations from influential women, and since Irene is blacklisted, she is forced to survive on her own. When the war ends, she returns to her work as a teacher, wanting to liberate herself from all hatred and to make life more simple by teaching love and peace. Without favoring one side or one class, she directs herself toward the most abandoned of beings, among whom is La Loba, a communist woman persecuted by the village. She had earlier had to intercede for Timoteo whom she had inspired and who later died in the war. Her ideas and the practice of them become one—a mission for her.

> Irene Gal is thinking now, like another time with Timoteo, which reality doesn't represent a comedy. Life also hurts her. She's always an open wound, and at the slightest contact she begins to bleed. For this it is easier for her to join the side of those who suffer, of those who live justly or unjustly scorned, of those who drag along the pain of some

> misery like a punishment, for the crime of having been born [p. 170].

Sexuality

Irene has sexual relations with Max the day she meets him. The fact that she is a virgin and has not told him fills him with disgust, for now he feels "responsible" for her. Max, who has lived in Germany, has a casual attitude toward women and when the two go to the country he asks Irene, "Do you want to go?" (p. 19). Irene doesn't answer, but gazes at him "childlike and bold, invitingly, like a challenge, as if she were telling him, "Do *you* want to?" (p. 19). She has bettered herself, but he, more reflexive, says: "I know better than you the society in which you have to live and . . . lastly, Irene, I will try to see that you will never regret it" (p. 21). Irene is a generous woman but also a woman with a feeling for her profession. When he asks her to join him in order to have her at his side, she prefers to teach in her little school. On the other hand, later when he is in jail, and is truly alone, she drops everything to be near him. She would even exchange places with him and sacrifice her life for him. During the following years, she lives in order to send him packages and letters and to wait to hear from him. When Bernardo Vega proposes marriage to her, she says:

> If Maximo didn't exist . . . if he didn't need me . . . if. Then certainly, I am sure I would marry him. I would quit, at last, being responsible for my acts and the acts of others. I could trust my own life to someone, let someone lead me, be a child again [p. 180].

This is the key to her personality that perhaps she does not want to recognize. Max offers her the possibility of having a man who will not guide her or tell her what to do. Although Vega is good, he is a strong man. As an "Indiano" he has made himself rich by his own efforts. He isn't prejudiced like the other local men and he knows that she is not a virgin. The only thing he hopes for is that she will, psychologically, offer him space "new, intact, reserved for him" (p. 190). Irene does not allow herself to be swayed because she, in spite of seeming to be a simple woman, has a very complex personality. Max tried before to model this girl, whom he believed to be "childlike and docile," but she has her own convictions and she fights for them. She is not free of sexual desires and upon feeling close to Vega, a virile and strong man, she has to control herself; many times she wakes up with "a violent desire which has ended in a flood of tears" (p. 187). On the other hand, she is aware that the day Max leaves jail, he will be an outcast within the community where she lives. She is too idealistic, however, and she transfers to Max her own qualities, makes him out to be a great teacher, a hero, a victim of the materialistic system against which she has rebelled since a child. Because of him, her wait is solitary and her sexuality heartbreakingly prudent. When at last he is set free, he is already 55 years old—she is 34—and is an exhausted man who wants to establish himself with a well-off woman and does not want to be a village school teacher. He reproaches her with, "Women bind you to an idea . . . " (p. 222). Because of the war, the political changes have destroyed their dreams, and he has left jail with the purpose of burying a past which no longer has a reason for being. He does not want to work on her project, "the Model Farm." Although he suggests to her that she might abandon everything and follow him, he knows beforehand that she could never untie herself from her students. While in prison, Max had a rich friend and he left with the intention of marrying his sister. At last Irene understands:

> And an electric current runs through her body. No . . . like cold sap . . . as if a vacuum was created within her. She felt a sensation that she had experienced before only two times in her life. The first when Maximo Saenz. . . . The other time in the hospital of Oviedo when someone told her that Maximo Saenz was condemned to death . . . and every time the vacuum sensation was stronger [p. 226].

The sexual act, death, and abandonment make her consider carefully the fact that Max is a coward because he can excuse himself and can attribute to the war his betrayal, not only of Irene but basically of his ideals. She herself is obliged to pretend an indifference that she does not feel because her pride hinders her. He offers to "pay" her when he knows very well that no price exists for a 15-year wait. She frees him from a debt and reaffirms that there is no reason for him to feel like a prisoner of his gratitude. He goes away—after a few hours—happy with not having to face a disagreeable scene. He recognizes that she is intelligent and a "great companion." They separate without a single kiss. She feels desperate, as if she were on the edge of a cliff: "For what do I want this useless life?" (p. 232). She is ready to take the step which carries her to the vacuum of death, but there is someone who detains her: the little invalid girl Babiana. She realizes that she has to keep on living in order to help forsaken children and that she has been loving a man of fantasy who has existed only in her imagination. Irene, at last, frees herself of her obsession that like a mirage has changed into an illusionary love through the years. At the end she alone is free.

Message

Irene is the Hispanic Penelope who patiently waits for a man to whom she entrusted her faith and her virginity. Max's odyssey, contrary to that of Ulysses, does not contain extraordinary scenes, but rather takes place within four prison walls. There her image of him changes. Faithful, she converts herself into a prisoner of a dream of love. She does not realize that having to face each individual crisis alone has matured her. At the end she has become reconciled with the realities of her children and of her community. She believes that Max is static and that he has remained the same, without understanding that Max has also had to arrive at some conclusions about his own life. Irene has denied herself another man and another close relationship because she believes that it is her duty to *wait* for the absent one. Although they had only lived together for three months without being married, she stretches out these memories for 15 years. Why did she wait for him so long? She herself had decided beforehand that Max was an incorruptible man, superior, a "soul-mate." She had continued creating an image of herself in this ideal dream of sharing herself with a man who would be her other half. Ulysses, upon his return, stays with Penelope only a very short period. Irene, according to Hispanic tastes, is no longer in the bloom of youth, and Max sees some signs of her aging. She has given up her chances of being married or having her own children because she believed that some day this "superior" man would accompany her. When the two meet, she realizes that they are two strangers. Now she will not have to await an absent Ulysses and she learns to accept the fact that her life has no more illusions. Her present is no longer tied to a fictional romance. What hurts her the most is that Max has turned against their youthful idealism in favor of the materialism that he used to criticize. The political goals for which he served so many years in prison have been a mirage. He goes out to join those against whom he previously preached. He ignores the woman who was his best disciple and who absorbed his teachings. Both of them represent a confrontation of ideals versus reality. Irene has succeeded in unifying the two. He has chosen the easier road and has sold himself to the world of materialism.

CONCHA ALOS

Concha Alós was born in Valencia, Spain, in 1929 and studied in Palma de Mallorca with the desire to be a teacher. She has worked as a television scriptwriter, as a fashion reporter, in a pastry shop, and as a teacher, and presently is employed as a writer.[1] Her book *Los enanos* won the Premio Planeta in 1962.[2] This prolific writer[3] has also published: *Los cien pájaros (1963),*[4] *Las hogueras (1964),*[5] which also won the Premio Planeta; *El caballo rojo (1966),*[6] *La madama* (1969).[7] and *Rey de gatos* (1972).[8]

Las hogueras[9] presents us with a married couple, Archibald Strokmeyer and his wife Sibila. Archibald is a very rich man; Sibila is a former Parisian model. Archibald has chosen to live on San Baulo island in order to have a more tranquil and studious existence. They have a chauffeur, Daniel Sanchez, whom they call Monegro. Archibald needs an appendectomy and meanwhile Sibila, who has become terribly bored with the island, finds Monegro the perfect accomplice for her plans to escape back to Paris to her modeling career. Monegro tricks Sibila, but when she goes to confront him at the police station, she forgives him. She, then, is left with Archibald and a dark and non-communicative relationship.

Family

Archibald is a foreigner and comes from a poor family. His father was animated, stubborn and a businessman yet he never was successful. Archibald, on the other hand, accomplishes what he sets out to do: make money. Afterwards, he wishes to spend the rest of his life in harmonious surroundings in the company of his beautiful wife. She owes him her comfort since he feels he has saved Sibila from a delinquent and sordid life. She comes from a humble family. Her father is a worker who, captivated by the extraordinary beauty of his daughter, raises her as if she were destined to become a queen. Sibila's mother is resentful because she feels like a maid to her daughter since her husband prohibited Sibila from undertaking any household tasks. When her father died, Sibila left home and became a model. She has an affair with a Cuban smuggler named Rosso until she tricks him and marries Archibald.

Two other characters in the novel are Monegro, who killed his uncle in order to rob him of his savings, and the local schoolteacher, Asunción Molino. Constantly comparing herself with her married sister who is mistreated by her husband, Asunción feels happy that she is single and independent.

Social Class

Among the poor on this island there are few differences. The local police, the teacher—although she has little money—and a few professionals belong to the middle class. Sibila and Archibald belong to the upper class and since they are outsiders, the normal rules of conduct of the region do no apply to them. Because at one time Archibald was poor. he has a great deal of compassion for those in need and he helps them financially when the occasion arises, yet he is personally bothered by the smell and the pleas of those who come to him for help. For him, freedom and happiness are only possible with money and thus he is ready to spend the rest of his life doing what he pleases without feeling any pressure from others. He never realizes the resentment that those who depend on him feel towards his wealth. Among these resentful people are Sibila, who feels "bought," and Monegro, who enjoys his automobile. The other person present on the island is the symbolic, phantasmal figure of Inglés de la Torre, whom the natives believe they can see and who they believe has power over them beyond the grave. He is as rich and powerful as Archibald.

Asunción Melino shows us the efforts that a teacher must make in order to maintain a level of life that is somewhat comfortable. She is thrifty and has carefully added to her studies, purchased a few books and permitted herself the luxury of living in a hotel that has hot water and meals. She, like so many public employees, lives from day to day, but at least she is happy because she does not have to account to anyone for how she spends her money and her time. Sibila, on the other hand, has all the money she wants from Archibald, yet she considers herself to be most unhappy:

> I live in a fortress filled with pillows. La Torre fortress in the cursed village of San Baulo. Hot water and a lot of food but always with the same view—the sun, the beach. . . . No one can see it. No person that could be a client at Xam's. Only a herd of swine: foreigners, fishermen . . . and Archibald [p. 146].

Sibila cannot identify herself with an intellectual like Archibald and has more confidence in those men who are physically strong, instinctively appreciate her body, and do not treat her as a fragile object. Rosso, her former lover, and Monegro are both men from the lower classes and both have criminal tendencies. While she tricked Rosso out of passion, with Monegro she is more generous, since she denies his part in the robbery and the authorities turn him loose. This man who almost died of hunger during the war is capable of making Sibila feel compassion even at the risk of losing her marriage and her respectability. Both Sibila and Monegro are like wild beasts trapped by society.

Sexuality

Sibila is a victim of her own beauty. Ever since she was a child she has been treated like a bit of decoration, a creature without the obligations others have. Even though her father was poor, he said, "Our daughter will never work. She will never be a slave to those lowly tasks. She will have servants. The whole world will bow before her, right, dear?" (p. 239). When her father dies, she still needs a witness for her beauty. As a model for an elegant firm in Paris she feels she has obtained the attention she needs, especially since Xam, the designer, uses her body in his creations. A symbiotic relationship develops between Sibila and the homosexual Xam. He says: "Your hips are marvelous for this gathered skirt. You see, Sibila, you are like sculpture. . . . Beautiful" (p. 61). Her dreams are fully realized when she feels the admiration of those who think her beautiful. When Rosso was her lover, he forced her to carry jewels through customs. "It will be easy. It will not seem strange that a woman as beautiful and elegant as you has such gems" (p. 145). But in reality, her life is not so wonderful, and Rosso's vulgarity and his demands tire her until she decides to denounce him to the authorities, since this is the only way she can free herself from him.

Archibald is the calm she needs to help her recover from Rosso, but she fails to realize that she has nothing with which to fill this calm. After the first months when she only eats and sleeps in an attempt to recover her strength, she one day opens her eyes and looks in the mirror and sees that she has gained weight and has grown lax in the care of her hair, skin and fingernails. Since Archibald married her for her beauty, now, according to her, "He never looks at me nor pays any attention to me" (p. 64). Archibald chose her at first as a recently found precious object but now he begins to see her as a human being, someone he can perhaps mold and educate. But his teachings are like monologues, since she thinks only of fashions, bars and of herself as a model. Archibald tries to get her to study the language of the island and even hires Asunción Molino to teach her, but he can never get Sibila interested in either the island or in books. While Sibila's intellectual laziness is evident, she needs sex as a form of tribute to her beauty. When Archibald becomes ill and can no longer satisfy her, she recalls:

> Rosso kissed me and said, 'Marvelous, beautiful. . . .' Drunk with desire, each millimeter of her body felt the caress of his lips. She would give years of her life to be at that moment kissed in that way. Kissed, bitten. Devoured by a voracious mouth. But her desire availed her nothing. She was alone, as desperate as a dog in heat, locked up in a dark room [p. 182].

While Sibila is capable of feeling compassion, she is also capable of resentment. The house, the servants, the money Archibald has given her are not enough. When she was with Rosso she could forget that she was an exploited woman and a jewel smuggler because whenever they went anywhere in public, everyone looked at her and envied her. Here in the island, she feels that she is wasting her beauty, that she lives in a prison. When Archibald can no longer have sexual relations and tells her so, she feels humiliated for having followed him everywhere trying to go to bed with him. She longs then for a Parisian brothel, where women can satisfy their desires with male prostitutes. The second step to infidelity is now easy. Excited by the sexual tales of the maids and by the masculine figure of Monegro, she feels that she is capable of finding satisfaction. While watering the garden with a red hose, she imagines that the hose "instead of being a brilliant plastic tube, was a dead snake" (p. 141). Since Monegro has access to the house as Archibald's chauffeur during his illness, she has the opportunity to see him. If she doubts for a moment, if her "being a woman" impedes her searching for a man, these inhibitions are soon forgotten; she has to do something in order to "quiet the devil within." She herself goes to see Monegro at his house, an act that causes her to break traditional patterns:

> Little by little she realized that what she was doing by taking the initiative was to confront, for the first time, the man's world. She knew that it was a very harsh world, full of traps, bright lights and rude, excessive falls. . . . She knew that it was a crazy world, a world where neither fear nor self-pity had a place. It was like entering a jungle [p. 188].

Sibila has from her youth learned that if her beauty attracts men, it also makes her vulnerable. The bear, the beast, the brutal man who bruises, bites and dominates her is the type that attracts her because only in this way can she feel completely possessed; it is almost a means of satisfying her frustrations. Even when she tries to struggle she does it only to succumb later to domination. While Archibald, with his delicate esthetic inclination, has not made her feel "devoured"; Monegro easily fulfills her wishes: "Isn't this what you were looking for . . . ? Well don't protest, here it is" (p. 195). She wishes to void her will and become a possessed object. To the question, "What would you take to a deserted island?" she answers, "A man." And when she finds Monegro she knows how to erase her boredom.

There is no doubt that Sibila is narcissistic and thus egotistical and vain. While still young and beautiful she is nevertheless a victim to her terror of growing old and ugly. In her there is a great desire to give, yet at the same time a great resistance to receiving even advice from men. Archibald wanted her to at least learn to drive a car or ride horses. Rosso treated her like a fool in front of the judges, like an idiot who did not even know what she was doing when she smuggled the jewels through customs. Sibila is not content because she wishes to take over the position that these men held. With Monegro, she has the opportunity to be kind, generous, human, and at the same time powerful, because he is poor and wants things he cannot buy. She then begins to dream of all that she can give him in order to make him happy, since Sibila still believes that there is a way to buy people. When she plans her escape back to Paris—taking money and jewels in order to have money with which to live on until she gets back her job as a model—she does so thinking that this is what a man would do in her place. Even in her rebellion she dares to think of herself as Rosso and Monegro would think of themselves. Monegro is taking her jewels to obtain money, but he decides to leave without Sibila because he is angry with her. Ironically, Monegro is stopped by the police for something else, and when they find the jewels they assume that he has stolen them. Here Sibila acts coldly, without reproaches and without tears—as she believes a man would act—and tells the police that "Yes, it is true. I gave them to him" (p. 276).

Asunción Molino is the other example of a woman who rebels against man's domination. Unlike Sibila, she is ugly. When she was young she had a boyfriend, and when he touched her breasts he told her laughingly, "Your virtue is lost" (p. 156). She pushed him and fled. At that moment she realized that she did not want to repeat the same story of all the women of the village who loose their senses over the first man who introduced them to sex. She wanted to control her own life— humble though it may be—and never be a creature of instincts. Thus, from then on, her relationships with men are platonic and as equal to equal. With great sacrifice she becomes not only a teacher but makes her single status work: she earns her own money, depends on no man and can choose the style of life that best suits her temperament. In her early studies at the Escuela Normal she had known Pablo Fontanals and for a time it seemed that they would marry, but he never proposed and they were separated by their work. Then she carried on correspondence with a former teacher, but the daughters of this lonely widower treated her badly when she went to see him. Asunción realized then that the daughters did not understand that the relationship was strictly platonic and she stopped writing. Her solitary life on the island continues, but when she compares her life with that of her sister who is married to a man "who follows the foreign woman like a dog" (p.

85), she is happy because at least she can take care of her money and does not depend on the pocket money of a husband. When Telmo Mandilego, the owner of the hotel, becomes a widower, he tries in vain to become her lover. She notices a peculiar trait in him: "Asunción could feel something mysterious in his face as he looked at her" (P. 86). She prefers to remain single rather than to marry only to appease her loneliness, but by chance her old friend Pablo Fontanals appears again, teaching in a nearby town. On weekends they get together to talk about books and they understand each other perfectly. Even at 35 she feels that they can get married and be happy together. She begins to imagine that at last she has found a compassionate man who loves her for what she is. When she receives a letter from him stating that he is going to marry another girl, she realizes the trick that he has played. Pablo has chosen a simple, ignorant girl "without complications and above all one who adores children, one who will take care of his old mother and himself, a delicate and sickly man." What Pablo needs is not a wife, but a maid for his mother and a female for his bed. Asunción, who believed that Pablo was an exception, now realizes that she was wrong: "She would be the misplaced person her whole life, the neutered cat who gets fat, the woman left seated at the dances" (p. 245). Experience has made Asunción change into an idealistic, intelligent, ambitious person and has given her a thirst for culture, but has made her resentful and a mistrustful spinster. While the word "spinster" is not to her liking, she realizes that it is applicable to her now since "she would now have to go through life without a man" (p. 85). She admits that "I have only succeeded in becoming bad, a resentful person with the most bitter thoughts—socially and physically inferior" (p. 172).

Archibald offers several clues to understanding why he and Sibila do not communicate. He married her for the same reasons a collector acquires another beautiful gem. After he takes pity on Sibila he idealistically believes he can help her:

> His wife. He. Two people without the possibility of communication. Archibald was drawn to Sibila out of greed, but also out of a deep and inexplicable compassion. There was a great difference between what Sibila was and what she thought she was. She considered herself a great model, a woman of the world, an elegant and exquisite mannequin

> and she was in reality an unhappy girl without any culture or curiosity. This was Sibila, aside from her beauty and her narcissism. Moreover, she was a person who did not know how to distinguish between the sordid and the noble. She was terribly confused, lost, without any notion of the correct path. He remembered the last night Sibila came to his room. He tried to approach her, speak to her as to another human being, but she withdrew into her little cell, her deep slavery to the flesh, and communication was not possible [pp. 230-31].

Archibald is a sensitive humanitarian and of great philosophical insight, but he can only see that his wife is full of contradictions. He believes that she is only a slave to her flesh, but he fails to realize that she compulsively needs the admiration of an approving public. As an art object she is vainly trying to free herself. The fashion house of Xam in Paris becomes a showcase in which she exhibits herself like a Venus. Archibald, who is involved in studying a medieval manuscript, is completely involved in philosophic questions and thus remains remote. He does not wish to judge Sibila because "history justifies everything that happens because it happens. Both the vanquished and the conquerors, the assassins and the victims, the executioners and the martyrs" (p. 222). After Sibila admits her complicity with Monegro, Archibald decides it is better not to speak:

> They had not exchanged a word, other than the brief mechanical phrases which their day-to-day living required. Afterwards, each clung desperately to the silence, knowing that silence was the only thing now that could sustain their lives. Not love, not ideas, not blood. Only silence to continue on slowly and silently onward, sustained by a dense covering of silence. A mass of clouds under which nothing exists [p. 277].

Message

The thesis of this novel comes from the opening lines of the *Alexandria* quartet by Lawrence Durrell: "We are neither strong enough nor evil enough to choose." Through four people who represent the extremes of man and woman the author has constructed a microcosm of dualities. Archibald and Asunción represent the rational side of life and Sibila and Monegro show the irrationalities of the flesh. Nevertheless they are all victims of their environment. Sibila has been molded by her father to live without doing anything; Asunción has learned from her youth to work. Sibila has always wanted to be the center of attraction, Asunción is so ugly that she even tries to hide the fact that she is a woman. Sibila obtains what she hopes will make her happy—a rich and compassionate husband. Asunción never finds a man who will accept her the way she is. Sibila is very ignorant, interested only in the physical and the sensual. Culture is a preoccupation of Asunción and she wants to be financially and spiritually independent even at the price of being a spinster. Sibila, on the other hand, risks the security of her marriage to satisfy her instincts and her need for rebellion. When the two women interact, Asunción as teacher and Sibila as student, both look at the other with indifference. Asunción sees a beautiful woman so egotistical that she does not even hear her teacher. Sibila sees a poor, ugly teacher who gives weekly lessons. Neither realizes that, in spite of their tremendous differences, they have a common cause that could make them sisters: both are looking desperately for an identity which is denied to them for different reasons. Sibila wishes to capture an immortal image of beauty, she wishes to live on untouched by old age, fat and ugliness. For her, men are only tools that she uses to give her what she needs (or thinks that she needs), but she is not tied emotionally to any of them. Sibila knows that Archibald, the intellectual, looks on her with tolerance and compassion. She wants to affirm her dominance over a man—no matter how low and vulgar he may be—and to use him as she believes men use women. Sibila sees her plans destroyed and must accept the fact that while she has broken all ties with men, she is still a prisoner of the inevitable human condition: old age, lack of communication and sterility.

Asunción has always sought her own identity, an identity which will save her from the fate of other poor women. She has made herself educated, self-sufficient and interesting in spite of her ugliness. She has idealistically sought spiritual qualities: understanding relationships, common interests and friendly companionship. More than sentimental attraction, she has sought her own image of the "exceptional" man. When she realizes that Pablo does not care for her she acknowledges her mistake. Her pride and dignity torture her, especially when she tries to analyze the situation:

> She knew she was happy next to Pablo, but she would have been happy beside her sister except that she thought her sister stupid. Moreover, she was never frightened when she was with Pablo and she was sure that if she were being caressed she would feel the same sensation as if he were caressing her with the walking stick he always carried [p. 246].

The author's thesis is that each character believes that they choose their path in life, or at least that destiny chooses it for them. In reality, this "destiny" is the design and plan of other people, and as a result the characters find themselves trapped by their own plans and expectations. Archibald provides the philosophical thread that binds the novel together, since his reflections bring together the seemingly isolated acts of the others into one pathetic solitary unit. In the work *Religiones politeístas de Asia,* Archibald reads that man develops psychological defenses to explain the arbitrary and unforeseen forces that he cannot control. It is as if the story were part of a great experiment in which all of the unforeseen and unexplicable events really do have an explanation. If we could come to know the laws of cause and effect that rule this ulterior reality, then all would appear clear. On an individual basis we can see that the auto-defenses each character has are—on an existential plane—their reason for existence: beauty in the case of Sibila, self-sufficiency in the case of Asunción, intellectual curiosity for Archibald, primitive "macho" supremacy for Monegro. With the title of the work, *Las hogueras* ("the fires"), the author condenses into one image an impression of life: "The desperate flight toward happiness which like an all-consuming fire destroys all and buries them in despair and loneliness, in the impossibility of escaping the daily and common routine of life" (p. 277). Like the brushfires of summer that take flame and are put out, the four protagonists try by different means to affirm their claim to happiness. These will-o'-the-wisp fires are deceitful and the victims suffer. Sibila is left with her rebellion still alive yet buried in the ashes of her subconscious. Asunción is like the dry plant who continues to shrivel without hope of water. Archibald will have to suffer in his solitude, since his search for God has become absurd, and even Monegro has seen his fatalistic outlook confirmed. He constantly repeats, "Each person is born with his destiny," and he sees the jail, the trap he has eluded for so many years, as a symbol of his own confrontation with terror. The author has thus shown us what each of the protagonists has sensed in "the weakness of their intellect and the power of their terror." They have all crossed paths, yet each has remained alone. Each has vainly tried to find love, but the fire has gone out almost as soon as it was lit because the dancing flames give light but they do not last.

Part II

Spanish American Novelists

GERTRUDIZ GOMEZ DE AVELLANEDA

Gertrudiz Gómez de Avellaneda was born in Camaguey, Cuba, in 1814.[1] Her father died when she was very young and her mother then remarried. Her stepfather became a hostile early figure in her life.[2] She preferred to show her affection for her brother, whom she later followed to Spain.[3] Her grandfather died leaving her and her mother without an inheritance. This seems to have greatly affected her, since one of the protagonists of *Sab* is a woman in the same conditions. In 1838 she traveled to Spain and remained there the better part of her life.[4] She wrote more than 20 works, among them six tragedies that made her famous: *Munio Alfonso* (1844), *El príncipe de Viana* (1844), *Egilona* (1845), *Saul* (1846), *Recaredo* (1858), *Baltazar* (1858).[5] Among her novels are *Sab* (1841),[6] *Dos mujeres* (1842), *Espatolino* (1844), *Guatimozín, último emperador de México* (1846), *La dama de Amboto* (1860), *El aura blanca* (1861), and *El artista barquero* (1861).[7]

Because of her passionate and restless temperament, her own life was much like a romantic novel. In her youth she was involved in amorous adventures in Cuba, interrupted by problems with the inheritance. In Spain, the great love of her life was a minor poet, Ignacio de Cepeda y Alcalde, whom she met in Seville in 1839. In spite of many separations and reconciliations, this love continued and was maintained through correspondence until 1854. (On the death of Cepeda, his wife inherited the letters and published them in 1907.) In 1844 Avellaneda had an affair with another poet from Seville, Gabriel García Tassara, by whom she had an illegitimate daughter. He not only abandoned her, but he also never recognized his daughter who died seven months later. Public censure and scandal ensued, but since Gertrudiz was still at the height of her dramatic career, her rebellion against the conventions of the day went overlooked. Carmen Bravo Villasante, her biographer, relates that when she was still in Cuba she was known as "la Doctora y la Atea" which shows diverse aspects of her personality. In 1846 she married Pedro Sabater out of friendship and compassion. Very ill, he died within three months of their marriage. She retired to a convent but a little while later she left to continue her literary career. She married colonel Domingo Verdugo in 1855 and both traveled to Cuba. There she was triumphantly received and even crowned in the principal theater. Her husband died in 1863 and once again she returned to Spain. Even though she continued to write, her health was failing and she died in 1873.

Her major novel, *Sab*, is of double importance. Historically, it is the first novel that denounces slavery in Cuba and is considered the *Uncle Tom's Cabin* of that country.[8] It is also the first novel by a Hispanic feminist writer that deals with the similarities between two social classes: slaves and women. One could even go further and say that Sab, the protagonist, represents all women.

In *Sab*[9] we find the family of Don Carlos, a Cuban landowner with five daughters. Carlota is the oldest and the most beautiful of them. Teresa, an unfortunate, illegitimate orphan, is her cousin. Sab, a slave who is protected by the family, is the illegitimate son of Don Carlos' brother. Carlota is pursued by Enrique Otway, son of Jorge Otway, a greedy Englishman. Enrique thinks that Carlota is very rich and asks for her hand, but when he learns that she has lost her fortune, he wants to break his promise. Sab, secretly and hopelessly in love with Carlota, has followed these developments carefully. Sab wins the lottery and the grand prize of 40,000 pesos, but he has Teresa pretend that Carlota has won it in order that she might have a dowry and thus marry Enrique, which she does. That same day, Sab dies and Teresa enters a convent. On her deathbed five years later, Teresa confesses to Carlota that Sab had made this tremendous sacrifice for her. Carlota is very unhappy with her lot as wife and daughter-in-law and finally realizes that the slave had been superior to the master.

Family

There are several levels to this novel which reveal differences not only between Catholics and Protestants, but also between legitimate and illegitimate children, and adopted children and substitute parents. Carlos' objection to Enrique is that he is a Protestant. Jorge, a Protestant, objects to Carlota's lack of money. Teresa, as the illegitimate daughter of a poor relative of Carlota's mother, has an inferiority complex which will not allow her to marry and so she enters a convent. Sab, whose mother was an African princess, must suffer as the illegitimate son of a younger brother of Carlos. Sab accepts his role of slave in the house, and the only family that accepts him as an equal is that of the Indian Martina in a nearby village. Teresa is white and Sab is a mulatto but both identify themselves with their illegitimate origins. Both are very conscious of their physical appearance and of their place in society. Between Carlos and his daughter Carlota there are great bonds of love and she is overly protected and pampered. Only after marriage does she realize that her sisters are now without a dowry. The women of the higher social class, without a dowry, are burdens on their families since there are no possibilities for them other than marriage or the convent.

Social Class

The great irony of this novel is that while Sab is a first cousin to Carlota, he cannot marry her because he was born a slave. They have grown up together, having the same lessons and reading the same books, especially since Sab is treated better than the rest of the slaves who have no family ties. On one occasion Carlota reflects on the lot of the slave:

> Poor, unfortunate people . . . they think they are fortunate because they are not beaten or persecuted and tranquilly eat the bread of slavery. They think they are fortunate, yet their children are slaves even before they leave their mother's womb and are then sold like beasts. . . . When I marry Enrique, no unfortunate person will breathe air poisoned by slavery. We will free all our blacks. What does it matter to be a little less wealthy? [p. 440].

As for Sab, his reflections on slavery are much more philosophical; the laws of God were perverted when men made laws to sanction the buying and selling of men. Sab also sees these same injustices in the case of women: poor, blind victims, "women, like slaves, patiently drag their chains and are weighed down by the yoke of men's laws. With only their ignorant and trusting hearts as guides, they choose a master for the rest of their lives" (p. 539). Sab feels that at least the slave may buy his freedom, but the woman can only be made free by death. Nevertheless, Sab is confident that there will come a "new reign of intelligence."

Social Class

Between the social classes there are many prejudices. Those of Hispanic descent consider those foreigners who have made their fortunes in commerce to be inferior. The foreigners believe that with money one can buy the "finest lady on the island." Economic conflicts play a large role, notably the lottery. Sab—in representing the women—is not interested in the fortune he offers to the person he loves. Enrique, on the other hand, is motivated only by the money of his future wife. Teresa could have accepted the money from Sab, but renounces it out of gratitude to the family who has cared for her. Carlota, ignorant of the source of the lottery, continues to believe that Enrique is marrying her out of love. When she later realizes her mistake, it is too late. Thus the author has a definite plan to use the lottery as a measuring tool for the various expectations of the characters of the novel. We must also note that Sab sacrifices his freedom; he could easily have traveled to another country and begun a new life. Even Teresa could have aspired to a better life, but for both of them spiritual values override pleasure and materialism. In several instances we see the *criados* as a special social class. This inequality becomes most evident when Sab is compared to a horse who is dying of fatigue and whose life is of no value to his owners.

Sexuality

Carlota, as the novel begins, is a young, innocent, romantic girl. Kisses and tears are the rule in her relationship with Enrique. She is gentle and kind in her treatment of Teresa and Sab. Blinded by her passion and believing that Enrique is marrying her for love, he becomes the center of her world. Not even the coincidence of the death of her brother in the city, the death of Sab in the fields, the entrance of Teresa into a convent and the departure of her father for her brother's funeral can cloud her wedding day: "What are all these, compared with your love. . . . I am yours! I love you! How very happy I am!" (p. 524). Only a few years later Carlota discovers that Enrique does not love her, that her father-in-law dominates both their lives, and that she is being treated "as a capricious child who asks for the impossible" (p. 529). Her "impossible item" is love, because even though she would like to continue as the impressionable girl of before, she cannot. The pain of the daily visits to Teresa at the Convent of the Ursulinas has helped her to mature. When she learns of Sab's love she becomes ill with sadness. She travels to his place of death and visits his grave every day. One day she disappears and goes to Europe with her husband and we never hear of her after this.

The sexuality of Teresa is very complex. When she arrives at the house she already has a well-formed personality: she is cold, reserved, unchanging. We learn that Teresa loves Enrique, but it is also possible that Teresa has experienced this love through Carlota. When she learns that Sab loves Carlota she becomes his confidante and indirectly gives him a bracelet with a portrait of Carlota: "It is a gift from Carlota which I value so highly that only to the person most worthy of my love and affection could I give it" (p. 520). Thus we are not too surprised when Teresa meets Sab late one night in a very private place and offers herself to him: "I will be your friend, your companion, your sister." Unfortunately Sab is only interested in Carlota and gently puts her off: "You are a sublime woman, Teresa. . . . I am not worthy of you" (p. 497). Teresa is the type of woman who lives a dream-like existence because there are no realities for her. Once, when Sab is about to reveal Enrique's true character to Carlota, Teresa stops him:

> Barbarian . . . who gave you the right to destroy her illusions, of taking her moments of happiness from her? What will you accomplish by destroying her dreams of love, which are her only reality? What will you give her in exchange for those dreams? Oh! You wretched man, anticipating her terrible day of awakening [p. 495].

The day Sab dies and Carlota marries, Teresa enters a convent. But even in the convent her interior struggles, which must be seen as her frustrated sexuality, do not cease. Ironically, it is only when Carlota tells Teresa of the poor treatment she receives from Enrique that Teresa is happy. Is Teresa the virtuous and sublime woman that all imagine? Or is she a malevolent woman who manipulates things so that Carlota learns the truth about Enrique? This last theory would seem to be born out by the conclusion to the novel. As she is dying, Teresa severs the last binding tie between Carlota and Enrique as she confesses the sacrifice of Sab: "He gave you the gold that caused Enrique to call you wife, but don't despise your husband; he is like most other men and there are even worse" (p. 531). After a pause, she gives Carlota a letter from Sab and adds: "Now, Carlota, are you tired of material existence? Do you need the poetry of suffering? Are you desirous of some hidden object?" (p. 530). Does Carlota represent profane love and Teresa spiritual love? Perhaps both are simply women who need to love. Teresa continues to think of Sab, who represents for her a world of love and virtue. Teresa, unlike Carlota, has always been wary of men, but makes an exception in the case of Sab.

Sab is a passionate person who is capable of jealousy, hatred and envy—even to the point of suicide. But he is also capable of sacrifice, generosity, love, dignity and heroism—even to the point of saving his rival's life twice. If Sab makes possible Carlota's wedding, it is because he is afraid she will die from love, just as he does in the end. When his heart can no longer stand the strain, he dies. Sab loves Carlota with loyalty and without thought of marrying her. Sab is also a rebel and often thinks of raising arms together with some other unhappy slaves on the island: "With a cry of liberty and vengeance I want to bathe in the blood of the whites; to trample their bodies and laws and thus die amongst their ruins, providing I can take Carlota with me to the tomb; life or death, heaven or hell . . . all is the same if she is with me" (p. 487). But Sab never rebels.

Message

Why has the author chosen a slave as a protagonist? His color represents an inescapable condition, even as does being a man or a woman. Being a slave signifies being a victim of the whims of men who judge by a person's color. On the island where we find several social classes, Carlota and Sab share the same destiny. Sab says:

> She must swear love and obedience to that man. She will give him her heart, her future, her entire destiny. . . . Respecting him will become her obligation. And he . . . he will take her as his woman like so much merchandise, by calculation, out of convenience . . . making a shameful bargain out of the most sacred tie, a most solemn endeavor. He will give his soul to her. And he will be her husband, the possessor of Carlota, the father of her children [p. 498].

Thus slavery and marriage are the same: "I think ghosts are passing before my eyes. Don't you see? It is she, Carlota, with her wedding ring and her virgin crown. . . . But a hateful, odious crowd follows her . . . boredom, repentance and further back that monster with the head of iron and a voice like a tomb . . . there is no way out! Oh, poor women!" (p. 538).

Two characters are the product of the author's own limitations as a child: her uncertain family life, her education, her lack of freedom of choice. Carlota's father refuses Enrique the first time he asks to marry her because he considers him to be from a lower social class. The second time he accepts because he now knows their true economic situation and is afraid his daughter will never marry. Sab, likewise, is not free to choose. The lottery gives him the opportunity to chose between slavery and freedom. Like a woman with a large dowry Sab can offer it to his beloved, but he cannot directly enjoy it himself.

Another point that the author tries to prove is that in spite of being a slave (which is like being a woman), Sab is far more noble than those around him. Sab is not blind, either, to the conditions of others:

> It is the men who have formed my destiny, yes, they have clipped the wings given me by God, yes they have built a wall of error and preoccupation between me and the destiny authorized for me by Providence, yes, they made useless all my God-given gifts. They have said to me: 'Are you strong? Be weak. Are you proud? Be humble. Do you long for great virtue? Drown your impotence in humiliation. Do you have an immense faculty for love? Well, suffocate your desires, you must not love any object that is beautiful, pure, and

> worthy of inspiring love. So you feel a noble ambition to be useful to those who oppress you? Well, bend under their weight and resign yourself to a useless and unacknowledged life, like the fruitless plant or stupid beast. . . .' Yes, men have imposed this terrible destiny on me, it is they who will have to appear before God—they will have to account for those evil deeds, they have perverted their immense responsibility [p. 537].

Sab also speaks for the author when he refers to the religion taught to women and slaves: "obedience, serve with humility and resignation and never judge" (p.533).

There is another reason why a slave may represent women. As the author herself has been vulnerable to great passions, she has also felt herself a slave:

> Is it possible, my God, that when I thought I was free of love's control, when I thought I really knew what love was, when I bragged of being an expert in love's ways, that I may have fallen victim, weak and defenseless, in the claws of an unknown, immense and cruel passion?[10]

Sab is controlled by his passion. The other men are calculators. Enrique, his father and the father of Carlota all plan and scheme and are moved by reason. To make the contrast between Sab and Enrique greater, she uses several examples. "Calculation, thought and convenience" (p. 528) are the three principle errors of men. When Carlota realizes that her life is one of solitude and not of love, she begins to detest men and their world. Sab, however, like a dog at his master's feet, is capable of humiliation. He has none of the characteristics the author considers typical of men.

Sab is dark, opaque, while Enrique is extremely white and luminous. Here the author refers to traditional occidental dualism (soul-flesh, light-darkness) which has always placed the woman in the negative role. Thus Sab from the beginning seems to have a stigma attached to him, and Enrique wins solely because he is so attractive. But Sab is the first to not be deceived by Enrique: "From the first, I knew that the soul enclosed within such a beautiful body was the resting place of pride" (p. 492). On another level, the author seems to indicate a possible allegory. Sab comes from African ancestry, traditionally associated with instinct, primitive irrationality, sensuousness and ignorance. Enrique is of English stock, admired because of its European cultural sophistication, civilized rationality, spiritual control and education. But careful examination reveals that Enrique is the inferior being and Sab the superior one. Step by step, the author has negated the *leyenda negra* of Sab, and, in reality, of womankind. She has thus indicated a new level of awareness for women; they no longer allow themselves to be tricked by the established doctrine of men. There are, however, noticeable differences between Carlota and Teresa. Carlota is a spontaneous girl, easily fooled by Enrique—even to the point of marriage. Teresa, a thoughtful and introverted woman, at first feels an attraction for Enrique, but quickly sees the difference between Enrique and Sab. She finally discovers that true beauty comes from the soul. We have already seen why Teresa allows her cousin to discover for herself the tricks of Enrique, and, only too late, the true value of Sab. Teresa ends her days in a convent, a place of no deceit, while Carlota ends her life in London, the place of mist, of the shadows of reality.

The liberation from slavery is a slow process and comes from within. Love can free or it can make one a slave. Love is the most beautiful and pure of human passions. If all women of this period suffer a traditional type of slavery, it is only through an intense love that they may obtain purification. Through generosity they overcome their own weaknesses and, like Sab, they are even capable of overcoming jealousy. Sab saves the life of his rival twice and Carlota grants him corporal freedom, but Sab does not leave, he is still tied by invisible bonds. He exclaims: "I have loved, I have lived. . . . I no longer live . . . but still I love" (p. 539). He has made his love a pathway to eternity. The material, physical body of his beloved means nothing to him. It is the invisible union of the spirit which he has accomplished by offering that which will make Carlota happy that is important to Sab. This union is in God, that is, in eternity; Sab has accomplished his freedom. According to the author, Carlota is still bound by the "chains of liberty" when she goes to the convent to complain of her lost illusions; she has not transcended, through her love for Enrique, the barriers which limit her to passive dependency. Perhaps the author has foreseen in Sab the inevitable summons of the body, through flight, into the universe, where there is no injustice or discrimination.

In closing we note that Sab has many characteristics which are similar to the biography of Gertrudiz Gómez de Avellaneda. Both had almost "unknown" fathers who died when they were very young. They both had four brothers and they dedicated all their love to a younger sibling: a brother (Manuel) or a small "near sister" (Carlota). Both are well educated, which separates them from others of the same station. When Enrique learns that Sab knows how to read, he muses, "Why so much talent and education in a man destined to be a slave?" (p. 425). Sab, like the author, is of a passionate nature and abandons himself to love. It has been said that the author began *Sab* between 1836 and 1838 and that what began as a novel against slavery ended as a romantic, psychological novel when she met Cepeda, her great love, in 1839. She did not finish the novel until 1841. These were the decisive years in the formation of Sab, the slave who represents, in the mind of Gertrudiz Gómez de Avellaneda, the feminine role in her society.

CLORINDA MATTO DE TURNER

Clorinda Matto de Turner was born in Cuzco, Peru, in 1852. During her childhood she was able to observe the life of the Indians on her parents' farm. Her mother died when she was quite young. She studied until she was 16 years old and soon after married an English doctor by the name of Turner. They moved to Tinta, an historic site, as it was the birthplace of the Indian rebellion led by Tupac Amaru. She began to write reconstructions of historical events, *Tradiciones cuzqueñas*[1] which first appeared in 1884. By this time she was already a widow and director of a newspaper, *La bolsa*, in Arequipa. Her move to Lima in 1886 was decisive in her literary career since she met many intellectuals in the capital and, more importantly, she became aware of the ignorance of the people of the city concerning the true conditions of life in the interior of the country. She tried, in particular, to denounce the abuses the authorities showered on the Indian population. In 1889 *Aves sin nido*[2] appeared, a work in which she shows not only the civil authorities but also the clergy as elements of oppression and corruption. Although the novel caused a great scandal, she had the support of President Cáceres who congratulated her: "For all you have done in fulfilling your duty as a writer to denounce grave crimes, especially those of the servants of the Church, about which I shall remind their leader, the Archbishop."[3] In 1891 her second novel, *Indole*,[4] appeared. Here a priest tries to seduce a married woman. This woman is under the influence of two men with personal interests at stake in her. While the priest wants to take advantage of his position as confessor, her husband uses his authoritarian influence to make her break her devout religious ties. So that he might forgive her for an error she has not committed, he asks that she give him her dowry so that he might pay his debts. Abused by two domineering men, she lacks the critical ability to choose for herself. In a conference the author presented years later she made references to this type of woman who is a slave to her husband, "who gave herself or was bound by preoccupations that held down the spirit, but always a slave."[5] In 1895 she published *Herencia,* a novel that tries to show that education is the basic factor in human conduct. Margarita and Camila, the two protagonists, represent the two extremes of women. The first girl has been educated by a virtuous and wise couple, Fernando and Lucía Marín. The second is the daughter of a rich aristocrat who believes only in money and a father who is a weakling. Both girls are reflections of their homes and continue the educational inheritance they have received from their parents in their own marriages. Although the author announced the appearance of three more novels in the flyleaf of *Herencia,*[6] they were never published. Perhaps they were destroyed when her house and printing shop were attacked by conservative forces. In exile in Argentina,[7] she published *Boreales, miniaturas y porcelanas,* in which she combined diverse writings, some of which were lectures given in Buenos Aires. Her last work, *Viaje de recreo,*[8] appeared after her death. She died in 1909, still in exile.

Aves sin nido has, as do her other novels, a double plot. The first plot concerns two Indian couples, Juan and Marcela Yupanqui, and Isidro and Martina Champi. The first couple is assassinated after suffering many abuses from the authorities. The second couple is accused, jailed, robbed and humiliated. It has been pointed out that this author is one of the first to have an "Indianista" intention, an attitude of denouncement in order to stimulate reform. I wish to leave this "Indianista" element to one side and concentrate on another intention of the author which has been completely ignored by the critics—the denouncement of the sexual exploitation of women. In the second plot of this novel appear two white couples, one of whom is Governor Sebastian Pancorbo and his wife Petrolina. They have a boy, Manuel, who we find out later is the son of a priest named Miranda y Claro. The other white couple from the important society of the capital is Fernando and Lucía Marín. After Lucía tries to protect the Indians, she and her husband are attacked at home and when the Yupanquis come to their rescue, they are killed. Margarita and Rosalía, the two small daughters of Juan and Marcela Yupanqui, are taken in by Lucía and they become part of her family. There then follow many incidents and complications. Towards the end of the novel, Manuel comes to ask for Margarita's hand in marriage. The climax of the novel occurs when it is discovered that Margarita is also the daughter of the priest Miranda y Claro and thus the two youths are brother and sister.

Family

The author places great emphasis on the conjugal relationship between Petrolina and her husband Sebastian Pancorbo. Although she is from the upper class of landowner and he from the lower classes, she endures all kinds of abuse from him. When her son Manuel tries to convince her to leave Pancorbo and to go with him to Lima, she resists the temptation. In order to better understand Petrolina's psychology, we must realize that she was pregnant when he married her. Publicly Pancorbo appears to be the father of Manuel, but there is a great deal of hostility between the couple as well as between Pancorbo and his "son." Once, when Petrolina complains about her disgrace, Manuel says, "Poor mother." She corrects him: "Poor women, you ought to say, Manuel, because for as happy as we may seem, there is always a worm that destroys us from within" (p. 167). Petrolina seems to accept the suffering that comes to her and meekly accepts her fate. There is a complicated relationship between Manuel and his mother. She, in order to pay for his education, must save whatever money she can and give it to Manuel so that he will not have to ask Pancorbo for any. And this happens in spite of the fact that all of the lands belong to his mother Petrolina. For his part, Manuel wants his mother to free herself from Pancorbo's oppression, but he cannot make her do so and finally he leaves by himself to continue his law studies in Lima

The other couple, the Marín family, has a pleasant marriage. He supports his wife's pleas to help the Indians. When she decides to take in the two orphans, he willingly accepts the added responsibility. When Fernando learns that Lucía is expecting her first child, he promises to take her to Europe. When she reminds him of Margarita and Rosalía, he promises to send them to a good school in Lima. This couple represents, to the author, the ideal marriage and, in effect, a rare bond of generosity and understanding does unite the young couple, especially since Lucía is not yet 20 years old.

The author also shows that unity exists in the Indian marriage relationship. The Indian women, Marcela and Martina, have more initiative in solving their problems than the men, who are depressed, reticent and pessimistic. It is possible that the author is trying to show that women are more practical when it comes to a confrontation with the harsh reality surrounding them. One thing that is constantly emphasized by the author is the white peoples' practice of taking the Indian daughters away from their parents in order to use them as hostages and merchandise in the payment of debts. In this way the author explains how many young Indian girls were "servants" to people living on the coast. In stark contrast to this, the treatment that Margarita and Rosalía receive from the Marín family shows that they do not have the same racial prejudices as other whites and that their sense of humanity and justice makes them the exception and not the rule among the rich white families.

Social Class

The action of the novel takes place in a small village in the mountains of Peru. There the division between the whites and the Indians is well marked. The upper social classes are made up of landowners and government authorities such as the governor, the mayor, priests and lawyers. The author makes clear, however, that these administrative officers have been named to these positions for having served the political party in power. Thus, these officials are only interested in gaining as much as they can from their short period of administrative power. Manuel says, "They look for employment, salary and an easy life" (p. 131). They all strive to become rich at the expense of the defenseless Indians. The village priest, Pascual, sides with the whites because he too exploits the Indians under the pretext of his ecclesiastical position. It is he who organizes the attack on the Marín family and he who expresses what the whole group feels: hatred for the Indian and the desire to terrorize anyone who interfers with their plans and their hypocrisy, since their method is to "throw stones and hide." He says, "It deals with the fact that Doña Lucía has asked us to intercede on behalf of some crafty Indians who do not wish to pay what they owe; and to do this she has used words that, frankly, like Don Sebastian says, if they were understood by the Indians, they would destroy our customs of allotments, enforced service, payments and the rest . . ." (p. 29).

The author also shows how men in administrative positions try to abuse women. Prefect Paredes would have been able to violate Teodora if her father had not made her take refuge in Petrolina's house. Father Pascual wanted to rape Margarita, Marcela's daughter, and insists that she be sent to be a maid in his house. Later we find out that the former priest of the town who had become a bishop, Miranda y Claro, had violated Petrolina, a woman from the upper class, and a poor Indian girl, Marcela. The words Manuel throws at the priest Pascual Vargas for his part in the conspiracy are well worth remembering: "Remember that it is not the habit that causes us to respect the man but rather it is the man who is to be respected, since the habit covers both good and bad priests" (p. 69).

The most helpless class is the Indians who are humiliated and poorly treated. They are forced to suffer whippings, jail terms, theft, slander and other humiliations. When Juan Yupanqui tells his wife Marcela, "I am older than you and I have cried without hope," he repeats the entire history of the injustices suffered by the Indian. And when Isidro tells his wife Martina, "Your hands and mine are free from robbery and death" (p. 132), he is also expressing the reproach of the innocent to the guilty. Martina herself later exclaims: "We are born Indians, slaves of the priests, governors, leaders, of all those who grasp the staff of the ruler" (p. 248).

The Marín family is rich. They are strangers from the coast who have come to the village for business reasons. Although they are from the upper class, the whites in the town consider them as traitors and will have nothing to do with them. Petrolina, who is from the upper class, married a man from the lower classes, but thanks to her influence he became governor. Manuel, who knows his true origins, does not identify himself with the upper class of the town. He acts like an outsider although he was born in the village. It is he who begins to investigate and to search for those guilty of the crime against the Yupanqui family. In the eyes of the upper-class people of the town he is a traitor, since no one knows that he is not Pancorbo's son.

Sexuality

Lucía is the protagonist who expresses the personality of the author. She is a wholesome and compassionate woman, very much in love with her husband and with many of the traditional attitudes of the Latin American woman. As the author says, she learned from her mother that the woman is born to "give poetry" to the house (p. 143). Naturally, she must use some of the traditional tactics to win the support of her husband. For example, when she asks her husband for money to help the Indians, she covers her true purpose and simply asks for a new dress, to which he says; and she replies:

> 'So, little one, you act like a schoolgirl, speak, but remember that if you use the money for something else, you will pay a fine.
>
> 'A fine, you always charge fines, my sweet, I will pay that fine'[p. 25].

Margarita does not say much in the novel and we only see her romantically idealized through the eyes of her lover Manuel. Petrolina is the one who has suffered, in her youth because of the violation by the priest, and in her motherhood because she has had to sublimate all need for kindness and affection. Her drunken husband's brutality only serves to make her feel less guilty, it is as if she were atoning for a hidden sin. She tells Manuel, "Remember that I am Sebastian's wife, and that I am bound to him . . . by gratitude, and you must respect him" (p. 112).

The author has very well-defined ideas concerning the celibacy of the priests. She says: "Let's not blame God, let's blame the laws of man" (p. 183). She believes that they would be better off married: "Yes, my God . . . you have made man sociable, you have placed in his heart the ties of love, of brotherhood and family. He who rejects this, he who flees from your work, curses natural law . . and will be abandoned" (p. 107). At the beginning of the novel we see the priest, Pascual Vargas, enjoying life and hypocritically using his concubine to learn of events in the town. Towards the end, however, we see this same priest in a weakened and delirious condition. He not only confesses his lust but also his abandonment:

> In this forgotten parish, I am a poor father to children who will not recognize me, and the memory of women who have never loved me is a poor example for my parishioners [p. 79].

He also suffers from guilt feelings and all of his repressed sexuality reveals itself. What is worse, hypocrisy makes him lead a double life, and in this way the author reveals to us the moral crisis of a man who has sworn vows of chastity that he cannot obey. The father of Manuel and Margarita, Father Miranda y Claro, is never seen in the novel because he has been sent to another town, yet the fact that he has become a bishop clearly shows that evil triumphs and that it is women who are the victims of crimes such as incest and rape perpetrated by priests. The author proposes, through the mouth of Manuel, a legal change; he is going to write his thesis on the need for priests to marry.

Message

The work ends with the words of Fernando when he discovers that Manuel and Margarita are brother and sister:

> Let's not blame God, blame the inhuman laws of men who take children from their parents, the nest from the bird, the stem from the flower . . . [p. 183].

The title of the work, *Aves sin nido* ("birds without a nest"), means "children without fathers." "Nest" cannot mean "home" in this case since both Manuel and Margarita come from well-established homes, but in both cases they are children without a father who can call them his own, and they both suffer from the dishonor of their mothers. Octavio Paz, in *El laberinto de la soledad,* speaks of a similar situation in "The Children of the Chingada" (page 79):

> The Chingada is the Mother forcibly opened, violated or deceived. The son of the Chingada is the offering of violation, abduction or deceit.

The author tries to show that both women were innocent. When Manuel is about to confess the secret of his birth of Fernando, he says: "First I must talk with my generous mother, upon whom I cannot cast . . . not even the slightest shadow of dishonor. Mother, dearest mother. . . . Fate placed me in your womb and later . . . oh, my presence has tortured your life" (p. 140). Likewise, in the case of Margarita, the author states through Lucía that "This girl was born by accident, not of corruption, and you know that between rape and lust carried out intentionally there is the same distance as between vice and virtue. . . . [I]n any case, you will find the knavery of a priest, nothing on the part of the woman" (pp. 280–81). The author has chosen two women from the extremes of society to show that each is a victim of a lustful man. Petrolina, the daughter of a landowner, believes in her father confessor. She is the victim of deceit and violation. Marcela, the daughter of humble Indians, is violated while serving as a maid to the priest. Her will is of little consequence because she is little more than a beast of burden who bears the violence of her masters. Both women quietly suffer the abuse. Since both become pregnant, each solves the problem according to her social position. Petrolina marries Pancorbo and suffers his punishment. Marcela marries Yupanqui who accepts her because he understands the ways in which the whites use their Indian servants. But the author does not confine herself to these two cases alone. Lucía comments on her impressions of the homes for foundlings in Lima:

> What has most caught my attention is the surprising number of orphans in the house for foundlings. Oh, Fernando . . . I know that the women of the village do not thus throw away pieces of their hearts. . . . I know there is no need to throw them out, just because social pressures require feigned virtue. Nothing, no family tie exists between the mothers and the children born by chance . . . or from crime. Fernando, I hope God will forgive my evil thoughts but this idea has arisen from my sad thoughts, remembering, without wanting to, the secret of Marcela [p. 176].

According to the author, the reason the women from the lower classes get rid of their children is because they do not want to face sacrilegious shame. If the position of the author seems too extreme, we must bear in mind that she is motivated by liberal political views that cause her to criticize a conservative and ultra-religious system. She supported the liberal policies of President Cáceres, but when the opposition candidate, Piérola, initiated a revolution against Cáceres, she had to suffer the consequences. Many years later, in exile, she compared the two candidates:

> General Cáceres leaned towards the liberal party, it was said that he was a Mason, and that during his first term the Jesuits were expelled; on the other hand, Piérola was a

> fervent Catholic and his promises to the conservatives were quite grand [pp. 41–42.].

It is impossible to separate liberalism from anti-clericism in Peru during this period. In *Horas de lucha,*[9] in a lecture entitled "Las esclavas de la Iglesia," Manuel Gonzalez Prada says:

> No one would be more inclined to reject religion than a woman, since it holds her back even to keeping her in perpetual infancy or indefinite tutelage. But it is not like that: she stands against her redeemers, the victim blesses her army and fights on the side of those who hold her captive. She will have nothing to do with the free-thinker and rejects as her enemy the reformer who comes to save her from oppression and disgrace, who proclaims the annulment of a marriage, not only by mutual design but also by the will of only one of the partners.

Matto de Turner maintained a constant, valiant, liberal position. As director of the magazine *El Perú ilustrado* she took up the cause of those persecuted by the ultra-conservatives. A good example of this is the case of the Protestant Francis Penzotti who was jailed for distributing material from the North American Bible Society in 1888. Matto de Turner not only interviewed him, but she also generated a great deal of protest against the Constitution of 1860 which prohibited any religious activity that was not Catholic. Her triumph came when Penzotti was freed by the Supreme Court, bowing to international pressures. In 1891 she published the story "Magdala" by the Brazilian Coelho Netto. The work was considered blasphemy against Jesus Christ and for this act she was excommunicated. Earlier, on the occasion of the publication of *Aves sin nido,* the Archbishop of Arequipa prohibited the reading of the work and even the Bishop in Lima denounced the author as being an "atheist and irreverent." With the publication of *Indole* in 1891, public furor sprang up and she lost the directorship of *El Perú ilustrado.* She and her brother then founded a periodical called *Los Andes.* In 1895 the liberal candidate Cáceres, who succeded Morales Benavidez, was elected president for a second term but an immediate revolution on behalf of the losing candidate Piérola brought about the persecution of the liberals, among them Matto de Turner. Her press was destroyed, her house was ransacked, and she had to flee to exile in

Argentina. In a visit to the Brazilian Netto which she describes in *Horas de recreo*, she gives her own evaluation of these events:

> It is true, Netto, but do not believe that everyone in my country was blind; men of great learning and open minds may be found there; it was a campaign led by those priests who took up their habit for commercial purposes, like the shopkeeper behind his cabinets and all this is over now; today they judge me quite differently in my country, and I myself judge the events with a different view; after this visit with you, I am off to visit the Pope; in religion as well as in politics the same things happen: there are true and false patriots; I respect the true believer, whatever his affiliation or creed [p. 25].

In 1908, one year before her death, she made a trip to Europe and was acclaimed in Spain as a great writer. In 1910 her book *Viaje de recreo* appeared posthumously in Spain. In her will she had declared that part of the income from the sale of the book would go as an endowment to any young girl who entered the orphanage the day of her death and the rest of the income was to be sent to Cuzco to be used for Woman's Hospital in her native city. Even at the end of her life she kept her interest in helping women as well as her desire to bring the gospel to the Indians. In 1901, still in Argentina, she translated several of the gospels into Quechuan and the American Bible Society paid for their publication. With this action she left behind ample evidence of her liberal thinking concerning freedom of religion and her interest in the modernization of the Peruvian clergy.

MERCEDES CABELLO DE CARBONERA

Mercedes Cabello de Carbonera was born on the southern coast of Peru in 1845 and was a witness to war between Chile and Peru.[1] When she reached maturity, she became the voice of reform for her country and in her novels she strove to reexamine national attitudes.[2] *Sacrificio y recompensa*[3] appeared in 1886, *Eleodora* in 1887, *Los amores de Hortensia* in 1888, *Blanca Sol* in 1889, *Las consecuencias*[4] in 1890, and *El conspirador* in 1892.[5]

Blanca Sol[6] her first naturalistic novel, appeared as a serial in *La nación* during 1888. After the first edition, published by Torres Aguirre, there appeared in 1894 a second edition with a prologue by the author in which she states the following:

> I have always believed that the social is of equal or greater importance than the romantic novel. To illustrate and study the imperfections, defects and vices which are admired, sanctioned, and esteemed in society is of much greater benefit than to study passions and their consequences. . . . And since we are dealing with a well-planned work and not merely an invented story, it is important to also study the determining factors of heredity, which are deeply entwined with education and poor example; it is important to study the atmosphere in which they live and develop those vices we wish to point out, all based on observation and experience. And if it is certain that this study and this experience cannot be gained except in the society in which we live and for which we write, it is likewise certain that the novelist need not copy specific people. If they are the result of experience and observation, the public will judge the errors in their conduct that become evident . . . [p. iv].

Cabello de Carbonera's thesis concerning the superior "social novel" appeared in a short work called *La novela moderna,*[7] and it is evident that *Blanca Sol* serves to illustrate the concepts of the author. Blanca, the protagonist, who belongs to the ancient, ruined aristocracy, has been spoiled to the extreme that she believes that nothing can be denied her. She marries Serafín Rubio, whom she does not love, simply because he is rich. She aspires to political positions for her husband that are beyond his ability. She meets Alcides, an Italian businessman, during a social function and he falls in love with her. After many romantic intrigues, Blanca Sol decides out of wounded vanity to recapture the love of Alcides after he marries Josefina, her seamstress. Alcides causes Serafín to go bankrupt and thus avenges himself on Blanca, whom he cruelly humiliates. At the loss of his fortune, Serafín becomes insane and Blanca becomes a prostitute to support herself.

Family

Blanca has been raised by her mother, since her father has either abandoned them or is dead. Her mother is a very beautiful woman who continues to maintain the appearance of money, thanks to the "gifts" she receives from a Mr. M. Thus Blanca from infancy has accepted a form of life based on vanity and luxury and is admired by the local girls who attend a school run by nuns. They are all impressed with Blanca's beauty and grace but no one thinks of "educating" her:

> What fault is it of hers if from childhood she has been taught to love money and to consider the glitter of gold more important than her social standing? What fault is it of hers if she has married a most ridiculous but much sought after man to save her family from a difficult situation [p. 181].

Blanca and her mother have a friendly relationship but her mother stimulates her daughter's desire to be the most beautiful and elegant woman of her social class. She doesn't help Blanca to see that the family life of a married woman will reveal other aspects of life that until now she has ignored. Blanca breaks off her relationship with a young man she loves when he loses his fortune, but she skillfully reveals that after her marriage they will be able to continue their relationship. After her marriage, Blanca's life centers around her social activities and although she has a child every two years, she has no interest in either motherhood or in having more than the five children she already has and therefore she places certain restrictions on her husband. Her ten years in the convent seem not to have created any feeling of guilt or obedience in her.

One person who serves as contrast to Blanca is Josefina. Like Blanca she comes from a ruined aristocratic family, her father having lost their inheritance through his incessant gambling. She was educated by her grandmother who is a woman in the old style. Josefina is a virtuous girl who makes herself responsible for the maintenance of her two younger brothers and her grandmother. Since the only work Josefina is capable of doing is sewing, she earns very little and it is only when Blanca takes her in that she has a secure job. As opposed to Blanca's mother, Josefina's mother is very religious and believes that God is testing them, but that he will bless her granddaughter because of her virtue. Josefina has no marriage plans and if Alcides had not crossed her path she would have remained single, and burdened with responsibilities, and her brothers would not have been able to attend public schools due to class prejudices.

Social Class

The idea of social class is a key to the understanding of the action and characters of the novel. The great social upheaval that took place in those years is best expressed by a witness to that period:

> A new uneasiness, deep, unexplainable, devours us, makes us uncertain, takes our desire away and threatens us with a future even more bleak; and this situation cannot change without making it worse, because it comes not from the nature of man but the nature of things, it derives its evil not from the men of today but rather from those of the past, that is, from those past thirty and their economic errors that have formed our way of being and our way of life[8]

While this is only an opinion, it is confirmed by economic data of the period wherein landowners lost out to foreign investments, business came to depend almost entirely on *guano* and social upheaval was caused by complicated governmental and political systems which sought to control dwindling urban resources. Some classes rose and others fell. The rich fathers of Blanca and Josefina lost all they had, leaving their families with an aristocratic name but little else. Other men grew wealthy, such as Serafin's father, a Colombian who thanks to his work and his avarice in business, left his son a great fortune. Serafín, however, is not sure he will remain rich since there are other "foreigners" who are manipulating the affairs of state and who are competing—thanks to the Constitution of 1860—with the freedom of industry. This is the period of the construction of railroads, government loans, depreciation of paper money and emigration. It is not strange, then, for the aristocracy to look upon their children as a solution to their calamities. Blanca is a good example of the alliance between money and a name. Likewise, Josefina and Alcides represent the mixing of the Spanish with Italians and other foreigners that had once been despised. If Blanca, after the bankruptcy of Serafín, descends to the lowest form of prostitution, Josefina by her marriage joins two classes—the ruined aristocracy and the lower class on the way up, as represented by Alcides. The essayist José Carlos Mariátegui defined this social change thus:

> The profiteers, both direct and indirect, began to construct a capitalistic class. A bourgeoisie was formed in Peru, linked and confused in origin and structure with the aristocracy.[9]

What Blanca says is significant when she realizes her ruin: "Wretched people, if I had my four million *soles* today, no one would dare ask for more virtue than my money" (p. 182).

Sexuality

There are various stages in the development of Blanca's sexuality. As a child she is narcissistic, she likes to be in the center of attention, the most beautiful and admired of the girls. In her youth, her coquettishness is used to achieve her end, a rich husband. Her boyfriend of five years is cast aside when her "catch" and his millions arrives. Now that she is married, she can acquire those European items that the industrial and artistic world had to offer: mirrors, mosaics, chandeliers, paintings. (This period coincides with the *guano* "boom" which takes the country by storm and during which all types of luxury items were imported.) In one area Blanca does her best to outdo the rest: titles. Thus she pushes her husband into politics, first as Minister of Justice and then even to consideration of the presidency of the country. She does not hesitate to use her beauty to obtain the popularity Serafín does not have. That is, Blanca flirts but never enters an adulterous relationship. Alcides—her long time admirer—thinks that she is "coquettish, dissipated, evil, but never adulterous, nothing but a flighty and simple woman" (p. 177). A third stage in her life is the impulse to play at sexual politics, wherein the goal for Alcides is her body, but for her the triumph will be her feminine pride in showing that no man can win or dominate her without her consent. There are two occurences of this "sexual duel." The first example is when Alcides tries to rape her, she physically resists, and he falls and is hurt. Blanca laughs and when her husband finds blood on the floor, she responds, "It was only a wounded dove" (p.76). Thus she is the huntress, Diana, the invincible. The second example is much more complicated since Alcides has made a bet in front of all his friends that he will win her over. When she learns of the wager, she laughs at him and ridicules him in front of his friends. The timely intervention of Josefina allows Alcides to hide some of his shame, but this is when he puts his plans for cruel vengeance into action. He begins by ruining Serafín financially and then he marries Josefina, Blanca's seamstress, as the greatest insult he could think of to Blanca's pride. Now Blanca's personality undergoes considerable conflict owing to the indoctrination she has received from her mother as a child:

> Try hard not to allow anyone to equal much less surpass you in elegance or beauty so that men will admire you and women envy you [p. 3]

Blanca, who until now has not been in love with Alcides, suddenly undergoes an emotional crisis which makes him indispensable in her life. When he announces that he is going to marry Josefina, Blanca calls him to her and says, "Love arrives when the beloved escapes," to which he replies, "Love leaves when the lover tires" (p. 120). She then begins to make moral judgments concerning marriage without love as being a form of prostitution sanctioned by society (p. 118) and refuses to sleep with her husband. There follows a series of incidents between the two couples. A letter from Blanca to Alcides is "innocently" returned to her husband and a duel is set, which out of practical concerns never takes place. Lastly, a note from Blanca to her husband in which she announces she is leaving him gives rise to an emotional trauma in Serafín that is so violent it drives him mad. He lives in the insane asylum obsessed with the thought of killing his wife. Meanwhile the creditors come and take almost everything, leaving Blanca with barely enough upon which to live. She, her five little children and her loyal maid go to live in several humble rooms. Now Blanca enters the fourth stage of her life. She goes looking for Alcides, but he gives her a long lesson on "morality" and tells her to look for another man with whom to "prostitute herself" since he now has a "beloved wife" who offers him "complete happiness" (p. 187). Blanca reacts to the hypocrisy of Alcides: "That is the last straw, that she, Blanca Sol, should cry and for what? Because a man, a miserable man, had decided to insult her. Cry for him! As if there were no other men on earth!" (p. 187). Her deflated pride becomes an open and declared war against the affected morality of men, social hypocrisy and the double standard. Until now she has maintained a somewhat romantic notion of her love for Alcides, even if she did not understand it well, and now she has a different, much more clear attitude. No longer will she try to hide her poverty but will openly use these same men who had been her "friends" in order to sell the only thing she has left—her beauty. Rejecting her previous hypocrisy, she puts on a dressing gown and invites the neighbors—girls of doubtful reputations and humble social standing—in to meet her former "admirers." These men, like Alcides, affect a rigorous morality at home but are themselves those who secretly frequent houses of prostitution.

We need to clarify an important point in the personality of Alcides in order to understand his morality. In the beginning, he tried to seduce Josefina by offering to become her "protector." She rejected the offer because although she was poor she was "decent." If Alcides marries Josefina later, it is precisely to prove that he appreciates "virtue." After having made public his wager with his friends as to the way in which he would conquer Blanca, a married woman, he does not later hesitate to preach of virtue to that same woman now impoverished, who returns and tries to rekindle his love. He who has robbed the innocent Serafín of his investments, does not vacillate one moment in sending the wife of his victim out to "work" as a prostitute. We must not think that the author is trying to excuse Blanca; there was at least one well-known case in the late 1880's in Lima of a high society woman who instead of acting as befit her social position, acted in a "shameful" manner. Nor does the author wish to excuse Blanca for Serafín's ruin, since public opinion also blames her for wasting her husband's money without considering that he lost his money in bad investments through the tricks of astute and unscrupulous foreigners like Alcides. What the author is trying to underline is a social thesis: Although Josefina is poor, she resists Alcides' temptation to "protect" her, she has thus merited a prize for her virtue. Like her grandmother, Josefina believes that "men do not value the women they have conquered" (p.108) even if they feign disinterest in their favors. The blind faith of her grandmother that "God will reward her virtue and will restore her lost fortune" (p. 135), shows that the author does in fact agree with Alcides when he says "happiness without virtue is impossible" (p. 157). The most surprising aspect is that Alcides the "lion," the "man of the world," the "conqueror," should marry a girl like Josefina who at 24 was, for her time, a spinster without a dowry, and with two small brothers and a grandmother who depended on her. The only possible explanation is that Alcides has planned a vendetta against Blanca for having humiliated him in front of his friends.

Message

This novel presents an allegory of the national situation of the 30 years between 1860 and 1890 in Peru. Blanca Sol represents *Perú*, the traditional child of the Sun. Blanca (white) is her name, but it also represents the traditional Hispanic colonial aristocracy of Peru. Her education in a convent is typical of other girls' from the higher social circles. Even without any money, Blanca and her mother pretend to be well-off. Serafín Rubio represents the descendent of the rising new social class. His father was a soldier who, from humble beginnings, rose to become a businessman. Serafín then joins forces with the poor aristocracy. Serafín is ugly and everybody continues to call Blanca by her last name "Sol," indicating that even after Independence the old aristocracy was more admired by society than were the nouveau riche. But Blanca Sol soon loses the austerity of her predecessors and succumbs to the elegance and decadence of French cosmopolitan manners. Blanca's attitude toward religion is also "modern"; she goes to Church, but does so out of habit and vanity and not because she is a believer.

Josefina serves as a foil to Blanca and represents the virtues of Spanish-Catholic domestic life: "For seven years Josefina has been enclosed in the narrow walls of her home, she lived without dreams, without more than her proud grandmother and her two small brothers" (p.91). The grandmother, even in poverty, "preserved the deepest faith, a type of fanaticism of certain families, who await fortunes that they once possessed and which, according to them, God took away only to test their unbreakable faith and which would be returned" (p. 90). The distinction that the author is making is one of ethics. Blanca has influenced Serafín to the point that he adapts to her extravagant modernity, her taste for expensive European goods and banquets and parties to gain political power. The only time Serafín protests is when Blanca loses 10,000 *soles* at the gambling tables. Here, the author criticizes the terrible vice of gambling, common among the wealthy Peruvians of the day. While Blanca achieves a cabinet ministry for Serafín, her presidential ambitions for him initiate the downfall of the period which is well captured by the author in her book *El conspirador*. An historical element which must be taken into consideration is that Piérola, a cabinet minister, proposed that the exploitation of guano be given over to foreign companies. Thus the Italian Alcides symbolizes the immigrant who makes love to Blanca—el Perú—who, although at first she ridicules and laughs at him, in the end offers herself to him as a victim of the economic errors, loans and financial catastrophies that occurred in that period. Finally there is no longer any need for Blanca to put on airs and she accepts her moral and economic bankruptcy. One might ask, who triumphs? Alcides, who—not content with ruining Serafín and mocking Blanca Sol—marries the poor, virtuous aristocrat who owes him everything. He feels like a magnanimous king, embodying the "miracle" the grandmother was waiting for, the foreign bourgeois who emerges after the crash of '79, altering the previous social hierarchy.

When Blanca Sol accepts her misery and ruin, she also accepts the truth. All the previous workings of social hypocrisy and illusory expectations—her husband's position, her passionate interest in a never-before-felt love—suddenly lose meaning when people no longer believe Blanca Sol to be favored by fortune. Another Peruvian of this period confirms what she must have felt:

> We are bankrupt. The most pessimistic predictions of yesterday have been exceeded. Our profits do not climb, as they did five years ago, to eighteen million *soles*, we will be

> lucky if we can maintain them at six million. We are fighting invincible difficulities. Each day that passes is a conquered danger, a complication overcome. We are reaping the consequences of our disaster. In five years we have not only lost the national treasury but, more dangerous, the private fortunes. This ruin has changed peoples' roles. Yesterday life went from top to bottom—now it goes from bottom to top.[10]

If Mercedes Cabello de Carbonera applied her theories of *La novela moderna* wherein she said "the truth, without conventions or compromises," she at the same time created a character who represents *Perú*, a Peru in most critical times. When the typical, traditional values are replaced by others which are much more opportunistic, Blanca Sol becomes the victim and not the villain. She never dreamed that a fortune could be so easily lost, leaving her in poverty. She thought the marriage to Serafín would solve a life-long problem but came face to face with a pathetic reality, She had always believed that her beauty was her only genuine attribute. Pride and vanity had made her forget the precarious, unstable situation in which she was living. She openly challenges the social norms of her day when she resorts to prostitution. Blanca Sol, like Lucifer, falls because of pride. The most beautiful and brilliant angel is brought to tragic depths. Her rebellion is wasted, futile. Social censure is harder on her not because she has been bad, adulterous or frivolous, but because she "had little respect for appearances; she openly and frankly challenged the conventions of the period without restriction" (p. 176).

TERESA DE LA PARRA
(Ana Teresa Parra Sanojo)

Ana Teresa Parra Sanojo, known by her literary name Teresa de la Parra, was born in 1890 and died in 1936.[1] Her family was of the Venezuelan aristocracy and thus her education was appropriate for her social standing: little instruction, a good deal of domestic endeavors, some music, religion and, at times, some singing or language instruction. She was of extraordinary intelligence and soon began to excel. Her publications and travels to Spain and to France widened her horizons[2]. Her novel *Ifigenia, diario de una señorita que se fastidiaba,* appeared in 1924 and was greeted with unexpected success. This was her only novel; later, in 1929, she wrote *Las memorias de Mamá Blanca,*[3] which is really just a long story. In spite of her small production, she attained much attention due to her lectures and literary contacts.[4] She was extremely beautiful and chose not to marry as a sign of her independence.[5] Once, in speaking of Bolívar's lover, Manuelita, at a conference, Teresa said:

> Doña Manuelita is an extremely interesting person, not only because of her picturesque character but also because she represents a violent protest against the traditional slavery of womankind who only have the not always open door of marriage as a future. She was a woman of action. She would not stand for tricks nor falseness in love. A daughter of the revolution, she only understood truth and the right of self defense. She represents the 'après guerre' woman of Independence. Her crusade was preached by example and she wasted no time.[6]

The novel *Ifigenia*[7] presents the case of a young girl who has been educated in France. At the death of her father she returns to her family in Caracas and there she must face the conventions that shackle a young girl from the upper social classes. Although both her grandmother and her maiden Aunt Clara have lost their money, they still strive to maintain the manners of their class. María Eugenia tries to rebel against all of the existing prejudices but she finally gives up. She marries Leal, a man she does not love, simply because of his economic position which will guarantee that she will not remain single and economically dependent on her Uncle Eduardo, whom she detests. Her only other alternative would be to run away with Gabriel, a former admirer now married to another, but she does not have the will power to do it.

Family

When María Eugenia's mother died, she went to Paris with her father. He, like so many rich Latin Americans of the period, lived off of his land investments, the proceeds from which were sent to him monthly by his brother-in-law Eduardo. She quickly learned that her father was a frivolous man, involved in many amorous adventures, and for whom a small daughter was a stumbling block: "in spite of his good intentions and fatherly interest, my presence, care, education and teachers were things that continually blocked his freedom and greatly disturbed his life" (p. 249). Finally, after having eight different instructors, her father decided to send her to a school run by the nuns of the Sacred Heart who would see to it that she left only on vacations. Since María Eugenia is raised almost without a family she concentrates all her affection on one of her classmates at the school, Cristina de Iturbide. Her friend Cristina is a Spaniard and somewhat of a mystery. Her family excludes her from all the social activities and the two girls discover that the reason is because Cristina is an illegitimate child. They also discover that Cristina's mother was a very famous opera singer, but they do not know her name. The two girls decide to "live through fantasy" and try to clear up this torturous and important mystery for Cristina. For María Eugenia this unknown woman is the image of a beautiful, rich, much admired mother who has defied convention and has had an illegitimate daughter. The fact that the Iturbide family has taken the girl away from her mother and has raised her according to their will in no way diminishes the "power" of this extremely fascinating, but unknown mother. The girls are separated when María Eugenia's father dies and she has to return to Venezuela. María Eugenia makes the trip in a style that gives her the impression of freedom and wealth—thus her meeting with the family is quite a shock.

Uncle Eduardo, her mother's brother and administrator of the ranch, and all his family seem provincial and mediocre to her. Uncle Pancho, her father's brother, is her favorite because he is very independent in his views. Her grandmother is very authoritarian and although she wants the best for her granddaughter she does not approve of the girl's "extravagances." It is one of her cousins, Mercedes Galindo, rich but married to a shameless man, who best understands her and stimulates her amorous and artistic fantasies. Aunt Clara, her mother's sister, is a good example of all that María Eugenia does not wish to be—fanatically religious, sad and abandoned by her lover, living without hope. Uncle Eduardo has made some bad investments and has lost her dowry, the grandmother's fortune, and María Eugenia's ranch; thus María Eugenia realizes that she is without an income and entirely dependent upon her uncle for her personal expenses.

Social Class

Both branches of her family are of old aristocratic stock who have come upon lean years. The grandmother explains that the reason they have lost their money is because "the men" have lived by spending money without thought of tomorrow, but she does not blame them: after all, it is the result of "their education, an evil that is very old and deep" (p. 74). No doubt this observation is directly aimed at Pancho and María's father who spent their last dime in Paris. The Galindos are also in this classification since the couple is going to Paris, leaving all their belongings in Venezuela in the care of administrators. Uncle Eduardo is a little different since he works his own land, but he does not have good business sense.

The novel shows us the great social changes that are taking place. Leal, María Eugenia's suitor, is representative of the new style of bureaucrat who is making a fortune out of investments and government contracts. Old, fat and dark-skinned, he is nevertheless accepted by the grandmother—even with her family pride—simply because she realizes that "In Caracas there is not much choice and each day it becomes more difficult to find a man without vices" (p. 285). Gabriel, like María Eugenia, comes from a ruined aristocratic family, but he has recovered his fortune thanks to his marriage to the daughter of a politician very similar in his dealings to Leal. This daughter, who is not light-skinned, is from humble origins, but her father has made a fortune thanks to his political friends and his dealings in petroleum. Gabriel, however, is unlike Leal; once he has regained his finances, he, like his aristocratic ancestors, goes to Paris to squander his fortune.

María Eugenia is prejudiced against those who are either not light-skinned or are not from the aristocracy; thus she despises her Uncle Eduardo's wife: "As for the old, ugly and ridiculous María Antonia, she is an upstart, or calling things by their names, a 'mulata,' full of the evil and the hatred of her race' (p. 149). The women of each of the different social classes have different moralities. A close relationship exists between María Eugenia and Gregoria, who was her wetnurse. Gregoria says, "I have always been glad I was born black and poor, first . . . because God wanted it thus and because I was black and poor I have always loved him who loved me" (p. 360). At other times she says "each color and each social rank has its own morality." In the Galindo household, French is spoken so that the servants will not understand. Uncle Pancho also has racial prejudices and he predicts that if Gabriel marries a "non-white" he will abandon her soon and if he does not divorce her, it is because divorce does not exist in Venezuela at this time. Thus when María Eugenia considers her upcoming marriage, her greatest preoccupation is having ugly children who might look like their father Leal. The author has captured, almost without intent to do so, the prevailing racial attitudes and at the same time has shown the great movement towards social integration between the impoverished aristocrats and the new rich who stem from the professional middle class. A good example is Leal, a doctor of law, senator, and director of the Ministry of Public Works. Pancho, meanwhile, without his titles, lives in poverty and has a nondescript job in the government. Family aspirations lean toward economic security, and the bureaucracy proliferates.

Sexuality

The first indication we have of María Eugenia's ignorance in things sexual is her lack of understanding of the term "illegitimate daughter." Her convent education makes the acquisition of such knowledge difficult and later this same ignorance continues at her grandmother's house. María Eugenia comments on the repeated expressions of the grandmother, "you don't know," "you ought not," "you may not," thusly:

> The ignorance of women about to marry, or rather the despotic care taken to make us ignorant of all that others know, seems to me to be one of the greatest abuses perpetrated by the strong on the weak. Yes, in the first place, it sows the path of life with mysteries which is much like digging deep holes in a road; it makes one terribly disoriented, we see things from a false point of view, we are surprised by things which can be very disagreeable and it creates, in general, a tie, a trap, used by others to more easily organize our lives to suit their views and whims. Innocence is blind, deaf, and paralyzed but it has been crowned with roses by human imbecility. It is a humiliating symbol of submission and slavery in which, like Uncle Pancho says, every honorable woman is accustomed to live after marriage [p. 152].

María Eugenia's first love is Gabriel Olmedo, whom she meets at Mercedes' house at one of the parties Mercedes organizes in order to have María Eugenia and her Uncle Pancho visit her. But this time María Eugenia is drawn only by the magical appearance of love for a man she knows only superficially. Her grandmother does not approve of this man because he "has evil thoughts," which Mercedes interprets as his being a free thinker, a ladies' man and a profiteer. Most importantly, however, her grandmother believes that Gabriel will not marry a poor girl, and thus to prevent things from going any further, she sends María Eugenia to Uncle Enrique's ranch. There she passes through a typically romantic period in which she tries to imagine Gabriel's love for her through poems and letters. She even dares to send him a poem hidden in a book which is almost an open declaration of love, but he never replies. Her aunt lets it be known that Gabriel has become engaged to the daughter of the Monasterio. María Eugenia then awakens to the reality of the situation: her grandmother was right, Gabriel has married for money. Until now she has been a rebellious child, full of artistic dreams of being a great pianist so that she could travel and do as she pleased. After this shock she represses her impulses and submits herself to the supervision of Aunt Clara, who tries to make her ready for marriage. Now María Eugenia is convinced that love is unimportant, that she should only "have a fiancé and marry him." When the grandmother decides that María Eugenia's period of mourning for her father is over and that she may now sit by the window, it is a veiled announcement that she now approves of María Eugenia's having a fiancé. María Eugenia invents a little rhyme with which to entertain herself while passersby look at her: "I'm for sale. Who will buy me? I'm for sale. Who will buy me?" (p. 276). Her grandmother is shocked and reproves her, but it is the truth. Leal passes by in his bright red car and he passes by so often that all are aware of his interest. As a man "of good intentions" he officially asks Uncle Eduardo's permission to visit his niece at home. María Eugenia feels nothing but revulsion for Leal, but he appeals to her vanity. She will not allow him to kiss her because she is a "virtuous" woman, which is a lie, and this provokes Leal to move up the marriage date. María Eugenia, who has always been proud of her beauty and her artistic and literary taste, is horrified to hear her fiancé say things like "those are women's matters," "men ought to act like men and women like women," or what is even worse, his male chauvinistic remarks:

> He hated romantic ideas; he hated poetry readings and even women like me, who pretend to be wise and learned; in his opinion, a woman's head was something more or less decorative, completely empty, made only to bring joy to men's lives and adorned by two ears whose only purpose is to receive and collect the orders that men give them [p. 315].

María Eugenia realizes that she is trapped and that the best she can do if she wants to marry is to be quiet. She is obsessed with the double standard however:

> If only I had been born a man. Then, Uncle Pancho, you would see what a good time I would have and how I would mind grandmother and Aunt Clara. But, alas, I am a woman, and to be a woman is the same as being a caged bird. They lock you in a cage, they take care of you, they feed you and never let you out while all the rest are happily flying all over. How horrible it is to be a woman! How horrible! Horrible! [p. 104].

The role of her cousin Mercedes needs to be clarified. She is very rich and has married a poor man of her same social class because of love, but her marriage becomes a disaster since her husband "has all the vices" (p. 173). María Eugenia is indignant when she hears Mercedes' complaints and advises her: "Don't you have your own money with which to live? Don't women in other places get divorces? You don't even have any children!" (p. 172). After Mercedes and her husband have gone to Paris, Mercedes invites María Eugenia to come and live with her, but their grandmother will not allow it. Mercedes gets a divorce in France a little while later and this brings her family's censure. The grandmother says "Once a high-born woman marries, no matter how disgraceful the marriage, she must suffer in silence, never neglecting her duty and never creating the grotesque and scandalous spectacle of a divorce" (p. 323). María Eugenia, while mentally supporting her cousin, also realizes that maybe her grandmother is right and that "a good son makes a good husband," and she overlooks what Leal is like as a man. María Eugenia has accepted the fact that "love does not exist" and that it is worse to be single. The test of her sexuality comes when by accident she meets Gabriel at her Uncle Pancho's house. She finds she is still attracted to him:

> Gabriel had such personal attraction and such a dominating influence that I, like a poor little dove fascinated by death, could only feel a mysterious and compelling desire to be swept up in the claws of an eagle from the top of this hill on which I live and be carried away to the vertigo of the heights, through the clouds, to the inaccessible peaks. . . . I do not know where . . . even if it was to there tear me to pieces, torture me, devour me in a bloody feast [p. 385].

María Eugenia is not sure of what she should do. Gabriel shows all of the typical complaints of an unfaithful husband: His wife is "detestable," they are incompatible, Venezuela has no divorce. After her Uncle Pancho's death, Gabriel proposes a trip to Europe. She weighs the alternatives and the night before they are to flee she looks in the mirror and sees her reflection divided into two and becomes frightened. A little while later when she goes to the attic to look for a suitcase, Aunt Clara appears to her. María Eugenia reflects: "Why? Why is this? What kind of a phantom was it that finally appeared that mysterious night?" (p. 428). If Mercedes is the sophisticated image she would like to imitate, Aunt Clara is an image of reality. María Eugenia notices her own beauty, "My only guarantee and my only reason for being," (p. 435) and she knows that it will disappear very quickly. Aunt Clara was once very beautiful but now she is a sad and bedraggled fanatic. Since there have been two deaths in the family, her grandmother's and Uncle Pancho's, her fiancé Leal wishes to get married right away and quietly so that they will not have to wait for the long years of mourning to end. María Eugenia allows him to decide for both of them:

> The sensitivity of my hearing allowed me to very vividly perceive the powerful metal of his voice and all of the protecting yet odious power of that soon to arrive despotism deforming the fragile beauty of my body, unconsciously and cruelly crushing the infinite desires of my heart, and making him the unpreventable owner and scourge of my entire existence [p. 435].

Although she could have refused marriage, her only other alternative would have been to remain single, and after her years of mourning she would have had neither youth nor beauty, and would then have to live like a poor relative, a "single woman," with Aunt Clara.

Message

The author makes reference in the title to the Iphigenia of Greek tragedy, the woman who was sacrificed to the gods, and to "the girl who wrote because she was bored." This girl, without purpose in life, will do anything to avoid a confrontation with her empty existence. The two elements of the title are related, since they present María Eugenia in her two stages: easing the boredom of waiting with writing, and her final decision between matrimony and spinsterhood—a decision involving dressing, being attractive, waiting, and following the accepted rules of society as a means of avoiding boredom. María Eugenia's reading and writing had alarmed her grandmother: "Your independence alarms me. Both your thoughts and conduct are too independent. Moreover, your ideas are truly chaotic; it is like having indigestion from reading too much" (p. 192). Then when María Eugenia learns to make cakes and broth, to embroider, and to take care of plants, then the waiting for a husband becomes more methodical and gains general approval. She once wrote a poem signed "Juliet," the girl waiting at the balcony, but she soon realizes that the "Romeos," like Mercedes' husband, are not so desirable after all. Mercedes confides in her:

> Even worse, you have to hide your arguments from everyone and you even have to defend that very thing which torments you because it is as much yours as is your own existence, since he has given you a name, a house and a second personality that is yours, yours, even if you hate it and become a martyr [p. 172].

Mercedes is trying to say that if Gabriel were María Eugenia's "Romeo," she would have to suffer similar tortures. On the other hand, with Leal it is a simple business transaction. María Eugenia asks, is it that a single woman is like a zero that acquires value with a husband, a number one, beside her? Her grandmother feels that it is indispensable that she have a strong will beside her to guide or rather dominate and educate her in life's ways: "Ah no! I could not die happy if I were to leave María Eugenia alone, without any help in this world," (p. 212) her grandmother says. She is beautiful and he is rich—a convenient exchange. Uncle Pancho is the only one who tries to make her see that marriage is not simply the buying of some pretty dresses, but that she herself is the one who will have to completely change, even to the shapely figure of which she is so proud: "I calculate that you will gain about ten pounds a month until you reach the normal one hundred and sixty pounds" (p. 241). Her life will also become deformed, a continual sham since her husband will no longer approve of anything she thinks or does. Under these conditions, which is reality and which is mere appearance?

The author, however, realizes that matrimony is only one of many crucial areas on which to base more definitive decisions yet it is also part of an entire structure that is reinforced by social norms:

> Terrible and ancient God, Holy Monster with seven heads called society, family, honor, religion, morality, obligation, conventions, principles. Omnipotent Divinity with the fierce egotism of man: insatiable Moloch, thirsty for virgin blood on whose altar thousands of young girls are sacrificed [p. 444].

The social dynamics of Venezuela are revealed through the various classes. The major difference is that a poor aristocratic woman like María Eugenia has family pressures that perhaps a man like Gabriel Olmedo does not have. Ambition is his motivation for marriage:

> I don't know how it happened. Perhaps, speaking sincerely, I cannot deny it, it is very likely that an insatiable ambition to become important forced me into this marriage . . . to arrive at being 'somebody' . . . these things are so complex and confusing: Of course, through my father-in-law's influence I finally got the concessions I was after, and with them my speculations were more precise and I have become rich . . . so rich, even more rich than I had wished to be, but ah, if you only knew the price I payed . . . [p. 265].

Moreover, María Eugenia does not have freedom of movement. Since she cannot leave unless accompanied, she cannot work and her life transpires within the walls of her house. The plight of women in the Venezuela of this period is very much like that of Venezuela under the dictatorship of Gómez (1908-1935). "Venezuela will be a place of peace and quiet, an enclosed island surrounded on all sides by petroleum, without an opinion, without movement, without windows on the future."[8] María Eugenia has had to renounce a love that would have brought dishonor to the family and social disapproval to her, but hers is no longer a clear decision and it is almost as if she allows the events to impose their will upon her. The words in Gabriel's letter coincide with what she herself thinks of her family: "They passionately want a good name depending on your behavior and completely ignore your intimate well-being" (p. 403). Her destiny appears to her in the form of Aunt Clara at the moment of her aborted flight. María Eugenia states: "I also thought of the invisible force that ominously leads to destiny, with its face always hidden beneath a blanket wet from tears, and in one word I summarized this absurdity, and desperate and conquered I whispered many times—"Ah, Life . . . Life . . ." (p. 331).

MARIA LUISA BOMBAL

María Luisa Bombal was born in Viña del Mar, Chile, in 1910. After the death of her father in 1919, the family went to live in Paris, where María Luisa studied drama at the Sorbonne. In 1931 she returned to Chile, where she continued her career working in "El teatro experimental." Her first book, *La última niebla,*[1] appeared in 1935 and was followed by *La amortajada*[2] in 1938. It was during this period that she spent some time in Argentina writing movie scripts for Sonofilm. After her return to Chile in 1940, she became involved in a passionate love affair that could have ended with her death or that of her lover: she attempted to shoot him, but missed, and no charges were filed against her.[3] She later married a French broker and went to live in New York. Her collection of short stories, *La última niebla,* was transformed into *House of Mist,*[4] a novel which the author sold to producer Hal Wallis in 1947 for $125,000.[5] An amplification of her novel, *La amortajada,* was translated into English in 1948 with the title *The Shrouded Woman.*[6] Since then she has not published any books or been involved in any literary activity.[7]

The Shrouded Woman is the story of Ana María, a woman who has died and who from her shroud contemplates those that come to say farewell. In front of her pass all the important events of her life and as each is evoked she begins, for the first time, to understand that life. When she is finally placed in the crypt, her family believes that although life has brought her much suffering, death will bring her peace.

Family

Ana María, the protagonist of the novel, lives with her widowed father and her brother and sister. Ana María feels a deep pity for her father who, since the death of his wife, has borne life with a dignified sadness. Her brother Luis also leads an unhappy life, having chosen to marry a mediocre woman rather than Elena, his great love, because the latter is too passionate and has a "past." Alicia, Ana María's sister, is also denied happiness, having married a very brutal man and having lost her only child in an accident. In this group of somber, unfulfilled people, only Zoila, the servant who takes care of the motherless family, is a positive, down-to-earth individual. Having raised Ana María, Zoila remains her lifelong companion.

A neighboring family, that of Ricardo, also plays an important role in Ana María's life. She and Ricardo have been in love ever since they were children; she calls his mother "Aunt Isabel." Isabel, however, has plans of her own for her son; she does not want him to marry Ana María and sends him away to Europe to study. Ricardo obeys even after finding out that Ana María is pregnant. The young woman thus feels herself to have been rejected by the only family that could have given her love.

Now it is time for Ana María to start a family life of her own; the once unruly and rebellious child has become a beautiful woman who marries Antonio, a rich and attractive man. Although she has not yet recovered from Ricardo's abandonment, she believes that this is her chance to find security, but again she is bitterly disappointed. She tries to compensate for her disappointment by immersing herself in the raising of her children, but even that proves discouraging. Alberto, the oldest son, marries María Griselda against his mother's wishes. Fred, the favorite son, marries Silvia, who later commits suicide out of jealousy over María Griselda. With her daughter Anita she is never able to share a close relationship. Ana María does not see her family objectively until she dies and only then does she realize her influence over them.

Social Class

Many social commentaries are to be found in the novel. Although both Ricardo and Ana María belong to the upper class, there are reasons for Ricardo's mother to oppose a marriage between them. Ana María, for example, will inherit only a small parcel of land. When Ricardo marries Sofía, a blond European, his family is satisfied because his children will also be blond, not the dark-haired children Ana María would have had. Ana María, in turn, will object strongly when Alberto marries María Griselda, the daughter of a nobody: "Alberto had married an unknown girl he had met in the town down south from where he made his lumber shipments" (p. 57). When she finally receives her daughter-in-law into her house many years later, she realizes the great injustice she has committed, for Alberto's wife is one of the most beautiful and angelic creatures she has ever known.

While injustices are done to people in more or less the same social bracket, servants, such as Zoila, are completely ignored. Zoila, nevertheless, sees Ana María as her own daughter. When she finds out that the young woman is pregnant she confronts her with the knowledge. "You are crazy," answers Ana María, trying to lie to her more from shame than from a desire to deceive. When she adds, "But what difference does it make to you?", Zoila answers "What difference does it make to me? . . . I, who am like your mother. To know what you have done, to know that you are a shameless . . ." (p. 28). It is Zoila, with the knowledge of Ricardo alone, who ends the pregnancy with the aid of an herbal concoction. Although Zoila is the strong one in all the family crises, she is always treated ungratefully and her services are always taken for granted because she is, after all, only the servant.

Sexuality

As an orphan, Ana María has more freedom than a girl from her social class would normally have—such as going out with Ricardo, who is several years older than she. When she tells him that she is pregnant, he puts the blame on her because girls, in his eyes, are supposed to be "good." She tries to hit him, but he just leaves. Here it is interesting to note that it is Zoila who accepts the blame for Ana María: "I am the one who is responsible. I don't know how to take care of you" (p. 28). Ana María thus feels more like the victim than the wrongdoer.

She carries this attitude a little farther in her first year of marriage. When Antonio makes love to her she is either passive or she rejects him completely. The shrouded woman would comment reflectively long afterwards: "Never did he know that she was struggling not only against his embraces but against the tremor which night after night those embraces made inexorably rise in her flesh" (p. 120). Antonio, a very intense man, views her attitude as typical of the inexperienced woman and in an attempt to calm her, offers her whatever she wishes. Her wish, however, is to leave, to return home to her father. This decision deeply wounds his pride, but he keeps his promise and lets her go. During the absence from her husband she begins to realize that "she needed his warmth, his embraces, all the encumbering love she had repudiated" (p. 128). After the passage of many months he does come for her, but his feelings are no longer the same and he never fully accepts her. She seeks for a means of "rehabilitating" herself in his eyes, but he is not interested in her. Soon afterward she finds out about his numerous love affairs and tirelessly tries everything in order to regain his love: kindness, violence, reproaches, silence. Sometimes when she feigns indifference she gains his fleeting attention and a compliment: "You are the most charming woman I have ever known, it is too bad you are my wife" (p. 134). On one occasion she follows him to a town where he has a lover and seeks a lawyer to testify to his adultery. The lawyer's advice, however, is that she should remember that he is the father of her children: "There are steps a lady cannot take without lowering herself. Perhaps your own children would criticize you later" (p. 137). She does leave, but later confronts Antonio with violent insults. Faced with this proof of her demanding love, he looks at her for a long time in silence and then he says: "How much you love me" (p. 138).

As Ana María's love for her husband turns into hatred, she becomes increasingly dependent on the devotion of her cousin Fernando. Left a widower by the suicide of his wife, he is someone with whom she can exchange secrets and confidences. Although remaining faithful to Antonio, she does use Fernando to discharge the resentment she has built up against her husband. At her funeral she is surprised by the realization that Fernando is relieved to no longer have to bear the brunt of her bitterness against Antonio. In the same way, it is only from the perspective of death that she can understand Antonio's nature. Because she had blamed herself for their first year of marriage, she had tried hard to get him back; now she realizes that he would have tired of her anyway, just as he tired of all his lovers. In her demand for love and devotion she had ignored the most basic facts about the nature of the two men who were the closest to her.

The author also shows that Ana María had lost another love she could have had, a different kind of love: the love of Sofía, Ricardo's wife. When Sofía comes to visit Ricardo's family, she becomes Ana María's best friend. It is a bond of friendship which Ana María is never able to experience with men, a relationship which includes "the joy of being able to give without fear" (p. 157). Sofía is sophisticated and could have been the one to introduce her friend to a new way of appraising love, but Ana María's love for Antonio keeps this from happening. She breaks off her friendship with Sofía when she hears rumors that Antonio and Sofía had been seen kissing on the bridge as he escorted her home. Sofía's explanation is revealing: "And I must tell you an absurd thing: I never felt as close to you as when that tall handsome man that was your husband held me in his arms making fun of me, as I had seen him do to you . . ." (p. 166). Ana María is incapable of allowing her great love for Sofía to overcome her feelings of insecurity which have tormented her all her life and which have caused her much suffering. She needs so much to be loved by Sofía—perhaps to forget Antonio—that when she feels betrayed by her friend her entire world collapses. Again, it is only from her shroud that she realizes the injustice she has done to Sofía by refusing her letters and her gestures of love. Freed of her jealousy and resentment upon her death, she appears to Sofía as a ghost and gives back her love.

There is a pattern of possessiveness that runs through the entire book. As the shrouded woman, Ana María can see that her son Alberto has also tried to overcome his insecurity by demanding that María Griselda be his alone, Still,

> it was in vain that in order to feel secure, he recalled and reminded himself of the many and intimate embraces by which María Griselda was bound to him in vain. No sooner out of his arms she seemed to live a life of her own, a life that seemed detached and apart from his own physical life. And it was obviously in vain that he could force himself on

> her, trying once again to impress on her his warmth and his scent. From his desperate embraces María Griselda would emerge more distant and as if untouched [p. 81].

Alberto, however, is not the only one to suffer from the emotional reverberations caused by María Griselda's overwhelming beauty. Fred's wife Silvia is so jealous of her that she commits suicide. Anita, Ana María's daughter, gives herself to Rodolfo in an effort to pull him out from under María Griselda's spell. When Alberto finally locks away his wife in her room, she becomes a symbol of that unattainable beauty that eludes possession. It is through this woman whom they all describe "as the most beautiful woman in the world" (p. 62) that Ana María finally realizes that love, too, cannot be captured; just as Alberto imprisons María Griselda and yet never possesses her, she never could have captured the love of Antonio by locking him up and keeping him to herself.

From her earliest years Ana María had wanted to love and to be loved completely and exclusively. She had even rejected God when yet an adolescent "because he never gives me any of the things I want" (p. 189). Throughout her entire life she was in love with love and thus never able to find it. When, as the shrouded woman, she says to María Griselda: "Oh, María Griselda! I am the only one who really understood how to love you. For I, and no one else, it seems, was able to forgive you for so great, so unbelievable a beauty" (p. 143). She is really expressing her very deep feelings about giving herself to love until nothing but absolute beauty pervades her universe. All her life she had repudiated God because he had not given her somebody capable of satisfying her great need and desire to love and to be loved. Even on her deathbed she refuses Communion from the priest, insisting that he "Ask God to perform a great miracle; that is, send me His Grace" (p. 191). The priest, who has known her since she was a child, says sadly: "Poor Ana María. Your whole life was nothing but a passionate search for that Garden of Eden, lost irretrievably, however, by man" (p. 188).

Message of the Novel

Ana María, when alive, searches for happiness and thinks that it is love which will make her happy. She desperately tries to avoid what she has seen in her family while growing up: a father, a brother, and a sister unhappy because they are unable to find fulfillment in love. She first seeks this fulfillment by force when she surrenders to Ricardo. After being hurt by his abandonment, she fights her love for Antonio in order not to be hurt again, but does fall deeply in love with him nevertheless. Her love, however, is too late, for she is no longer loved by her husband. Like so many people around her, she is unhappy because she loves with every fiber of her being and yet receives no love in return. As happiness is equated with loving and being loved, and unrequited love is a predominant theme in the novel, it seems that we are being told that the search for happiness is but a futile one.

Ana María, when dead and reviewing her life from the perspective of the shroud, sees something very clearly which before she had not seen at all: the existence of two kinds of love. One of these, possessive love, is a destructive love which sunders the very relationships which it has forged. It is this love which Ana María had experienced with Ricardo and Antonio. Even now, looking about her, she sees it destroying her children and their spouses as they try to capture it, lock it in a room and live happily ever after. The other kind of love, a selfless one, had been around her until her death. This love is made up of the memory of the beloved, thus it can never tarnish, never disappear or be taken away. She now sees that Ricardo continued to love her after their separation, that Sofía continued to love her after their estrangement, that she herself continued to love Sofía even while fighting against it. Her son Fred also harbors this selfless love, for he will go on loving her until he dies. The only really new love which she discovers is that which is born within her daughter Anita as she cries by her mother's lifeless body. Ana María realizes that death can also be an act of love and that from now on she will continue to live in Anita's consciousness.

Another discovery of the shrouded woman as she reviews her life is that the search for love is sometimes only a way of covering up problems which we do not want to face, such as insecurity or fear of old age and death. She sees her own insecurity and her fear of leading an empty life. Because she had made love her lifelong purpose, her *raison d' être* (for even her hatred of Antonio was but another aspect of that possessive love), she had left herself vulnerable and groping for an identity of her own. She had made her husband the center of her life because she had wanted to believe that he was superior, a man beyond the threat of destruction. When, however, as the shrouded woman, she sees him standing in front of her, she thinks:

> He is crying, crying at last. Or perhaps is he only crying for his youth he feels gone with this dead woman; perhaps is he only crying for those failures the memory of which are now arising, unavoidable, before this first assault. But she knows that the first tear stands as an open channel for all the others; she knows that sorrow and perhaps also remorse have at last made a breach in that stony heart, a breach through which in time they will infiltrate with the regularity for a tide that mysterious laws impel to strike, to corrode, to destroy. . . . And as his tears appear, slip and fall, she feels her hatred abating, evaporating. No, she no longer hates.
>
> How could she hate a poor being, destined as she herself had been to old age and sadness. . . .No, she does not hate him. But neither does she love him. . . . Now nothing matters to her anymore. It is as though neither she nor her past have any longer a reason for being. . . [p. 141].

Life is attachment. Death is detachment. When people are alive they create desires, they make believe that they are living intensely. When people are dead they cease to care and thus can face their lives such as they may have been: full or empty, intensely lived or passively suffered.

Death is an element present in the novel from the very beginning; the rigidity of the shrouded woman's body is not unlike the rigidity of the young Ana María on her wedding night. The author does not seem to have a sad, terrible or even tragic sense of death; she seems to view it rather as a new or deeper state of awareness. Fernando, for example, describes his wife shortly before she commits suicide:

> I still cannot explain the reason for her decision. She did not seem depressed or sad. There was nothing about her that seemed unusual either. Yet from time to time, I re-

> member having noticed her staring at me as if she were seeing me for the first time. . . . [p. 141].

Death is like a memory, a sometimes imperceptible legacy that remains a vital part of the living people left behind. With the new awareness given to her by death, the shrouded woman addresses these words to her weeping daughter: "No gesture of mine brought out what my death achieves at last. You see, you see how death can also be an act of life" (p. 178). In the penultimate sentence of the above quotation, Ana María is expressing a concept found earlier in the novel: the concept of a "second death, the death of the dead" (p. 91). This seems to be, for the author, an immersion into the bottomless depths of the universe. Little by little the shrouded woman loses her consciousness as Ana María and begins to feel a submersion into the cosmos and a disintegration into an amorphous existence wherein neither her individuality nor her personal aspirations subsist. After her burial,

> she felt innumerable roots, born of her body, sink into the soil and scatter like a spider web through which the constant vibrations of the universe rose to meet her [p. 91].

SILVINA BULLRICH

Silvina Bullrich was born in 1915 in Argentina. Her literary production is quite abundant.[1] Her first novel, *Su vida y yo*, appeared in 1941; later came *La redoma del ángel* (1943), *La tercera versión* (1944), *Bodas de cristal* (1952), *Teléfono ocupado* (1955), *Mientras los demás viven* (1958), *Un momento muy largo* (1961), *El hechicero* (1961), *Los burgueses* (1963), *Los salvadores de la patria* (1965),[2] *La creciente* (1967), and *Mañana digo basta (1968).*[3]

Bodas de cristal[4] is the first short novel of a collection of three. The narrator is "the wife" for whom no other name appears, which alone signifies the importance of her matrimonial role. She is completing 15 years of marriage—her "crystal" anniversary. She rejoices at having to resign herself to the infidelities of her husband. She also rejoices at being ten years younger—he is already 45—since she remains relatively attractive. The third and most important reason for her rejoicing is that she should always be pleased with her role of "legitimate" wife, given that even though her life is"full of surprises of men and women lying in ambush who could destroy our laboriously maintained edifice," (p. 13) she still has the hope that she and Luis will be united as the other women tire of awaiting a separation. This is because divorce, even though an alternative to a bad marriage, is in their case too full of problems, both of them being too conventional to risk their home and child by extraconjugal pressures.

From the first years of marriage to the present, the wife remembers the greatest torments that have threatened her home: the amorous affairs of Luis with Elena, Susana and Isabel. Their lives circulate within the same circle of friends and therefore the wife knows in detail, and at times personally, each "adventure" of Luis. At the end, she is happy that she never has been able to be independent, because thus she has never tried the experience of a separation. This old-looking and tired Luis will at last be hers in the last years. Perhaps he sees in her the only permanent woman of his life.

Family

The author, who in other works such as *Los burgueses* tries to give us a picture of all of the bonds within an extended family, limits herself in *Bodas de cristal*, to just the nuclear families, as much for the main characters as for the lovers of Luis. He, his wife and their son constitute the characteristic family of the professional middle class in Buenos Aires. The wife has always been "faithful" to her family. She has always been a simple cog in the machine, never the owner of the machine.

The concept of tradition in a family mixes the spiritual and material ties into a meaningful whole, as if the young couple in some way will continue living according to some of the values of their forebears. This relationship becomes a custom and a necessity inasmuch as when Luis or the wife thinks about their respective families, they feel a sentimental adhesion to a collective group which has made them what they are in the present, such as Luis and his role of male among many sisters. The wife says, "I do not want to judge him too severely. I know that he is not entirely guilty for what he has done. ... [H]e had that curious impression which only the Argentinians and the Japanese have, that his sex gave him the dignity of a god" (p. 112).

Luis is vain with a vanity that extends to his son, his wife, and all who have anything to do with him. When his lover Elena asks him for a son, he tells her "if you only knew what a bother they can be." "But you seem delighted to have one," she says. "Of course. Lucho is a very exceptional boy" (p. 47). For Luis "lack of morality" is an illness of the times in others and he never includes himself because he considers himself to be "exceptional."

Social Class

Even though Luis still has "the cattle ranch" he basically makes a living by being a lawyer of some success. As he tells his wife, they can live well as long as they don't "put on the airs" of the very rich, such as trips to Europe and, in his case more appropriately, maintaining a lover. This is an interesting facet of the novel because it shows that the women who are Luis' lovers are of a special type: women who are "passing through." Luis always looks for women who will not be financially dependent on him, either because they are divorcées or married to rich men. Although he feels liberated from any "responsibility," they are looking for a source of support after having either abandoned their marriage or having been abandoned in it. In the case of Elena, she has been ruined by her husband and then abandoned. Little by little she has learned to administer the little property that remains to her in the country in order to have some monthly income but, since she maintains her mother who continues living as when they were rich, Elena suffers quietly. She has learned to solve her problems alone because she cannot count on Luis:

> 'I am the man,' said Luis. By that he did not mean to say, 'I am here to protect you, to fight for you, to ward off the blows that are meant for you.' He meant to say, 'I am in the world to enjoy you, for you to lower your head, for you to understand that the most cold-hearted is always the strongest' [p. 58].

Susana's case is one of a woman who had married when very young a rich man twice her age and who now wants to divorce him because he is an alcoholic and of a vicious temper. Therefore she seeks out Luis as a lawyer for an Uruguayan divorce. She realizes that although she is rich while married, if she leaves her marriage all that will change. Luis explains to her that—because there is no divorce in Argentina—she will be at the mercy of her ex-husband's generosity. Her only alternative is to work, but in the high social class women are not prepared to earn a living. Susana compares her life to that of the male and comes to the conclusion that her parents educated only her brothers. They assumed, after all, that she would marry a wealthy man within her own social class. Nobody ever thought that she would need to work. If her marriage fails then she is out alone to face life.

Susana asks the question, "What rights do women have?" and Luis pragmatically answers: "It is not a question of rights, it is that you do not have any means of living separated from Andrés" (p. 69). This is the most blunt reason for advising her not to seek a divorce nor a separation, but it leaves things just as they are. After all is said and done, he is there by her side, even though Susana, like Elena, cannot count on Luis for anything but sexual pleasure. If Susana were more resigned she could, like Elena, remake her life on a smaller scale with a smaller income, but Susana is a girl from the upper class with definite tastes, and she prefers to commit suicide rather than wait patiently while her life slowly declines in style and while her lovers treat her like an extravagant woman who cannot adjust to the reality of her lonely life. In Susana can be seen the characteristics of the girls of the upper class who speak various languages and whose work could be as translators or as sales clerks in large and expensive stores. Like Susana, they constantly compare themselves with their brothers. She realizes that it is the "system" that is unfair to women. Her brothers within the upper class always find jobs or "influence" and are able to live well. In the family situation of Susana one realizes that everybody has counted on her marriage to a man of her own social class which will "guarantee her" against any misfortune. What nobody has counted on is that among this "new kind of woman" there are some who do not resign themselves to a marriage of appearance and who do everything possible to get out of it. For them, a cruel reality awaits. They are not professionally prepared and they are accustomed to the luxuries of "their class":

> It lives its life in an altogether up-to-date European fashion, although many of its habits and customs, virtues and vices included, are more exotic and graceful. The lives of these magnates lie in smooth and pleasant places. Each will own an establishment in Buenos Aires that ranks little beneath a palace. In his own winter he will frequently seek the European summer, in the hottest season he will return to the cooler surroundings of his own *estancia,* and should time chance to hang heavy upon his hands, he will buy a new race horse, or dabble just a little in politics.[5]

Susana belongs to the pre-Peronist aristocracy, and her husband is one of "those magnates."

To this same social class belongs Luis' next lover, Isabel. She perhaps is much more cosmopolitan than the others because she and her husband live the greatest part of the time in Europe and only return to take care of financial matters, which have been affected by the rise of Perón.[5] Isabel is much more free in her married life, since for her lovers are like an adornment or a way of making life interesting. She realizes that Luis is a "primary man" who is not even a particularly good lover because he is always afraid that his lover might require some "obligations" from him. Like other Argentinian men, Luis "went along bound to his customs, to his customs of a pitiless master, to his inalienable rights as a sacred male" (p. 104). In this way Luis only recognizes a few responsibilities toward his wife. Yet even though Luis acts with the superiority of the male, he has given to her the responsibility that goes along with being the legitimate wife—that of saving the marriage. She admits that he has given her a gift the day that "upon choosing me he chose his life, his present, his future, he foresaw his son. It is as if someone should loan us all of his fortune without asking for a receipt" (p. 29). That is why the wife adds: "I suppose that there are no infallible weapons to retain a man, but maybe the most infallible is being his wife, and even more likely the only possibility that a man has to retain his woman is by being her husband" (p. 28). This redundancy explains the morality of the middle class regarding the indissoluble nature of marriage. The entire system rests on the idea that the man, even though he may have many adventures and lovers, never will believe to have seriously chosen any other but his "legitimate wife."

Sexuality

The wife, for her part, candidly relates her "art of being a woman":

> Until the day I met Luis my life was limited to studying; once my studies were finished I dedicated myself to restless social activities. Life was easy, the days were happy, the nights were disturbed by vague desires that we tried to kill by endless dances. We were going, smiling, toward an inevitable end: marriage. And when one marches toward something, everything one does acquires meaning. Later I met Luis and the distant goal rapidly drew near. . . . And later that time outside of time, those interminable kisses on

> the lips, that patient desire, prolonged, unsatisfied, unbreakable, languid without end nor beginning, without dismay, without hope, that desire that would die of weariness and be reborn of its own exhaustion. The arms of Luis and our mouths united in a common silent scream, in a common murmur, in a hope....
>
> I remember that the first time I found myself alone with Luis I thought: 'This is my life. This will be all my life. I have nothing more to dream, nothing more to hope for' [pp. 19-21].

At 20 years of age she feels she has finished her "search" for the rest of her life; emotionally, however, she still is susceptible to sensing that at any moment she might lose everything, and from that comes the long "career" which awaits her of apprenticeship to her own tactical defenses: "I had to learn one by one the manners of the humiliated" (p. 80). Threats, tears, scenes of jealousy, and despair are her weapons until she arrives at the role of "the understanding woman" of relative cordiality, since she pretends to ignore what goes on, a tactic through which her husband is made to feel very uncomfortable, but not she. Of course one of the most typical reactions of a humiliated woman is to look for her own lover. As she knows herself to be pretty and has within her reach various diligent friends, it is easy for her to take up with Felipe, but after one encounter with him she realizes that her desire for revenge has not yet liberated her from her own scruples. She feels shame at having experienced pleasure with Felipe, because she continues to think about Luis. She decides to end the relationship because for her it is only "physical," and she explains that Luis has turned out to be the strongest and has triumphed because he is "the least sensitive, the least pure, the least loyal" because he is able to overcome his body-soul duality and she is not:

> Until my meeting with Felipe I had thought that I lived as a prisoner of prejudices; now I knew that I was a prisoner of atavisms. It was useless to argue, to want to compare the sexes: they (males) acquire strength from the unlimited inferiority of their instinct. We (females) weaken ourselves in the infinite superiority of choice [p. 94].

It is interesting to note that in the opinion of Isabel she has liberated herself from the atavism of women "who attempt to fill with love all the emptiness in their life in this continent of disoriented men," and we have the explanation that the wife just as much as the lovers needs to justify her relations with the man whom they share. It is not enough that they give themselves up; they need to convince themselves that they do it only for "love," for a "great love." Because of this conception of love, both Elena and Susana go to destructive extremes. When Elena realizes that Luis is using her egotistically she wants to separate from him, even though their relationship has lasted for seven years, because she "gave herself for love, tremulously, indefensive, conquered, dazzled, dominated by that man as agile as a cat" (p. 53).

The case of Susana is much briefer because she is more impatient. Susana, whom Luis believes to be "above sentimentality" and a typical "modern woman" with "something boyish about her," is the one who kills herself. Susana represents this woman who "appeared to believe that the day in which she would resolve to fight she would tear down the barriers, open doors, and leap over principles." She, however, like other women before her, was conditioned to believe that only "exalted emotions" justify giving herself to a man. Luis ignores that Susana would like to fight against a system of injustices, but more than that he ignores that she would like him, as a man, to be honest in love, but also realizes that he is not able to change. She believes that for a man or for a woman there is nothing more humiliating than to share a loved one with another, because love is an instinct which cannot accept "games." Her decision to kill herself in the way she does is symbolic of her frustration with love and with the system. She runs her sports car into an empty truck parked near a cliff. For the first time in her life, Luis goes through a period of regret, but still is not able to understand why she killed herself, because in accordance with his beliefs, "Women were happy thanks to him and perhaps never very distressed. The proof was that they never wanted to leave him, women like to suffer; it is the only way they have of feeling that they are alive" (p. 74).

The sexuality of the wife continues to diminish, and what she calls "maturity" is a sort of patience mixed with expectation. Upon learning of the death of Susana she comments: "Now I knew that Luis had killed Susana and had prostituted me. Each commits suicide in his own way, Susana had chosen the more pure and brave route. And soon I was asking myself how Elena had killed herself' (p. 83). The wife finally arrives at 15 years of marriage with no desire left to rebel because, as she says:

> If one were able to rebel only on the inside I would, but I have noted that rebellion draws me from myself and causes me to commit acts which I later disapprove of. Rebellion causes us to stand erect against the entire world and also against ourselves, on the other hand resignation at least leaves us at peace with ourselves [p. 97].

This sense of tranquility, peace and agonizing conformity is what seems to predominate in the wife. What ends up being more interesting is that Luis, from his own point of view, believes himself to be a "good husband," not perfect but "almost perfect." After intercourse they appear to be satisfied, but she observes:

> Last night, like a hundred, like a thousand, like an incalculable number of times, I thought I sensed rejection in him. I always had told myself that that rejection was incurable and it had always been remedied the following day. For many years I thought that with those rebuffs Luis wanted to proclaim his rights as a man. Now I was beginning to realize that those rights actually belonged to him, that they formed a part of his instinct in love and in life [p. 118].

She prefers not to think too much. The book ends when Luis is asleep as though he were dead, and she is contemplating him. Her words, "only his fingers slowly gave signs of life" (p. 118), accentuate a contradictory image: that of the now passive man at the mercy of the woman who is the spectator, attentive of her husband in whom only the fingers, as though they had acquired a life of their own, are moving, the only organic vestige of his vitality. It is undeniable that this man is more than a "macho"; he is a "sacred macho".

This novel presents one of the most incisive studies of the Hispano-American "conquistador," from his sociological causes to an explanation of his perpetuation in the system. The novelist presents various approximations of the conqueror to the conquered, and of her to him. For the first time, wife and lovers appear to be tacitly united above the traditional animosities. It is as if the author is focusing on the novel from the point of view of a "sisterhood" of understanding. One woman is like all women, in that one is not the triumphant and the other the conquered; all are bleeding and suffering for the same man. The wife is an extremely intelligent woman for not blaming anyone, but rather analyzing the circumstances and the typical development of the occurrences. She modestly says: "By chance I am saved by my lack of initiative, my lack of effectiveness in confronting life. Now I know that when the woman is too effective the home is endangered" (p. 116). Her case is typical of the many resigned women who must live in the system. She is not certain that Elena, or Susana, or her cousin Gloria—who is her confidante—are better than she, since they are opposite in every way: starting with the implied sentence of imprisonment to those who love them. The true ineffectualness of all these women is the same weakness which is common to all of them: their need to love in order to have their lives acquire meaning. All of them come from the upper class—with a few economic differences—or the upper middle class. All of them have been indoctrinated with love, marriage and children as their reasons for existence. The great emptiness that Luis fills in all their lives—with the exception of Isabel—has little to do with Luis, who is egotistical and vain. The emptiness is the result, as the wife illustrates, of being a small part of a machine and of finding oneself without any usefulness outside of that machine. Even Susana, who appears so modern, so independent, so dynamic, needs to believe that it is not worth living if there is only the possibility of dishonest love affairs, and if there is not a true passion between a man and a woman. Susana kills herself because she feels the emptiness of the system that has formed her. The inequality, the double standard, the uselessness of all her activities appear in the hypocrisy and in the injustice of the established order, and she is not able to adapt herself to an order that has deceived her.

Elena is another who desperately seeks love. She, who wants to be the great passion in the life of Luis, at last is convinced that she is and has always been alone in her love; Luis has only been a projection of her needs and desires. Elena, however, does not have the strength to remain alone once she breaks off with Luis. She needs the constant presence of a man who at least will give her the sensation of being alive, the feeling that time has not become detained in a repetition of trivial acts. Her grief appears masochistic at times; she seems to represent the woman that Isabel talks about: the Hispanic woman with a "vocation of grief" who advances as if hypnotized toward the man who is destined to torture her.

Isabel is the only woman who does not have the idea that a woman only lives for a man and for a great passion, but she has to be on the defensive with Luis, who is too slow for her sort of sophistication. She, who has been educated in Europe and who has had other lovers, is intrigued by this type of man:

> The Argentinian still has in his conscience the old taboo of the sexual act. He feels it is only permitted in marriage. He is only permitted it with his wife; if he falls in love with another, he lives torn between his love and his preconceptions. . . . [I]t is inadmissable to say that he is the best lover in the world. He is neither gentle nor generous. . . . No man who feels committed to an infinity of mediocre adventures can be passionate. It would be spreading himself too thin. Moreover, love for them is a rite; these savages of the pampas can do nothing without employing the rituals of the Indian medicine men. They are solemn, silent and grave; they clearly show that they are satisfying an ancestral appetite in our arms. They do not laugh, they do not mess up our hair nor their own, they comply with the mysterious commands of the species. Over there, in Europe, the greatest ambition of a man is to be the ray of sunshine in the life of a woman. Here, love falls upon our heads like a great storm cloud [p. 105].

Message

The author presents ways for increasing consciousness of the mechanisms which those who have become trapped by society employ to accept or deny the system with greater clarity—mechanisms which provide more than one route out of a psychic prison. Another element which clearly shows up as a message of the author is the need for women to be prepared to confront life with their own weapons, and to not feel themselves a victim incapable of living a free and honest life.

CLARA SILVA

Born in Uruguay in 1908, Clara Silva died in 1976.[1] Well known as a poet[2] for her works *La cabellera oscura (1945)* and *Memoria de la nada* (1948), her first novel, *La sobreviviente,* did not appear until 1951.[3]Other collections of poetry followed: *Los delirios* (1954), *Las bodas* (1960), *Preludio indiano y otros poemas* (1960). Her most recent novels were *El alma y los perros (1962)*[4] and *La habitación testigo (1967).*

La sobreviviente[5] is a novel that presents the world as it is seen by the lone protagonist, Laura Medina, a young Latin American girl who passes through some of the great cities of the world: Florence, Paris, and a Latin American capital, possibly Montevideo, in the 1940's. At twenty, her purpose in life is to seek her vital relationships with the people and things that surround her. Without a normal plot, the novel presents chapters with titles such as "The Room as Witness," "Morning," "Purple," "The Body," "I Am Laura Medina," "A Boy of Solids," "Separation," and "City." The protagonist vacillates between God and nothing, sensuality and spirituality, poverty and wealth, love and indifference, masculinity and femininity. Existential problems fill the novel and cause the protagonist to abandon her position as spectator and become a participant in the anonymous, collective unit. This requires her to compromise herself, submerge, unite herself with the whole, the masses. The techniques used are subliminal and two constant literary devices are the stream of consciousness and the interior monologue.

Family

In several of her recollections she appears as an only child, so alone that she invents her own friend to accompany her. At times *La Otra* appears who is her other self, a facet of her personality with whom she carries on a dialogue. Frequently *La Otra* reproaches her for not acting: "If they had allowed me to be as I wished, I would have made of your life—which is really my life, you understand... mine—a long process of pleasure" (p. 144). To Laura's question, "Why do we not have any brothers?" the answer is that perhaps it was necessary there be no other children, with the implication that it was a premeditated act.

Her mother is "the woman of the tresses" who appears with an image of the Virgin above her bed. She is a violent woman and causes terrible scenes with her husband. Her mother also appears as a "chess queen" who has been previously conquered by her life and its destiny, her game being sin and death. Her woman's condition marks her as another Eve. This woman harbors resentment against God for having made her a woman and her resentment surfaces when in a fight with her husband she spits on the Virgin and exclaims, "Take that, God!" (p. 102).

The author is rather vague as to her family which appears surrealistically in the form of visits and reunions which her mother calls "bitter family matters." Moreover, there are other people present in these after-dinner chats—the Dead.

> 'Yes, the dead, they are never lost. The candles burning night and day in the corners sustain their souls, they are summoned by these candles. Their tears, desires, take the form of the dripping wax. It is like walking through the silence of souls in torment [p. 148].

The girl also remembers an absent father who comes from time to time late at night accompanied by the sounds of chains and squeaking doors. She describes her return to her childhood home many years later as "an enormous black breast of a wetnurse, full of heavy milk and warm with fear" (p. 149).

Social Class

This novel is very precise in the description of the rich and the poor. Laura, the protagonist, is poor and earns a miserable salary at the Medical Institute, yet she has attended the University and could be called "an intellectual." Although she despises the bourgeoisie, she wonders what it would have been like if she had been one of those rich women who are so empty and nonconsequential. She comes to the conclusion that it is not merely a question of having been born here or there; she has had to confront her individuality in an innumerable series of psychological circumstances: rebellion, problems, sensitivity, everything that has "made her what she is" (p. 109). She cannot avoid being a spectator, spying on the rich. Once she is invited by a lawyer, a former friend from secondary school, to a reception he is giving for a poet whom she greatly admires (and who is probably Neruda). She describes the atmosphere thusly:

> Shadows, many shadows circulated amongst the mirrors. Diplomats, painters, writers, scholars, official poets. But this small minority was disappearing beneath the terrible pillars of the bourgeoisie, whose resplendent, flourishing ornaments were matronly, clothed in the essence of money, name and virtue. Money, jewels, famous names. And some foreign names. Everything came to them without effort. They supervised the welfare services, the kermises, and the social-literary parties. The high social level, the unequality, the misery, brought prestige to their names and caused them to make headlines in the social colums of the newspapers [p. 85].

She realizes that she is between two worlds. Through her reading of Nietzsche, Baudelaire, Gide, Huxley and so many others, she belongs to the exquisite world of the "elite", but at the same time she shelters the seeds of noncomformity. Her literary studies go beyond intellectual stimulation and come to a basic idea: her desperate search for a theological position when faced with the injustice of God and her own lack of faith. "Is the source of some peoples' faith and other's lack of it to be found in heavenly hierarchies or is it in God's injustice?" She sees this spiritual exile as a frontier that transcends even social relations among men. Thus throughout the novel there is a dilemna between two systems—one with faith in a Christian God and one Communistic, omitting God entirely. She herself vacillates between these two extremes. Laura uses three symbols of spirituality which she has seen attacked and destroyed: the saint of peace—Gandhi—who has been assassinated; the persecuted poet; and the lonely, tormented girl. This last symbol is very significant since it applies not only to her own reality, but also to women without economic, social or family protection who become victims of masculine exploitation, since the male is in a dominant position when the woman works for him. The men try to force sexual favors from the woman by promises of work or better positions. She uses the visual comparison of a compass at whose center we find the man and on the outside the women—like so many points and without autonomy.

This novel shows us the misery that exists in the streets and the houses and at the Institute where she works. These people who pass by her daily are the poor of the city. She realizes that some of the children are treated even worse than the dogs and she is concerned about these children's future. They, too, will have to choose—even as she—between the red and the gold, between two economic systems.

Sexuality

In this novel we are given a carefully detailed dissection of Laura's sexuality. She suffers from a duality that causes her to constantly separate sensuality and spirituality. The essential dichotomy between body and soul is presented in a fragmented way, like the following example when she is with her lover on the beach:

> I am in the mouth of the bull. His porous tongue licks me. The bullring is a well, full of red stains. The horses gallop, their guts in the air. My clothing is stripped from me. I exhale a stench of rotten milk. I am tired. I shall lay down in the throat of the bull and sleep [p. 28].

Following this moment comes the part she calls "separation," when, following their sexual coupling, both parties feel like strangers to each other: "Do you love me?" he asks and she answers "Perhaps I love myself" (p. 29). The explanation for this reaction of disgust is that she considers that during the "terrible and miserable" act she has left her soul behind, like a careless angel. In other words, her spirit and body were separate, even during the sex act. She also tries to interpret her lover's attitude:

> He had already demanded the 'maximum submission' from a woman; now he looked at her with his desire satisfied. And Laura felt that from his high, irritating pedestal he looked at her with a calm assurance that she, without him, was nothing more than a 'thing,' an empty force, a sterile jewel [p.58].

If she perceives this male pride in him, it is because she herself feels inferior—something which has been taught her through the Bible, with the idea of original sin, and through what Church literature reveals about the condition of womankind. Using many Biblical quotations, she shows how the Church Fathers sustain dogma against women, and in one instance she gives the example of King David who could take any woman as if she were a slave. But it is personal experience that has caused her loathing of sex and of the sexual act and that causes her disgust. The most objective case that illustrates her resentment is that of her friend Mariusa, a beautiful and very feminine girl. She is seduced and used by her lover:

> He had only the hint of a soul. He was empty. His worldliness was evident in a sea of vanity. She did not want only his body, she also wanted to reach his soul. But he constantly rejected her. Their intimacy was exhibited to his friends. His frivolity caused her to take her wherever there were men, men and bright lights. Like a racehorse. Words caressed her. Silence. Time passed. No promise was kept. At last she fled . . . [p. 126].

Pregnant and alone, Mariusa has an abortion and afterward she felt dirty, broken, sacrificed, ready to die:

> 'Let's go to bed,' that phrase, that cry, persisted, followed her. . . . Woman's fate. With her mouth, breasts, belly, from the beginning she brought with her her own destiny. Her designation: matter, carrier of sin. The virus of sin extended in the savage miasma of matter. Ah! [p. 126].

Thus, for Laura Medina, the sexual act always leaves her full of frustration and she even doubts that she knows herself. "I seem to be two strangers, thrown apart from themselves" (p. 59), she tells her lover and instead of feeling happy, she always feels alienated, anguished, not calm. When *La Otra,* accuses her of being frigid, "Last night, while you gave yourself, dispassionately, analyzing the very act, I, like a beggar in the shadows, in your shadow, fought to act, to leave. But you suffocated me, drowned me. It was horrible. With him, you were alone" (p. 143). Laura cannot accept the other accusations of *La Otra* that she is hard and egotistical, because she does indeed love, but she is not capable of a "gross, brutal, careless life" (p. 144). This may be the justification of her attitude. It is not that she is so different, it is because she can better see the other facets of sexuality and is not ready to accept that everything can be reduced to instinct. She looks for fulfillment within herself since she does not find it in her companion, makes a creed out of her own self-love, and even kisses herself. When he asks her, "Why do you kiss yourself?" She answers

> 'You have found me out. I love myself . . . I sustain myself. . . . Out of love . . . ? No, from my senses. Like those artificial ulcers which, in a prophylaxis of the soul, turn men into paranoids, in order to ignore the dramatic problems within. Who can leave one's own body? And give of one's self? To whom, if it were possible? [pp. 130–31].

In this question she implies that it is not any particular lover but rather the entire masculine sex that she faults. She has not found a man in whom she can fully and completely confide. Once in the course of the novel the question is asked that if men could choose a feminine archetype to represent all time, whom would they choose? The protagonist believes they would choose Marjorie Bloom, a body without a soul, like a whore from the Apocalypse. She does not believe that men would choose "a woman with body and soul, with her weakness, contradictions, dreams, helplessness in a life directed by men" (p. 129), because in this last instance what she suffers is from having been conditioned by the masculine system to feel inferior, divided, alienated and despised by the other sex because she is an instrument of their pleasure.

In a world where sex by itself does not create bonds between two people, the author wants to know if there is still the possibility "to be happy in such a harsh, sad, miserable reality" (p. 158). Silva makes a comparison between herself, Laura Medina, and the women who were violated and carried off during World War II. What could she hope to find in a world without faith in God? And if she herself does not believe, what other alternative is there but to organize love like a sociopolitical system? Is there any hope that a woman might at last find her place and sexual justice in a system that is not economically exploitative?

Message

The title indicates that the protagonist survives. Survives what? We might imagine that there has been a shipwreck and that the boat with its passengers has sunk. Some of these people have been saved. Taken from a world view, the boat is the Christian system which, with its values, has been tossed by the storm of exploitative capitalism with the obvious consequences for those who had faith in its promising destiny. Laura Medina has, from her youth, experienced pain, anguish and conflict and basically has not been able to maintain her faith in the face of constant, suppressive attack. But, if this is the system she must live under, her worst conflict comes when she tries to escape the subjugation of the flesh. In a poem with the same title[6] Clara Silva carries on a dialogue, supposedly with Christ, and says:

> Tie me to your heart.
> Don't let me fall to earth
> With a darkened mirror in my hands
> And blind, in the night,
> I harass myself
> Looking at me . . . surviving my body,
> That went to look for your crown in the dark dust
> [pp. 372–73].

Although this poem was written nine years after the novel, it indicates that Silva has overcome the temptations of the flesh. Her obsession with the sordid world that surrounds her—wars, class hatred, sexual exploitation—causes her to wonder "And I, where am I going?" She realizes that even in the midst of this misery she always has a choice:

> 'I am in the middle of my ideas. I can choose the future. And leave behind, in the ashes of the fire, the ardor, the hurry, the terrible uncertainty. A great cause calls me to action. A creative mystic puts men together and controls

> them. It organizes them for love.' But here, Laura, carried away by the enthusiasm of her thoughts, suddenly stopped, as if she had stumbled. 'Organize love? Organize love?' [pp. 158-59].

Choosing where to bestow her love is difficult for her because she herself is incapable of the reciprocity that love requires. She reproaches herself many times for being too romantic. Thus there is a clear protest that comes out in her message:

> To whom should she give her heart, if not to herself... ? Could she upbraid her listeners for their egotistical, desperate and proud sensuality in which the heated reciprocities of body and soul, mine and yours, were like pretty decorations on the allegories of the past, leaving the body and its desires alone, standing like sparkling but empty armor? Had she arisen, with her self-awareness, with her woman's experiences, her muddled woman's condition, to give a valuable and human sense to sexuality? [p. 130].

This "valuable and human" sense is what makes her survive since even though she seems to have drowned in desperation, there is still something that keeps her afloat: the belief in her responsibility to be a human being. She believes that the intellectuals protect themselves with books, that they have forgotten how to live outside of themselves, of their own dreams and sensations. What is needed then is to give one's self, not to a man but to a cause. She refuses to give herself to any man because they have made a clear division between themselves and women:

> She, too, was an object in its place. Woman. He assigned her everything. But in this 'everything' was one flaw: her woman's condition. Without him, she had no future. Or, at least, he thought he could give her destiny a profound sense of direction, like a diploma embossed in red letters. He was the creator, she the substance. And he persued this substance, not for herself, but out of pure desire. Did it please him? Thus they all went, almost every woman, looking desperately and blindly for the strange world of the men [p. 61].

On the other hand, when she chooses a cause, she does not do so for intellectual reasons and it does not even matter what that cause is. The real thing of importance is the act of committment. She believes she has been poisoned with the drug of egotism. From her anguish, her confusion of body and spirit, will come a new woman. She believes that out of the loathing, resentment, and sexual fears a new woman can emerge as if miraculously resurrected, a new woman able to face life clearly. The act of committment will free her from her egotism, will unite her with those who suffer. She says:

> In the morning I was once again innocent and intact as at first. I will be happy. Will I be happy? I will become part of the great army of the world, taken into the collective whole. I will give myself. To whom . . . ? Why . . . ? It doesn't matter. It is necessary. I will commit myself. I will step down or up to others. I will unite with their flesh. I will unite with their wounds. I will smell their odors. I will be happy with them. I will sustain their hopes with my despair. I will help them with my helplessness. I will nourish their faith with my scepticism. I will disappear amongst them. I will be nothing more than a number [p. 161].

This unexpected development in which she accepts these things she has rejected for so long—the masses, the crowd—is a type of conversion. In the poem "Orilla del naufragio," Silva also expresses this sudden gesture that combines committment and rebellion, the impetus of the soul to find a destiny for the earthly body, and the search for universal value that transcends the egotism of individual instinct. She says:

> You have given me the craziness of your kingdom. I feel your breath on my discouraged face; I can no longer turn back, I can't. I leave behind the broken, scattered history of my life, an empty chair on the shore of the shipwreck, from which arise, yet, the last gropings of the drowning man.[7]

The death of the novelist has forced me to search out her more intimate friends in order to find more details to help clarify many questions that only she could answer better. I believe the best answer as to the creative process of Clara Silva is her own as follows:[8]

> The sexual act is sad. Man looks perhaps for God in it. When he return to reality, he is filled with melancholy because he realizes he has not found what he sought. I do not

know how to explain the apparent contradiction between this fullness of life of which I have spoken and my pessimistic view of matrimony. But I believe it is difficult to enter into ideological or conceptual explications of what has been written. I feel that a writer in general and I in particular, work not with concepts and theories, but rather directly with our intuitions of our own reality. Problems of an intellectual or philosophical nature which arise from my work are best handled by the critics.... Look, I read not long ago and I don't remember where, that the tree and flower know nothing of botany, they are things whose essence lies in themselves. An author, likewise, cannot explain to others, even to himself, those things. His thoughts are on the work itself. The author is like nature, in certain ways things are 'created.' Each thing is a mystery unto itself. The critics are in charge of the interpretation. It is a pity that so often they are wrong.[9]

MARTA BRUNET

Marta Brunet was born in 1897 in Chillan, Chile.[1] *Montaña adentro,* a collection of short stories that first appeared in 1923, made her famous.[2] Her other books include: *Don Florisondo* (short stories, 1926), *Bestia dañina* (a novel of the same year), *María Rosa, flor del Quillén* (short novel, 1927),[3] *Bienvenido* (novel, 1929), *La mampara* (novel, 1946), *Humo hacia el Sur* (novel, 1946),[4] *Raiz del sueño* (short stories, 1948), *María Nadie* (novel, 1957),[5] and her last novel, *Amasijo (1962).*[6] Her literary activities have been interspersed with diplomatic posts in cultural affairs.

María Nadie[7] is narrated by María herself, an independent, single woman who leaves her home and goes to the capital, Santiago, after finishing high school. She finds work and all goes well for her until she meets Gabriel, a man who wants to have a good time with a girl who will submit herself to all of his whims. At first she is excited with the prospects, but she soon realizes that he is egotistical and inconsiderate. When she becomes pregnant, he forces her to have an abortion. She makes a break from him and goes to a little town where she is determined to make a new life for herself as a postal employee. She soon discovers that the hostility of the women in the town and the lust of the men makes her life miserable. She becomes friends with two small children, but their mother's jealousy and violent temper threaten her and she decides to leave. But where to go? Her experiences as a free spirit in a society that does not accept single women causes her to have some doubts. One alternative is to return to the family she detests. The novel ends without any answer.

Family

María suffers through a childhood that is economically tight and made even more unhappy by the methods her parents use to climb the bureaucratic ladder. Her mother is beautiful, intelligent and a clever manipulator of her father, who is a mediocre, timid and unimaginative employee:

> This same man, without hiding her manipulations and even turning them into everyday conversation, squandered his great wealth of comprehension, generosity and good feelings on his wife and family. He understood all, he had a smile for everything, great cordiality, he never denied anything to anybody. Whatever his wife wanted was law. Whatever the children wanted, as long as mother said 'yes,' was law. At what point did generosity stop and cynicism begin? Where did affection turn into mere accommodation? [p. 118].

The great "confusion of affirmations and negations which had neither beginning nor end" (p. 123) cause her much concern. If it is the wife who uses her personal magnetism to enable her husband to gain new positions, it is he who pushes her into doing it. Perhaps María refuses to accept the continual moving from place to place: "A new life, new furniture" explains her mother each time they change places, each time gaining more money, but also more debts and new school for the children. María knows that with two brothers and two sisters she will not be able to continue beyond high school even though she has the ability, because her parents will not be able to support her. With her commercial training she can only aspire to some office position, but at least it will provide a life without hypocrisy and servitude. Her first job in the capital shows her how others live. Gabriel, her lover, belongs to an emigrant family from Europe which has made some money. Gabriel gets a good allowance from his father as long as he is single and he has no desire to back himself into a corner and marry. María finally realizes that he never introduces her to any of his friends and prefers that she know nothing about his family.

On the provincial level appear the families of the two children María befriends. One is the Reinoso family, with father, mother and Cachito. After their first child, the father has decided he no longer loves his wife and prefers other girls. He becomes platonically involved with María when she arrives in town. The wife is resigned to "letting the men do as they will." The other family is composed of Don Lindor, his wife Petaca and their son Conejito. He is very lazy and lives off of his wife's work while he spends his time with every servant woman in town. His wife's jealousy makes her ill and the son realizes that something is wrong. He begs his father:

> Please, don't make Mama suffer. . . . With that Don Lindor's house of cards fell. He had been sure Conejo knew nothing of his wanderings. He felt miserable, uncovered, nude as it were, not knowing what to do, wishing to throw himself on the ground like a dog and cry from humiliation or perhaps dig a hole with his hands and bury himself forever. My God! What to do, what to say to Conejo . . . ? [H]e had said these carefully chosen words out of a desire not to hurt his father but to protect his mother, to be both partial and impartial, of course he could no longer remain silent, pretending not to know or that he hadn't heard anything, and suddenly convinced that he could not leave his mother alone to face disaster [p. 97].

Social Class

María is very much aware of the various characteristics that set her apart in her society. In the capital, since she is an "employee" she is ignored by Gabriel as socially inferior. In the village she is "blond and white" and has an education, and is therefore much above the farm girls and uneducated men. Since childhood she has learned what makes one job better than another, as her parents are experts in moving up the ladder of public service. When she meets Gabriel at a wedding, she immediately realizes he is a well-off bourgeois. She feigns a sophistication she does not have by allowing him to make love to her that first night without telling him she is a virgin. He is wary, owing to his rich bachelor status, and does not want to be trapped by a girl who might use her maternity to tie him down. Even though he never offers María any money, he buys her a series of useless gifts that show his lack of understanding of her needs and desires for books and records. She, although from a lower class, has much greater artistic taste than does he with his vulgar and banal ostentation.

We see in this novel a good overview of the social life of the town of Collocollo. Reinoso and his family belong to the middle class of government workers. Lindor and his family belong to the lower class, since both he and Petaca have been servants, but Petaca, thanks to her labors, has been able to open and manage her own restaurant. Petaca is obsessed with her little son's having the proper doctors and medicine, since he is a sickly child. Petaca's insecurity and her animosity toward any pretty woman—she is very fat and ugly—is shown in the incident at the theater where she insults María when María stops to talk to Conejito. The author also has tried to show the loneliness and limitations of the women from the different social classes.

Sexuality

María remembers that during her youth both the servants and her school companions had "a tremendous obsession with all that was sexual." It has not been difficult for her to remain a virgin, since her disposition for reading and her literary interests have protected her from temptation. When she arrives at the capital she lives alone and seems content to do without a sexual relationship. When Gabriel appears on the scene, she, perhaps in an effort to free herself from the prejudices of her education, gives herself to him. When he discovers her virginity he exclaims: "How could I imagine that you, so pretty and so small, could be intact . . . ? Go on into the bathroom, don't be so messy" (p. 142). She is now confused: "Has she begun to see the other face of happiness? Has she been kicked out of paradise, with a threatening finger pointing the way to suffering?" (p. 142). Although at first she is very much in love with Gabriel, their relationship is very chaotic. He comes to visit whenever he wishes and when she tries to regulate his visits he objects. He does not treat her as a human being but as a domesticated animal. He calls her by many nicknames, throws her into the air, and plays with her as if she were a doll. Possibly because of her sexual ignorance, she becomes pregnant. He wants her to have an abortion but when she resists, he forces her to have sexual relations with such violence that she begins to bleed. He then takes her to a clinic where he sees to it that she has the abortion and leaves her there for a few days. When she comes home, he begins to visit her again as if nothing had happened. When she refuses to have sex with him, he says:

> 'It is a pity. We got along so well. If some day you want to again, call me. I don't think you will but don't wait for me

> to call. It is you who are throwing me out. It is you who will have to call. I am telling you that seriously. . . .' And then he left [p. 155].

María then analyzes the reasons why she wanted the baby: for her, the child would have been the only thing really hers and she had wanted to start her own family line. When she realizes she is at the mercy of a cruel and unfeeling man, she changes her name from María Lopez to María Nadie and leaves the city without telling him where she is going. She eventually finds her way to a hidden town in the Andes. There she wants to be left alone. In her solitary walks through the countryside she meets the two young boys with whom she begins a friendship. She believes she can transcend the vulgarity that surrounds her by imagining all sorts of beautiful things. Petaca insults her by suggesting her friendship with the boys is something else: "It isn't enough that she play with all the men, she also has to take up with the boys" (p. 110). María realizes that while she has really tried to create a new life, the atmosphere that surrounds her is completely negative. The men here act according to the code of the *macho* and the women react with jealousy and insecurity. All the women of the novel, in fact, are represented as being frustrated, jealous, gossipy, spying and filled with hatred. One day María sees a little cat trying to get into a closed house and she identifies with it: Should she go back to the old family home or should she continue on alone?

Message

For the author, María typifies the woman who tries futilely to liberate herself. *María Nadie* transcends a purely regional interest, and the novel becomes depictive of the single woman in the great Spanish American capitals. One of her best critics states:

> In the second period of Marta Brunet, that period which we will call 'Boanaerense,' we find a hidden and sordid vision much deeper than her previous period in Chile. It is a movement that comes to life in her, that possesses her, and in a certain way makes her its victim, of which she is not sufficiently aware but which she feels and experiences, even against her will. Moreover, each time Marta alludes to her novelistic creations she insists on the independence of those

> characters she throws into the world and insists that they walk by themselves, as they wish and wherever they wish, abandoning the author and leaving her alone on the outside. . . . A feeling of inevitable solitude runs through both worlds, the exterior and interior, in a continuous flow, the only bridge between them. Here the author begins to know herself.

María Nadie presents the case of a girl who through her education, social position and ideas could have reached relative security if she had done what 99 per cent of the girls in her position did: stay at home, work until a husband came along, and then repeat the same cycle as her parents—respectability and mediocrity as a "decent woman" for the rest of her life. If her marriage were not perfect nor her dreams realized, at least her social group would have supported her to the extent that she would never feel completely alone. Family, friends, relations, subordinate classes and superior classes form a typically Latin American symbiosis which lends itself well to the changing of her name from María Lopez to María "Nobody." But the author has shown another alternative and also the price María must pay for her independence. Since she is young and beautiful it is easy for her to obtain the attention of men and the rivalry of women. María wants to rebel against the middle-class prejudices of her parents and falls prey to her illusions. She wants to have full confidence in the man she loves, but common sense tells her that this man is not worthy of her and only exploits her emotions. She feigns indifference—both are free to come and go—but she feels that she wants to give herself exclusively to him as long as he does likewise. Although she is reasonable in her spending and in her daily activities, she has one extravagance: she wants to confront the world with a child that is "completely hers." When Gabriel tells her "you must be sensible and do things as they ought to be done" she rebels. In spite of her middle-class upbringing and knowing the social pressure against a "single mother," she wants to raise her child, even if it means losing her job and having to do menial tasks in order to feed it. She does not even consider the possibility that Gabriel will set her up in a house and will support her and the child, since she is now convinced that he is irresponsible and seeks sexual pleasure and nothing more. There is no communication between them. For her, physical pleasure is not sufficient to keep them together and yet she is not strong enough to break off the relationship completely. Only after his brutality and the abortion does she decide to flee, changing her name beforehand to María Nadie.

There are two other women in the novel who are very different from María but who are also victims of masculine instability. Reinoso's wife Ernestina is from the same social level as María. When they were married following the conventional courtship she was still a virgin. He too was sexually ignorant and after their first child he no longer loves his wife because she does not provide that "incomparable happiness described in novels." He begins to make up for lost time with every woman he meets while she, with the passivity of the escapist, exclaims "as long as he leaves me alone" (p. 32). When Reinoso falls platonically in love with María, he "continually enjoyed his intimate thoughts full of humiliations, interminable monologues referring to the young woman of the golden hair . . . without her ever finding out about it" (p. 86). Petaca's situation is much more bitter. She, in spite of working in the kitchen, maintained her virginity until her wedding night with Lindor. When she realizes that he is always looking for sexual adventures with other women she develops a tremendous hatred for both sexes. About men Petaca says: "You unclean, hollow shells of men . . . you only know how to talk about whores. Beasts, worse than beasts" (p. 39). In general, the author has a very pessimistic view of the relationship between the sexes. In her other novels we find *machismo*, homosexuality and feminine aggressiveness, as well as many other facets of human behavior displayed by those who do not know how to resolve their bitter unhappiness.

ROSARIO CASTELLANOS

Rosario Castellanos is one of the most important Mexican writers.[1] She was born in 1925 and grew up in Comitán,[2] in the state of Chiapas, which has a large Indian population.[3] She studied in the capital at the Universidad Autonoma, graduating with a master's degree from the College of Letters and Philosophy.[4] She practiced journalism and teaching, and in the last years of her life held various public positions, among others one in the Central Office of the Instituto Nacional Indigenista,[5] and also that of ambassador to Israel, where she died in 1974.[6] She wrote poetry, stories, novels, essays and newspaper articles.[7] Her works are numerous and other collections of essays have appeared posthumously.[8] Among her novels and stories we have: *Balún Canán* (1957), *Oficio de tinieblas* (1962), *Los convidados de agosto* (1964), *Ciudad real* (1969), and *Album de familia* (1972).[9]

Balún Canán[10] means "nine stars" in Tzeltal, the language of the Indians who inhabit the region where the novel takes place. The work is narrated by an unnamed seven-year-old girl who lives with her family in Comitán. The little girl has a "nanny"—an Indian maid—who introduces her to the Indian legends. The first and third parts of the novel are narrated by the girl, but the second part is written in the third person. The girl, her six-year-old brother Mario, her mother Zoraida, her father César Argüello, and her Indian nanny live in a house in Comitán. The greatest part of the action takes place on the *hacienda* of the Argüello family where conflicts develop between the whites and the Indians when the large landowners raise obstacles to the implementation of the land-reform laws on their plantations. An Indian named Felipe is the instigator of the Indians who demand that Argüello build them a little school. César appoints his nephew Ernesto as teacher. A crisis develops and the Indians kill Ernesto, who was going to ask for help from the authorities. César goes instead. Meanwhile the nanny warns Zoraida that the witch doctors have condemned Mario—the Argüellos heir—to death. Zoraida desperately tries to counteract the sorcery, but it is useless and Mario dies.

Family

The Argüellos have been the owners of the Chacjtajal hacienda for several generations. César is the father and takes enormous pride in his family name. Mario is the only son and the mother Zoraida has placed all her hopes on him. She does not treat her daughter with the same consideration, which is why the girl looks to her Indian nursemaid for affection. The mother, for example, scolds the girl for reading the family books: "Do not play with those things, They are the inheritance of Mario. Of the male" (p. 60). The little girl begins to find in the cosmogonic world of the Indians the answers to her questions, and thus begins to understand the Indian race through her nanny. When the mother gets rid of the woman, she says upon leaving: "I am with you, little one. And I shall come when you call me" (p. 74). For many years the girl searches for her nursemaid among the many Indians she sees and at last exclaims: "Even if I find her I'll not be able to recognize my nanny. It has been so long since we separated" (p. 292). The relationship between the mother and the father is quite typical of that setting, given that he, because he is a man, has many women. César Argüello explains to his nephew that, of course, his wife knows what is going on:

> She would have to be stupid to not recognize such an evident fact. What is more, all ranch women figure that their husband is the biggest stud on the place. What saint could Zoraida have prayed to to be the only exception? As for the rest, there was no cause for anger. Children like those, women like those, they mean nothing. The legal one is the only one that counts [p.81].

Zoraida understands that it is because of her son that she is able to keep her place of supremacy in the life of her husband and her despair is great when the maid tells her of the decision of the Indian witches. Zoraida exclaims: "If God wants to prey upon my children . . . but not the boy . . . not my son" (p. 252).

Other important relationships are those that we see between the three Argüello sisters who are cousins of César. Francisca, the oldest one, took care of Matilde, a recently born baby, when their mother died. From that day on Francisca broke off her engagement to Jaime Rovelo and dedicated herself entirely to the baby and to the running of their hacienda. Once grown, Matilde goes to the city to live in the house of her cousins. The other sister, Romelia, who is separated from her husband, also lives in the city. Matilde, once a spoiled child on the hacienda, becomes a "relative" who has to help in the house to earn her room and board. She feels inferior to her cousin César and asks him to reaffirm his wish to have her in the house and to have her submit a "soplada," a superstitious ritual of the region. When she and Ernesto, who is an illegitimate son of César's father's brother, have sexual relations, nobody finds out. She makes it known to César and Zoraida when Ernesto dies. She asks César: "Aren't you going to kill me?" His only response is "Go!"—and she submissively leaves without anyone's knowing what becomes of her afterwards. The man has absolute control over the lives of the women, the only exception being Francisca who is completely independent. When she closes her door in César's face she tells him:

> I don't want you to judge me to be worse than I am, César. We were raised like brother and sister and I owe you many favors. But the Indians would lose confidence in me if they see me opening the doors of my house to you. Nobody has passed through them for months [p. 220].

Social Class

An extreme case of victimization by artificially created social barriers is that of Ernesto, César's nephew. In spite of being white and well-educated, he is considered inferior by the rest of the family:

> During the time he had spent near César he had learned that dialogue was impossible. César did not know how to converse with those he did not consider to be equal to him. Any sentence passing through his lips acquired the aspect of a command or a reprimand. His jokes seemed to poke fun. And moreover he always picked the worst moment to ask questions [p. 144].

The fact that Ernesto is illegitimate places him outside the Argüello family circle. Not only he, but also his blind mother are victims of abandonment when they most need family: during the years of his childhood. Nevertheless, when he is grown and the Argüellos need him, they call him and order him about. When he dies, nobody is worried about what may happen to the old and blind mother.

Another important social distinction is the one that exists between Zoraida and her husband César. She comes from a lower class and married him when she was very young. He was much older and lived alone. She says that she has always felt like "a bought hen" (p. 91). Zoraida has a great deal of gratitude for her mother, whom she maintains even though "she has to scrape it together from what César gives her to spend" (p. 91). Zoraida, however, feels very insecure in her social role and this causes her to vent her frustrations on those who are beneath her. She strikes the nanny and on another occasion verbally attacks a cripple whom she had helped, the reason being that she feels inferior without her son because César treats her like a sex object instead of a companion. He often ignores her and never discusses his business with her. His phrase: "That is man's business" is his best put-down for Zoraida who at times would like to say something, but he shuts her up with:

> 'I don't care what you think. I know what I should do. And stop moving around. It makes me nervous.' Zoraida stood still, filled with humiliation. César had never permitted himself to speak like this to her. And even less in front of strangers. Her pride wanted to protest, to avenge herself. But she did not feel sure of herself in front of this man and the fear of ridiculing herself silenced her [p. 130].

The work puts much emphasis on class conflict. The dominant social class of the old-timers, the landowners, feels threatened by the laws that protect the poor, especially the Indians. There is also a social change that follows the Mexican Revolution: even among the same rich class they cannot trust one another. Jaime Rovelo explains that his own son, who is a lawyer, has become a defender of the Indians, and César's cousin Francisca has taken the side of the Indians and closed her doors to her own family.

Among the Indians themselves there are conflicts and changes. Felipe, who is married to Juana, is the leader of the rebellious Indians. Juana still feels uncertain about her position, and during the rebellion considers crossing over to the side of the enemy, becoming a maid in Comitán, and renouncing her Indian language in favor of Spanish. This is the position in which the nanny finds herself, because by serving the whites she has been rejected by her own kind. Also, when she tells Zoraida about the curse of the witch doctors, she is betraying her people in order to forewarn her masters.

The child begins to recognize the distinctions between the upper class, to which she belongs, and the servants, peasants and Indians of the surrounding countryside. But because the only person of another social class whom she knows well is her nanny, she begins to perceive the injustices of the masters over their subordinates. According to Indian legend the gods made the rich and gave them the name "men of gold," but they also ordered that rich man could enter heaven unless "a poor man led him by the hand" (p. 30). The child begins to see the poor Indians as the means of salvation. Compassionate, she cries when she sees a bloody crucifix because it reminds her of an Indian who was killed for having been loyal to his masters. When the child discovers the image of Christ, she exclaims: "I'll never be able to escape from here, never. I have fallen into the black pit of hell" (p. 42). She knows that she belongs to the social class of the oppressors and she is afraid. Through conversations with the maids, both she and her brother begin to realize the hypocrisy of the whites regarding their religion. Later she steals the key to the chapel so that she and her brother will not fall into the trap of the Christian world which she associates with the social class. She hides the key in a trunk which belonged to her nanny and which she left behind when she was sent away, as though it possessed the sacred power to save her young charge. That night she dreams that Mario's kite is like "a fixed and resplendant star" and that she and her nanny see coming toward them one of the heavenly guardians which is the wind, and they remain "holding hands looking at each other forever" (p. 247). This is symbolic of her desire to belong to the social class of the Indians and to adopt their religion.

Even though Felipe is an Indian, he is convinced that if his people could learn to read they will be equal to the white race. In this part of the country the Indians have been prohibited from speaking the language of the whites but since Felipe knows how to read and write, he knows that there are laws in the country which require the owners of the haciendas to build a school for the children of the workers. Argüello and Rovelo discuss the problem. They decide to pretend to obey the statutes while making fun of the spirit of the law, thus Ernesto is made into a teacher for the Indians, although he does not understand them nor they him. When Ernesto gets drunk and hits one of the Indians, the crisis is touched off and the Indians rise up and burn one of the sugar mills.

The owners then come to the conclusion that they have no other alternative but to hire *ladinos* (mestizos or "acculturated" Indians), but now they will have to pay the minimum salary, transportation, living expenses, food and schooling. They also realize that the *ladinos* who return to the town to hold a public office, such as Gonzalo Utrilla, are dedicated to getting revenge on the upper class which humiliated them earlier. Utrilla says to César: "Fortunately these are no longer your times, don César. Suppose that things had not changed. The government pays me a living. On the other hand, from the rich I never received anything" (p. 134).

Sexuality

The young girl of the novel experiences a sisterly love for her nanny who also expresses affection for her, in spite of the fact that she feels that a curse of her race follows her:

> 'Say nothing, child. I came from Chactajal so that they would not follow me. But their sorcery reaches far.'
>
> 'Why do they wish you harm?'
>
> 'Because I have been a servant in your house. Because I like your parents and Mario and you.'
>
> 'Is it bad to like us?'
>
> 'It is bad to like those who order you. Those who possess you. That is what the law says' [p. 16].

The nursemaid, also out of love for the children, tells Zoraida that Mario has been selected as a victim of the sorcerers in order to break "the bridge" of the whites. Zoraida strikes her and it is then that the loyalty of the girl goes toward the wretched Indian and not toward her mother: "Silently I drew near to the nursemaid who remained on the floor, destroyed, abandoned like a thing with no value" (p. 233). This same woman is the one who has initiated her to the grandeur of Indian cosmogony and who has even presented her to the Indian gods in a ceremony entitled: "I come to give you my child":

> Open her understanding, widen it so that she might know the truth. And restrain her from using the whip, knowing that each whiplash records its mark on the back of the executioner. And thus may your likeness be hers, as salve spread over the wounds [p. 63].

After the Indian nursemaid is sent away from the house, the girl still has her brother Mario, but he becomes mortally ill. When he dies, she deposits the key to the chapel in the cemetery with him and entrusts them to "the family guardians," in order that they may be good to him and keep him company. She knows that she is now truly alone because her nanny and Mario, her only two loves, are far away. To keep herself company she writes the name of Mario on the walls of her house and on the tiles in the garden. In the incipient sexuality of the girl one observes resentment against her mother for the rejection she feels due to her sex. Also there is somewhat of a sense of guilt for the death of Mario, something inexplicable which perhaps arises from infantile jealousies.

In the sexuality of the women in the novel there is a conduct which is incomprehensible and which the popular mentality attributes to *Dzulum,* a powerful Indian god who forces women to obey him. In the case of Francisca Argüello, she suffers a mysterious persecution and is found at the bottom of a ravine: "When she came to she said that she had had a vision. Among the Indians there arose the opinion that she had been dragged down by *Dzulum.* And if he had not carried her off it was because she made a pact to serve and obey him" (p. 116). From that moment on she is bewitched, paints the walls of her house black, and assumes the role of leader of the renegade Indians. Even Matilde is afraid of her and goes to live with her cousin. The strange thing is that Francisca acquires prophetic powers. Matilde explains this to Zoraida: "The Indians come to consult with her. And when she tells one of them: 'Maybe such a thing will happen,' it happens" (p. 116). Francisca, who had even given up her plans to marry Rovelo in order to raise Matilde as her own, becomes neglectful of her—"She fled from her to recite spells and curses by herself" (p. 117).

The situation of Angelica, another member of the family is much simpler: She runs off with her lover. In the case of Matilde, when she goes secretly off to her house out of shame, the people say that *Dzulum* has carried her off. Matilde is a woman in whom sexual frustration, class pride and an extreme inferiority complex causes her, when mature, to undertake to lose her virginity, which she had retained due to the social conventions of her class. When she and the girl narrator and Ernesto go together to the hacienda Chajtal, an opportunity presents itself in which Matilde feels her desire to know a man sexually become inflamed; she goes freely to Ernesto's room. Ernesto tells us about what went on there:

> All I did was kiss her and she froze up like a paralytic, as if in a seizure, she fell backwards, stiff, cold, pale, as though dead. I carried her to the bed and laid her there. I was frightened, word of honor. I grabbed her by the shoulders and shook her and shouted: 'Matilde, Matilde!' She said nothing to me. All she did was to begin to tremble, and to cry, and to beg me not to hurt her, to say that she was afraid, that I was going to cause her pain. As for me, why would I lie to you, as God is my witness, not the slightest evil intention had crossed my mind. Oh my guard I began to think and think. That Matilde would say that I was not much of a man if I left her in that state. What's more she began to defend herself, to struggle. She even began shouting, but I covered her mouth. That was all we needed, to be found there together like that. I told Matilde that to quiet her down. She paid no attention to me. She obeys no one. Because of the way she was brought up she is used to getting her precious way. What she needs is a man to keep her in subjection and make her trot along in place. But it is obvious that I am not that man [p. 163].

She feels a mixture of tenderness for this man who is younger than she, but at the same time she feels that she has lowered herself because he is a bastard of lowly position whom she has no wish to marry. But she herself feels inferior because she is no longer young and she knows that men have their certain code:

> After all, what had there been between them? They made love like two beasts, silently, with no vow of love. He had to despise her for what had happened. Now he could find no respect for her. Matilde had given him all. But that never pleases a man. He pays for that with insults. Cheap women can keep a man only when they are young. And Matilde was not young. Other women wait their turn and would not be as stupid as she had been [p. 142].

One day when they go together to the river to accompany the girl, Matilde jumps into the deepest part of it, but an Indian saves her. Ernesto worriedly whispers into her ear, "I dreamed about you every night" (p. 158). For a second both of them are seen to be vulnerable and without their masks, but she rebukes him by saying that she wants to kill herself because she is pregnant by him: "Because I don't want your child to be born. Because I do not want to have a bastard" (p. 159). Ernesto, who has suffered all of his life because of his illegitimate origins, now feels only hatred for her, and his intentions of marrying her vanish: "I was not going to go backwards, I had not planned to leave her dishonored. But after what she did I could not even dream of asking her to marry me. I am not so bold. Let her take responsibility for her child" (p. 164). Matilde goes to the witch doctor to seek an abortion. Ernesto's words weigh heavily on her mind:

> Do not mention the name of my mother. Don't you dare compare yourself to her. Do you think you are better than she? More honorable? Why? Because you preferred to wither away as an old maid rather than sacrifice yourself for a son? She sacrificed herself for me. And I am not ashamed that she is my mother. I am not ashamed that we are seen together in the street even though poorly dressed and without shoes. And even though she is blind [p. 124].

Matilde has made her decision and the only witness is Ernesto, who in an excess of hatred becomes drunk and beats up an Indian boy, which sets off the chain of events that lead the Indians to assassinate him. At that moment Matilde confesses her guilt and waits for César to throw her out of the house, which he does more because of his position than because of any desire to punish her. She also feels guilty for the death of Ernesto: "I killed him. I was his servant. I did not allow his son to be born" (p. 216). A few months later, Zoraida asks Romelia, the sister of Matilde, "What could have become of Matilde?" she responds: "If no animal of the forest ate her, then she must be serving as a servant for some ranch" (p. 238).

A case of a marriage without children and in which everybody considers the wife to be sterile, is that of Juana and Felipe, the rebel Indian. Among the Indians there is sufficient reason to annul a marriage if the woman has no children. Nevertheless, Felipe stays with Juana because he has other worries: the rebellion which she does not understand and which comes between them:

> No, it was not jealousy. Jealousy is a human emotion, common to anyone. And Juana would have known how to put up with it, dissimulate it, feel it. If Felipe had wanted another woman, Juana would have had in front of her an equal adversary and could have fought with the same weapons and would have won, because she was the legitimate wife even though she had no children. And if she had lost she would have been able to accept it. But this was not the case, and the true one was cruel. Juana could not understand it and she would beat her head with her fists and ask what she had done to be punished in this way [p. 179].

Both Juana and Felipe are outside the norm for their race and yet they lack the ability to communicate and draw together. Their separation is made even greater because Juana feels frustrated in her role of a married woman in her community. She is not able to understand him in the same way that Zoraida cannot understand César:

> He becomes bored with me because I do not know how to converse. He was educated abroad. When we were sweethearts he would visit me at night at my window. And he would try to explain to me the phases of the moon. I never understood him. Now he hardly ever talks to me. I

> don't want to be separated like Romelia. You seek companionship everywhere and find it with no one. If you get fixed up and go out on the street, they say that you are a whore. If you stay at home they think poorly of you. Thank God that I have my two children and one is a boy [p. 92].

Another type of frustrated woman is Romelia, but for a different reason. Her husband is lazy and "useless." "There is a reason I am separated from him," she says. Yet Romelia is a hypochondriac who at last is advised by her doctors to return to her husband, which she does because "I prefer to live in my own house, however modest it may be, and not be shut up in some strange house" (p 254). It might be that that reason is a bit secondary, since her husband does not communicate with her. What Romelia wants is to "have her house" because she does not have the patience to watch Zoraida in her desperation and madness trying to save her son from the effects of the witchcraft that has been used against him.

The only woman who appears to accept her place with resignation is Amalia, "the spinster," who wanted to become a nun but was prevented from doing so by the priest because she had an ill mother. She is the only one who, because of her faith in Providence, is able to shower attention on those who need it, as in the case of Zoraida:

> Listen to me, please, Zoraida. The priest is the only one who can save Mario. He would recite exorcisms so that the demon would go away from this house. Because it is the devil, everybody knows that. Even doctor Mazariegos. Why do you think he refused to even attempt an operation on the child? Because he knows it would be in vain [p. 277].

Message

The women of the novel are creatures who are pursued by fear. Once that they fall into "the trap" they have to suffer their personal hells. The social conventions have been so deeply engraved in these women that they feel guilty even when they are not. Even the little girl suffers this fear. When they ask her to look at her brother for the last time she turns her head: "No, I could not stand to. Because it is not Mario, but rather my guilt that is rotting in the bottom of that coffin" (p. 283).

In the case of Zoraida there is also a sense of guilt. Her daughter describes her: "There she is on her bed, the bed on which her son died, twisting and moaning like a steer when the cowboy wrestles it down and the mark of slavery burns into its flesh" (p. 285). This "mark of slavery" is her fate as a woman, almost as if to say a cow, hen, procreator. In her condition as a female she feels useful when César recognizes her as "the legitimate one," but without her son she loses her role, which is to provide the continuation of the family name Argüello. The little girl suffers also because she feels useless being a woman and because she intuitively senses that her mother would have preferred that it be she whom the sorcerers select, but she does not even serve for that revenge. The case of Juana, the Indian, is not so different from that of Zoraida. She has been indoctrinated to be a mother and the fact that she is not important to her husband does not change the situation. She feels useless, with no function within society.

The author also shows the diverse forms that repressed sexuality can take. Matilde does not give herself either out of love or through instinct; her motives are a mixture of boredom, emptiness, loneliness, and a desire for emotional nearness. Because she cannot understand herself she is caught up in a web of her own weaving. Her surrender is one of a condemned woman, abandoning herself without joy but rather with a terror of sex, of the man and of the strength which she attributes to the male. It appears as more of a rape, even though she chooses the rapist, because Matilde does not have the honesty to rid herself of all the social roles which have been placed upon her for being an Argüello since the day she was born. Unlike the mother of Ernesto, who came from the lower class, she does not feel herself to be strong enough to face the world with an illegitimate child. Nor does she believe that Ernesto will marry her because of their age difference. Marriage does not seem to be a solution for these women who are trapped by their role as a sexual object. Those who marry often do it simply to have their own house as with Romelia and Zoraida.

Love for both of them is an outward show; their men are unfaithful to them when they want because for them sex is like food, a natural satisfaction for a man. Having children is not a responsibility for the men, let the women find a way to take care of their bastards. Through Ernesto, the author shows all the suffering of one of these children and makes clear the social injustice against the mother, who like so many other peasant women, has to go hungry to enable her children to survive, with no help and suffering public condemnation. It is evident that this is a novel of feminine protest, even though there are many other important aspects to the work. The conflict often oscillates between individual reality and social appearances. If the woman breaks one of the rules she feels sentenced to cleanse herself of her guilt. Angelica and Matilde both go far away from their homes and, even though the populace says that *Dzulum* carried them off, everyone knows that the inescapable destiny of the dishonored woman is anonymity, where the family names fade away and the victims do penance.

The author presents a gamut of women of diverse ages, races, social classes, and economic conditions. From the little girl, to the spinster (still a little girl) like Amalia, to the old maid like Matilde, to the one with a bad marriage like Romelia, to the one with the good marriage like Zoraida, to the sterile woman like Juana, to the mature Indian woman like the nanny, and to the independent woman who is outside all regulation like Francisca Argüello, all have something in common: A psychic alienation, a lack of identity. All have been marked from birth and at best attempt to find themselves in some moment of suffering or of catharsis. None of these women is happy, none is able to control her destiny. It is the priest confessor in the case of Amalia and *Dzulum* in the case of Francisca who is the "controller," but both are women who seek in faith and in fanaticism a way out of their trap.

The author also selects problems that are common to any Hispano-American woman in a provincial rural society of religious and racial mixtures. Comitán and Chajtal are two typical places where the women do not have the opportunity to study, to work, to find themselves, to live alone or to seek an alternative to their loneliness. The lives of all of them are hanging on the consequences of their feminine actions. If they have, like the little girl, the sensitivity to consider the feminine trap, perhaps they will in the future be able—as the author does in her personal life—to free themselves of their chains and openly defy society.

Occupying herself with the testimonial value of the Mexican novel the author here makes a comment which seems to me to be applicable to her own novel, even though she was referring to *Al filo del agua* by Agustín Yañez:

> The story is that of a town, of any town of Mexico, in the last years of the dictatorship of Porfirio Díaz. Isolated, superstitious, oppressed by the rigid moral norms and by their nearsighted economic institutions; *a town of women in mourning* in which live, even that which is legitimized by ecclesiastical blessing, is like a stigma that causes shame to those who suffer it; in which happiness is nothing more than a prelude to catastrophe; in which all desire is frustrated, all impulse is checked, all vital strength made bloodless, slowly yet steadily, until it is extinguished, in spasms as useless as incoherent. And if not extinguished it has no other way to manifest itself but in madness and death.[11]

Rosario Castellanos is the spokesperson for the necessity of feminine liberation in Hispano-American culture. She did her work conscientiously, and in each of her works reveals a system that has alienated men and women, rendered them unable to communicate. She notes various aspects of this, including hypocrisy, the imposition of strictly masculine and feminine roles, and especially the anguish, emptiness and hostility among women who apparently have respected the system and pass for exemplary women. She also depicts the conditons which have been arbitrarily imposed and which create incomprehension and resentment among the same women. Of course when the two sexes interact, other elements of "conditioning" come into play: "Customs have enclosed the Mexican woman in a very restricted area and have made objects of them."[12] Because of that they are presented like puppets who are manipulated so that they never leave their place and so that they play their role well.

BEATRIZ GUIDO

Beatriz Guido was born in Argentina in 1924.[1] She has written several novels,[2] among them *La casa del ángel* (1955),[3] *La caída* (1956),[4] *Fín de fiesta* (1958), *El incendio y las vísperas* (1964),[5] *Escándalos y soledades* (1970),[6] and three collections of short stories: *Estar en el mundo* (1950), *La mano en la trampa* (1961)[7] and *El ojo único de la ballena* (1971). The fact that she has written for the movie industry and is married to a film director has added a cinematic perspective to some of her novels.[8]

Her novel *Fín de fiesta*[9] takes place between the years 1930 and 1945, and begins with the domination of the political leader Braceras and ends with the appearance of Perón on the Argentine political scene. One protagonist is Mariana, her sister is Julieta: both are granddaughters of Braceras. They are orphans, and ever since their parents died in a shipwreck (along with the parents of their cousins Adolfo and José María) they have been in the custody of their grandfather. Another boy who lives on the ranch, Gonzalo, is the illegitimate son of Braceras. Felicitas, a maid and housekeeper, is in charge of the boys' education. The girls have a German governess, Fräulein Elise. Gustavino, their grandfather's right-hand man, also plays an important role in the education of Adolfo. The narration begins when the boys begin to discover their sexuality, and continues when they are sent to a Jesuit school in punishment for Adolfo's rebellion against his grandfather's orders to kill Gustavino. The girls are sent to a private school and enter into their social life. Julieta marries a neighboring doctor and Mariana develops into an extremely beautiful girl who is pampered by her grandfather. Adolfo and Mariana are reunited when he is 18 and she is 17 and they at last consummate the sex act after many years of frustrated passion. This is a period of political changes, and little by little Braceras is eliminated and finally dies. The grandchildren—now adults—are forced to make some decisions about the future.

Family

There are two pairs of girls and boys, all children of two sisters who were the daughters of the Intendente de Avellaneda, otherwise know as Braceras or "Braceritas." The two mothers and their husbands were traveling to Europe for a vacation when the boat sank. This family tragedy binds their children together until they grow up. The surnames are important, since the children belong to two powerful families: the Braceras family—rich landowners—and the Aguirre family—their grandmother's aristocratic family from the city. The fathers of these children do not seem to have much influence on their lives. Thus when José María becomes identified with his father's side of the family, it is simply an association made with his interest in sports and horses. On the other hand, Adolfo is from the beginning identified with the Braceras family, as he is daring, interested in politics, and keen-witted. Mariana is like her grandmother: delicate, beautiful and elegant. Julieta, on the other hand, is like her grandfather, fat and ugly. Even her grandfather himself approves of her early marriage: "He is ugly enough for this fat girl" (p. 160).

The ties between the two brothers are very strong and they are inseparable in their youth. Their loyalty extends even to self-sacrifice, as José María accepts the punishment of a boarding school with Adolfo even though he knows that his true passion lies in the open air and the ranch. Their emotional ties only separate when José María travels to the United States with a polo team and marries an American girl. There is a similar bond between the girls. When Julieta marries and almost goes insane following each of her frustrated pregnancies, it is Mariana who accepts complete responsibility for her sister and tries to save her. There is a larger family sphere of influence which is not well-defined, and thus Gonzalo, son of a country girl who drowned, will be cared for by Braceras (who is the boy's real father) as long as Gonzalo obeys him. We even suspect that Felicitas, the maid, is Bracera's concubine or that she had been earlier in his life. Gustavino becomes a substitute father for Adolfo and their relationship is more intimate than even blood could make it. Likewise, Felicitas the maid considers herself "like a mother" for the children. Mercedes and Maria Mercedes, their aunts on the Aguirre side, consider the girls to be their own daughters. This extended family has the grandfather as its head, and he makes Mariana his favorite and only tolerates the rest because they have the same name and blood. While the others look on Gonzalo as a poor relative, between him and Mariana there is a bond of sympathy and comprehension that lasts throughout the years. He does not expect too much of anyone and he is most helpful during the crises which happen in this chaotic family life. Towards the end of the novel, when he is the parish priest in the area of the grandfather's ranch, he is forced to postpone decisions out of fondness for his cousins even though he realizes he is compromising his spiritual life.

Social Class

The grandfather is an all-powerful and astute *cacique* who manipulates the town; Adolfo remembers him thus:

> 'The town,' my grandfather used to say, 'must be driven like cattle. When they refuse to cross the bridge—five cents a head for those who cross over to Avellaneda's side. One peso a week, every Saturday, is what it costs me to see that they do not wake up to reality.' I had heard this very infrequently but it was impressed indelibly on my mind. I thought that my grandfather viewed the town of Avellaneda as he did 'La Enamorada': a vast expanse of land inhabited by ignorance of misery. A vast land of noncommunication. Over there, beyond the bridge, the Federal Capital. On this side, a great feudal land known as the province of Buenos Aires [p. 62].

The grandfather's authoritarian attitude is typical of the *cacique* of his day, but his tactics extend to his grandsons to whom he gives money so that they too "will not open their eyes" to reality and so that he can drive them in whatever direction he pleases. He also is very typical of the landowner whose roots are in the soil and who looks on the cosmopolitan aristocracy with disrespect. Once, when speaking to Adolfo about one of his political defeats, he says:

> After all, you have my name, that ought to mean as much to you as it does to me. I am not talking about your brother because he will stay away forever. He prefers not to come

> back. I have known many people like him, without family ties. They would rather be 'gigolos' in France than to care for their lands at home . . . [p. 216].

The grandfather uses people of poor repute for his questionable deeds, and his interactions with them are carefully hidden. He allows Gustavino to deal with these criminals, prostitutes and paid politicians. Unlike the grandfather, Gustavino has his own "macho" rules which direct his conduct. On the other hand, the grandfather is treacherous and very Machiavellian. At first he approves of Gustavino's taking Adolfo with him on his political adventures because he wants Adolfo to take Gustavino's place one day. Nevertheless, he does not hesitate to betray Gustavino when it is convenient, and when Adolfo shouts"murderer!" at him, the grandfather knocks him down. While he has the appearance of an educated man, he is a barbarian and the Aguirre aunts recognize it. The upper social class is tied to the Church, and although the Aguirre family is the more religious of the two, the grandfather nevertheless chooses a Jesuit school in which to educate the boys. He does so out of custom because he knows that the Jesuits will prepare the boys to be rulers with methods that are not as brutal as his. Likewise, he chooses European schools for the girls in order to refine them and even allows the Aguirre women to supervise and introduce the girls to fashions, high society and travel. He is a typical corrupt official, his forefathers killed the Indians for money and he relies on official help from the authorities whom he bribes. During World War II he sells meat to Europe and does so through a monopoly. When this monopoly is discovered, he has his men kill the legislator who revealed it and then has the nerve to show up at his funeral. Adolfo makes Gustavino realize that he can no longer blindly serve his grandfather. This dandy, "dressed in black and with a handkerchief around his neck," begins to feel pangs of conscience and says:

> It is one thing to kill the Valenzuelas and quite another to kill a Senator in the Senate because he wanted to uncover a few Imperialist thieves [p. 192].

When Gustavino tells "Braceritas" that there was no need to kill the Senator, the grandfather has the Valenzuela brothers kill him because he will not tolerate insubordination.

Adolfo goes through a crisis of rebellion against his grandfather, and even when he is away at Jesuit school he uses his free time to make friends with students who are unaware of his name. During a student protest, the other students discover his identity as a "Braceras" and they reject him. He realizes that he is a marked man and cannot change sides, and so decides to do what the other youths of his class do—enjoy himself. He goes to dances, has a girlfriend, drinks, goes to the races and avoids social conflict. He says of his girlfriend Cecilia Araoz, "I was interested in her because I was free at the moment" (p. 180). His grandfather pays for all of his expenses and those of his brother José María, who lives in Buenos Aires. When José María begins to be noticed as a champion polo player, his grandfather charters a plane to fly the team all over. The activities of Adolfo and his brother are the "status symbols" of the wealthy class and as Adolfo says, "I took full advantage of the benefits."

While the boys are engaged in political life, the girls are directed to the social life they will lead. Particularly for Mariana—since Julieta has married a country doctor—life is dancing, trips to Europe, drives in the country, boyfriends and all manners of distractions. The women of the upper class are all waiting for marriage. A dialogue between Cecilia Araoz and Adolfo reveals the differences between the sexes:

> 'You must do something.'
>
> 'And you, what do you do all day?'
>
> 'I am different.'
>
> 'Why?'
>
> 'I am a woman. . . . What can women do?'
>
> 'I don't know, something' [p. 181].

Matrimony and maternity, together with social activities, are the feminine goals. Julieta has married a fanatical Catholic and all her pregnancies end in spontaneous abortions. Nevertheless, her husband insists that she continue to try and he even decides that if there is a choice between the child and the mother, the doctor is to try to save the baby.

There are racial distinctions among the servants. Elise, the German governess, has certain privileges. When Gustavino chooses a lover he chooses a French girl whom he cannot understand and needs Adolfo for his interpreter. The Padilla girls, daughters of farm workers, are sexually initiated early and later become maids in the main house. We can see some changes in the aspirations of the poor. Ramona Sánchez, a prostitute protected by Braceras, wants her son to go to the Police Academy and more than likely she will see it happen. This is a period of great changes and expectations.

Sexuality

Mariana's sexuality is influenced by an incident that takes place in her pre-adolescence. Elise insists the girls bathe nude in the pond and Adolfo hides in a tree to watch. Mariana sees him and runs crying to her grandfather. He only half listens to her story, thinks that Adolfo has raped her, and shouts, "You wretched person, you have scarred her for life! Forever! You deserve to be raped yourself" (p. 18). He then beats Adolfo with his belt, which also determines Adolfo's sadomasochistic attitudes later:

> I hoped the whipping would never end; it was as if I were already choosing between pain and shame; between humiliation and the blood which was running out of my nostrils. And perhaps for the first time I wished my father were alive or that José María were older than I so that they could defend me [p. 18].

That same night he avenges himself on Mariana by giving her a severe beating. From that moment on he takes the role of the executioner with her as the victim. This will be reaffirmed later, when in the moments of his most passionate desire for her he arranges to humiliate her:

> Mariana was part of myself. It was like digging deeper into my wounds. She was the image of my humiliation, of my

> heroic dreams, of my infamy and cowardice. And also the image of my surrender . . . [p. 182].

For both of them their grandfather becomes a person whom they hate and love at the same time. The grandfather cannot hide his love for his granddaughter, he passes hours "caressing her hair" (p. 208). Thus a hidden rivalry develops between the two men over Mariana and this creates an evil passion in Adolfo. For a time, Adolfo concentrates all of the love his grandfather denies him in Gustavino; subconsciously, Adolfo is learning to become a "man":

> With each passing day he felt a strange feeling grow towards Gustavino: admiration, kindness and pity were all mixed together . . . as if they both were victims of unknown circumstances. They ought to act more like dandies, if they wanted to be tough. . . . If he wanted to be a politician, he ought to imitate one; his pity for Gustavino arose from the fact that he thought that one paid a big price, at times, to become a man [p. 94].

As for Mariana, although she has not been violated by her cousin, she nevertheless suffers as a result and begins to fear everything sexual. When she learns that her cousins and the Padilla girls are involved in sexual games, she asks Gonzalo, the only one she trusts:

> 'Gonzalo,' asked Mariana after a long silence, 'will you ever kiss a girl?"
>
> 'I don't know; I would have to be very much in love to wish to kiss one.'
>
> 'Of course,' answered Mariana, 'you don't kiss for the act of kissing, like the boys do with the Padilla girls: they do it merely to kiss' [p. 87].

She is really talking about the sex act itself. A few years later, when Mariana and Adolfo feel compelled towards each other by a deep passion during the pre-Lenten carnival, Mariana surprises Adolfo rolling around on the floor with one of the Padilla girls. Once again the sexual act separates the two, since she is horrified. They do not see each other again for three years, when she goes with her aunts to visit the boys at the Jesuit school. When Mariana is on her way to a dance and Adolfo cannot attend, he tears her dress and insults her: "I am not interested in girls with your reputation" and she replies, "If you are referring to the boys with us, you are wrong . . . at least they don't hang around with murderers like you do" (p. 153). Later, during Julieta's wedding, Adolfo gets drunk and declares his love for Mariana. She discovers the dirty trick Adolfo has played on Gonzalo by locking him up with one of the Padilla girls so they can have sex, and Mariana once again flees, horrified. Later she takes a trip with her aunts to the United States and has nothing more to do with him until Julieta has an emotional breakdown and Adolfo sends her a cablegram asking her to come home and care for her sister. Mariana realizes that Adolfo is more interested in punishing her than in Julieta's health and she says "What are you waiting for? Do you want me to go crazy too?" (p. 197). Even though all the cousins now live under one roof on the ranch La Enamorada, they hardly ever speak to each other. Mariana finally looks for him when Julieta is about to give birth. When the child is born dead she cries, "Never a son!" (p. 202). That same night, Mariana and Adolfo make love for the first time. He describes her gestures as she crosses her arms over her breasts and her face becomes flushed. Her fear he takes to be a sign of love. When he discovers that she is not a virgin he says, "You must really have laughed at me thirty minutes ago. I thought of you like a schoolgirl. I never thought you were a whore like the rest" (p. 204). When she leaves the room she berates him, "If you had not locked Gonzalo up with Rosa Padilla at 'La Enamorada,' I would still be in your arms" (p. 204) and she hints that he is to blame for her loss of virginity.

If Mariana were to tell her own story, we would find that she hesitates between her fear and hatred for sexual things and the attraction her cousin holds for her. She also associates maternity with insanity because she watches Julieta suffer. She asks that Gonzalo have Julieta's husband sterilize his tormented wife, but he refuses, and when Julieta has another stillbirth she goes even more insane. Although Julieta wishes to poison her husband, she repeats over and over, "Abortion is a sin." Once again Mariana goes to Gonzalo, the village priest, so that he might arrange special permission for sterilization from the Church, but Gonzalo says, "I cannot find one argument to destroy her husband's reasons" (p. 211). From that moment on Mariana says:

> 'I will not wait another moment, I assume the responsibility. All of it. I condemn my self, not you.' she said angrily to Gonzalo. 'If they don't wish to come with me, I will go alone . . . anywhere. With money everything is possible' [p. 212].

After the operation they all feel relieved. Julieta throws her husband out and her grandfather pays him to have the marriage annulled and to leave Julieta.

Another fear enters the house: death. Braceras, the grandfather, has lost the support of his followers and they ask him to retire, so he stays on the ranch with nothing to do:

> He would spend the entire day on his black horse, riding in the fields near 'La Enamorada,' much as José María did. At dusk he would sit on the west side of the house, as quiet as a statue, waiting for the sun to set [p. 207].

Adolfo, when he sees his grandfather's defeat, takes sadistic pleasure in accompanying him while he waits for death; the hatred which Adolfo felt during his school years and which the Jesuits never could destroy has increased. All of the ideals the Jesuits tried to teach him—love, children, family, social, and moral stability in politics—have been for nought, since Adolfo has never been able to free himself of his desire for vengeance. When his grandfather dies in October of 1945, the military leader Perón takes command. The only people who attend the grandfather's funeral are a delegation from the Central Committee, the Aguirre family, Felicitas the maid, and some prostitutes and nuns. With the fall of a class, represented by the grandfather, the clamor of the rise of the proletarian masses can be heard. Adolfo decides to abandon La Enamorada and takes Mariana to an apartment in Buenos Aires. She now submissively reclines her head on Adolfo's shoulder and thinks: "I cried for the first time, for the three of us [including Julieta]. There we were, shocked, uncertain, not knowing what to do in the next few hours, the coming days, next year" (p. 218).

Message

This novel clearly shows the importance of sexual roles. In Latin America, principally among the middle and upper classes, there is a great deal of emphasis on "sexual" models which are to be imitated. In the case of the boys, the "men" are urged to do certain things the girls are not allowed to do. The maid Felicitas emphasizes this when the girls play with their cousins; some things are only done by "tomboys." From a very early age the boys go to houses of prostitution or "play" with the maids or local girls. Nevertheless, when Adolfo looks at his naked cousins he causes great concern to his grandfather, for whom the virginity of his granddaughters is of great importance. Mariana could have been taught to be free of prejudices by her German governess, who allowed her great freedom, but she has a great fear of sex and is obsessed with the possibility of rape. Gonzalo's case is an exception, since he does not act like the other men, nor does he want to go near the prostitutes, nor does he mistreat the animals. When he is sent to the seminary the boys laugh at his habit, and later they play a trick on him with the Padilla girl which he bears with resignation. Only Mariana seems to understand that Gonzalo is not effeminate but that he, in reality, has a finer sensibility than the others.

The author also shows the homosexual tendencies of the men which they themselves do not realize and which appear because their imitation of masculine models causes a psychic transference which affects them emotionally. Felicitas, the most observant of the group, says to Adolfo when he follows the grandfather everywhere: "I don't like to see you alone, following him around the house. Don't you have a girlfriend? Why aren't you with her? Have you taken up politics again?" (p. 196). Both Gustavino and the grandfather are the center of political and manly ambitions. Gustavino, because he is younger, is the one with whom Adolfo has more in common. When Adolfo thinks Gustavino will die from a shot in the chest, he takes the slug out with his own teeth and he remembers, "He took one of my hands and placed it on his cheek. I withdrew it immediately" (p. 102). Adolfo is the most vulnerable because he has no mother and the only men who treat him with affection are his brother and Gustavino. Much of Adolfo's inability to communicate with Mariana is due to his early experiences when he witnessed the relationship of Gustavino and the French prostitute. When he observes them he says:

> He understood at that moment, all at once, the weakness of man when confronted by a woman. He understood, without an explanation, that Gustavino was looking for something, something that she had hidden. Something that only he, a boy behind a screen, was able to clarify. And he saw that lascivious, dark man, his grandfather's servant, leader of firing squads, loosen his belt and sit down powerless in a chair [p. 67].

The relationship between Adolfo and the other women is one of "lusty women" on one hand and inaccessible lovers like Mariana on the other. The fact that she is inaccessible to him for so long causes him not to be able to hide his resentment when he discovers she is not a virgin when they make love for the first time. The "double standard" has allowed him to do as he wished and his surprise is a little forced when he states that he has treated her like a schoolgirl. Mariana is not very experienced in these matters and shows the same terror she did as a child. Although the novelist presents this scene from Adolfo's point of view, we can see that Mariana has been forced to lose her virginity—with some other boy—simply to avenge herself or perhaps to try and experience what she believes the Padilla girls must enjoy. Here she imitates a feminine model, something she has always disliked and her first sexual encounter with Adolfo is disastrous. Mariana's sensitivity is also directed by the affection of her grandfather, who takes pride in her feminine beauty. The Aguirre women, her aunts, also stimulate her vanity with dresses, dances and ideas of feminine elegance. Mariana has been educated for the express purpose of "pleasing" and thus her education has been artificial and useless in spite of the fortune her grandfather has spent. To marry a man of her status is her only alternative and Adolfo could have been the expected boyfriend were it not for the sick relationship that already exists between the two. When as an adolescent he brutally beat her, she did not try to defend herself and remained kneeling down. He takes this as if she were asking his forgiveness, but she was thinking all the time, "I hate him so much, one day I will kill him" (p. 25). Many years later their meetings affirm his obsession with her beauty, but he cannot avoid punishing her because Mariana represents his other self, the person he wishes to be so that his grandfather would love him. At the end of the novel Adolfo, Mariana and Julieta abandon La Enamorada and he thinks of selling the ranch. The ending of their passion is ambiguous. Mariana seems to have given in and thinks "all will begin anew" (p. 219), and thus gives us a clue to this war between these two people motivated by a misunderstanding of the adult world and by the violent repression of natural curiosity, a curiosity that would have been understood in a different spiritual climate.

ELENA GARRO

Elena Garro was born in Mexico in 1917.[1] Her dramatic works began to appear in 1958 and she combined them into a volume entitled *Un hogar sólido.*[2] According to one critic, they constitute the best of the theater of the absurd in Mexico in recent years.[3] In 1963 she won the Premio Villaurrutia[4] for her novel *Los recuerdos del porvenir.* Her short stories and essays appear in the major European journals.[5]

Los recuerdos del porvenir[6] has as its narrator the village of Ixtapec and its memories of the events that took place during the presidency of Obregón and the uprising of the *cristeros.*[7] It deals with the times when military troops took over several towns in order to keep the peace. General Rosas, his beloved Julia, and his officers and their girlfriends live in a hotel. The general is a very jealous man, and when the stranger Felipe Hurtado comes to town, the General's vengeance becomes evident. On the other side, the leading families are engaged in helping the priests to flee so that they don't become prisoners. The Moncada family, Isabel and her brothers, is involved in this struggle. When they are discovered, the consequences are tragic: Juan Moncada dies and the other families are punished. Isabel goes to live at the hotel with the General in a desperate attempt to save her brother Nicolas. In a mythical ending, the novel ends with Isabel turned to stone and the town in decline: "I am only a memory and my memory will last" (p. 9). Time is cyclical and the future is but the repetition of the past.

Family

Martín and Ana Moncada have three children: Nicolás, Juan and Isabel, who is the youngest. She is a beautiful and imaginative child who feels a great, almost incestuous love for her brother

Nicolás. In order to separate them, her father sends the boys to another town to work so that Isabel will work at getting married. Her mother does not understand Isabel and continually repeats, "the boys are different," as if she is surprised that the boys are so unlike their sister. Their father is a dreamer, a thoughtful man who spends his life in speculation about time and about those things which go on around him. For him Isabel is the product of the best and worst of both him and his wife, the depository of all their secrets. He also feels the same strangeness that his wife feels towards their daughter saying, "I look at her as always: a strange and enchanting being who shares our lives but who jealously keeps a deep secret" (p.30). With this "deep secret" the author is alluding to the possible incest between Nicolás and Isabel. Joaquín and Matilde Moncada, Isabel's aunt and uncle, have no children of their own. They are the ones who take in the stranger Felipe Hurtado and protect him until the end, even though they will suffer the hatred and reprisals of General Rosas by doing so. Other important family relations are those of two widowed mothers with their children: Elvira Montufar and her daughter Conchita, and Lola Goribar and her son Rodolfo. Mrs. Montufar remembers her husband as a tyrant, "I never met a man so conceited," she says alluding to his enslavement of her to iron his clothing. Out of vengeance she had him buried in a sheet "so that he might learn." Conchita is a sweet and timid child who is secretly in love with Nicolas, but he does not feel the same way. Her parents have taught her not to speak and she looks at the world with patient resignation. Her maid Inés will be the one to betray her. Lola Goribar has such a fondness for her son and he for her that they are even happy that the father has died and left them alone. Rodolfo "felt himself bound to his mother by a kind and unique love" (p. 67). She protects him and will allow no girl with marriage on her mind to get near him. Little is known concerning the families of the other protagonists, General Rosas and Julia, and Hurtado.

Social Class

After the Mexican Revolution the landowner class suffered the most, as witness Dorotea, the poor, pious woman in town, who lives almost like a hermit. The professional class has been maintained and has a dominant role in the life of the town. Doctor Arrieta and the

Moncada family belong to this class. There are other examples of people from the middle class who have become rich following the Revolution. Rodolfo Goribar has not only persuaded the new government to give back his land, but he has also by means of bribes been permitted to invade the land of the Indian farmers who have acquired lands during the Agrarian Reform. Rodolfo is protected by his two bodyguards and has an understanding with the officers. Money is the only thing that matters to him and he is ready to betray his class and to exploit the Indians as long as he gets what he wants. His mother is very religious and hypocritical and knows very well that everyone hates him, but she pretends that Rodolfo never does any wrong.

The lower class is made up of townspeople and lower still are the Indians. The order in which the violence and cruelty of the military descends upon the civilian population is as follows: "The women, the dogs in the street and then the Indians" (p. 63). Among the women of the lower classes we find the prostitutes and the owner of the local brothel, Luchi.

In a class all by themselves are the officers and their girls. They are "outsiders," and as they are the ones who run the town they demand obedience from everyone, rich and poor alike. But their women are not "decent" women; they are generally thought of as having bad reputations, even though they have a conjugal relationship with their men and some, like Luisa, Antonia and Julia, belong to the upper class in their home towns.

Sexuality

The major protagonist is Julia and after her, Isabel takes her place. Julia is so extraordinarily beautiful that she lights the imagination of the whole town with her presence when General Rosas takes her for walks in the town square to the weekly open-air band concert. All wait on her hand and foot and the General himself cannot control the sexual admiration of the men who look at her. He is eaten up by jealousy and strikes her without reason. Julia does not love the General and it is quite likely that he has carried her off or at least forced her to come with him. She takes refuge in psychological distance. She is "indifferent" to the man who sexually subjugates her, but whom she does not deign even to reject because she is above it all: "Look at me he said, And Julia looked at him through her almond eyes and she favored him with a blank stare" (p. 119). He senses that he cannot "see what was going on inside of her" and thus although she is his, she remains "intact." It is as if her psychic space could never be occupied by either his violence or his pleas. We become convinced, from the moment Felipe Hurtado enters the hotel in whose garden she is walking, that Julia has known and loved him before, in some other town; they speak briefly, as if they have known each other before. They never speak again until she comes to see him one day at the Moncada's house to beg him to go away because Rosas is going to have him shot. There they spend hours together and we are not told what happens; it is possible that they make love. Julia leaves and a little while later the General and his soldiers arrive and take Hurtado prisoner. That same night Julia and Hurtado are killed and their end is cryptically explained:

> A shepherd entered town. He said that dawn was breaking in the countryside . . . only in Ixtepec was it still night. In his terror he did not know if he should cross over that border of light and shadow. He was still in doubt when he saw a rider go by carrying in his arms a woman dressed in pink. He was in black. With one hand he held the girl and with the other, the horse's reins. The woman was laughing. The shepherd said good morning to them.
>
> 'Good night,' shouted Julia . . . but we never hear of the lovers again [p. 145].

The soldier's girlfriends are seen through them, thus Rosas' passion best explains what Julia means to him and why he is not satisfied with owning her body:

> He tricked Villa and went over to Carranza and his nights remained the same. Neither did he seek power. The day he met Julia was, for him, like having touched the stars over the Sierra, of crossing their luminous circles and upon finding Julia's body he forgot all but her radiance. But she did not forget, and in her thoughts she continued to repeat the gestures, and remembered the cries, the streets, and the men that came before him [p. 78].

The people of the town commented that "the more he loves her, the farther away she moves. Nothing amuses her: not jewels, not treats. I have seen her boredom when he comes near. I have also seen him sit by her bed and watch her sleep" (p. 96). Gregoria, the local healer, feels that Julia will have a bad ending, because when a man loves a woman this way, the woman is always the victim. Rosas realizes this later when he is drunk and almost out of his mind because of the crimes he has committed against Julia, Hurtado, Nicolás and others. He asks himself: "Why did I always kill that which I loved? My life is a continual fraud; my destiny is to wander alone, luck has left me" (p. 289).

Another example of frustrated masculine passion is Captain Daniel Alvarez who steals a young girl, Antonia, by order of Colonel Justo Corona. The terrified girl begged the Captain to save her even if it were to be for himself, but he paid no attention. Later he falls in love with Antonia and is killed by Corona. These women are like objects that at times, like mares, pass from one hand to another. Such is the case of the twins Rafaela and Rosa, the girlfriends of Colonel Cruz. They do not seem to mind and they are happy to be together, to allow the same man to possess them and to enjoy all his gifts of candied fruit. But even these girls rebel against Cruz when he attacks the priests. They exclaim, "You will pay for this! You think everything can be arranged in bed!" (p. 230), and they make a fruitless attempt to escape. It is interesting that the girls, who are called "my pleasure" by their lover, wish at times to be "decent" or at least to participate in the life of the town, but they are like prisoners and must stay. The prostitutes are paid to provide pleasure but they realize, like Luchi, that the men come to them to vent their real feelings, which they cannot do with their virginal brides-to-be. Luchi exclaims "Of what worth is the life of a whore?" and "We whores are born without mates" (p. 99). For her, life is a horrible, continuous bore and the obsessive presence of the "murderer who watches from the remote corners of her memory" (p. 225) is with her always. But even among all these women of ill repute there is great faith in the Church and thus, paradoxically, it is Luchi who becomes a martyr to the cause of the *cristeros*.

In contrast to all these women who have become prostitutes and concubines, we have the case of Isabel Moncada. She has been protected by her family and it seems as if she will follow the conventional pattern of life of her social class and family position. Ever since she was born, Isabel was associated in her mother's mind with pleasure because, as the midwives say, "One can see in her beauty that she was conceived with pleasure" (p. 239). In order to understand why Isabel later becomes the "black sheep" of the conservative classes, we must understand that Isabel and Nicolás, since their youths, "were accustomed to ugliness and had invented an unreal world. Behind the appearance of this world was the true one, the one that she, Juan and Nicolás had sought since childhood" (p. 153). Moreover, the teenagers had grown up in a world of revolutions, of excitement concerning what was happening in other parts of the country—not in *their* town—and they wanted to escape the monotony of their lives. This is well reflected in the phrase Nicolás often repeats, "I no longer fit in this body." Likewise Isabel, who has been by her parent's side and with the same circle of friends who visit them every day, finds her imagination heightened by the one fascinating person whom she knows: Julia. Julia represents to Isabel a complete break with convention. All the girls comment, among other observations, that Julia sleeps in the nude and that she wears all the gold the General has given her. It is only natural that a girl like Isabel would exclaim: "I wish I were Julia!" (p. 95)—and with her great imagination she does this easily. Hurtado's arrival at her uncle's house adds a romantic dimension to Julia. She is no longer only the General's lover, but she is also the unattainable lover of this troubadour who has followed her from afar and who is content to look at her from a distance. This impossible love that ends so tragically is basic to our understanding of Isabel. The theater presentation that Hurtado and the Moncada brothers prepared was the foreshadowing of what would later happen. The performance of this play is cut short by Hurtado's assassination, but the Moncada brothers immediately set to work to plan the two priests' escape, using the same elements of suspense. Isabel plans a dance to which she intentionally invites all the officers of the army. She will be the hostess and decides to wear a red dress. While all are dancing, the men—Nicolás and Juan as leaders—will evacuate those in hiding and will take them to where other Catholics can continue to hide them. But no one takes precautions against treachery and the servants pass unobserved; the Montufars' maid is in love with one of the soldiers and she betrays the conspirators. The officers attend the dance, but do so in order to paralyze the conspirators while the soldiers break up the conspiracy. Juan dies in the struggle and Nicolás is taken prisoner. We must remember that between Isabel and her brother there has been such intimacy of feelings that when she learns that the plan has failed, she knows her brother will be shot. This is the moment when she decides to give herself to General Rosas. As in the opera *Rigoletto* and so many other works, the woman sacrifices herself sexually in order to save the only love in her life: "I always knew what was happening. . . . So did Nicolás. . . . We had been waiting for this day since childhood" (p. 207). Their father intuitively anticipates his family's disgrace: "He covered his head, he did not want to see Isabel. It would be better if she hadn't been born" (p. 207). To this father, wrapped up in his philosophical meditations, his daughter seems like a stranger who owes him her life. On the other hand, the mother sees in her daughter a continuation of her lust, for she remembers the scene at her birth:

> It is easy to see that they made you with great pleasure. Even then Ana blushed in her delivery bed and Martín looked at her with longing. Everyone would know of their lust thanks to the brightness of their just-born daughter. She bit her lip. Isabel had come to life to denounce her. She promised to live more correctly and she did so, but Isabel continued to show the lustiness of the night she was conceived [p. 239].

Since her mother has always seen her own sensuality in Isabel, something which she has always thought reprehensible, she sees her own feelings materialize in Isabel when General Rosas utters one simple phrase "Are you coming?" Isabel follows him to his house without even thinking twice and her mother exclaims, "She is a bad girl" (p. 239). Even General Rosas cannot explain it:

> How could a decent young girl be in his bed after what had happened to her family. Francisco Rosas tried to imagine what was going on within Isabel but he could understand neither the frowning forehead nor the somber eyes of his new love [p. 251].

The moment he returns to his room and finds her he almost repents of having taken her from her home, but his desires for vengeance against a town which favored Hurtado and his tragic love for Julia makes him decide that Isabel will stay. "Now they will learn that I fill my bed with that person which most pains them" (p. 246). Isabel does not matter to him, since he continues to think of Julia, and Isabel even disturbs his memories of her. When he comes face to face with Nicolás, Nicolás reminds him so much of his sister that he begins to detest Isabel, but even then he does not shun her. He promises Isabel that he will save Nicolás and he prepares a plan in which the youth will be allowed to escape. Nicolás refuses to follow the plan and since there is no other alternative, he is shot. Thus the General is forced by circumstances to confront the brother and sister who represent the same thing; he feels the two have become part of life "by force." It is difficult to understand from the narrative sequences of the book why Isabel would go with the General when she did not love him—and at only a slight hint from him. If we look deeper into her thoughts, we can more fully understand her.

> Isabel did not like the differences that were established between her and her brothers. She was ashamed that the only future women had was marriage. To speak of marriage as a solution was to reduce oneself to merchandise that must be sold at any price [p. 22].

Isabel has always been a nonconformist, a rebel, an individualist. Marriage did not interest her. She had already planned and imagined her escape from "that enclosed town, like the chamber for rotting bodies." She wanted to leave with her brother and not with some husband that would be pleasing to her society. Neither the town, the soldiers nor her parents understand why Isabel goes off with the General. They all believe that it is because she is sensual, in love with the General, or weak. General Rosas himself says to his officers: "All women are whores" (p. 248). The only one who shows understanding is Nicolás, and he does so by refusing to flee and save his life. He makes the supreme sacrifice for her because she cannot go with him, having herself chosen a kind of slow death: being a concubine to a General who for her is despicable and who also is the murderer of her lover. But the novel does not end there. Isabel runs to the scene without being able to stop the execution. Gregoria, the General's maid, follows her and explains that Isabel was turned to stone as a punishment and as a witness to her madness. The plaque that Gregoria places in front of the stone says the following:

> I am Isabel Moncada, daughter of Martín Moncada and Ana Cuetra de Moncada, born in December 1, 1907, in the town

> of Ixtepec. I was changed to stone on October 5, 1927, before the astonished eyes of Gregoria Juárez. I am the cause of the misfortune of my parents and the death of my brothers Juan and Nicolás. When I came to the Virgin to ask her to cure me of my love for General Francisco Rosas, who killed my brothers, I repented and preferred the love of the man who was the ruin of myself and of my family. Here I will remain, alone with my love, as I remember the future for centuries to come [p. 295].

Message

At the end of the story, Gregoria explains that she pushed the stone and placed it at the feet of the Virgin. This would seem to confirm the public opinion that Isabel deserved to be punished—changed to stone—and in order to pay for her sin placed close to her who is symbolic of all purity, the Virgin Mary. But we must not forget that we are told this tale from the point of view of men and women who do not know and who cannot correctly interpret Isabel's actions. What the author has really tried to do is to reconstruct the legend of the "fallen woman," the story of Eve who is the cause of mankind's problems. Thus Isabel causes her family to bury themselves in life, her brothers to die, her social class to feel shame; even the local prostitutes choose her as an example of "what one does not do." But the author makes clear that Isabel is not the only one. Nicolás confesses to the judge, "No one was an instigator. Isabel, Juan and I made plans and executed them without the advice of anyone, with our own free will. . . . Yes, I am a *cristero* and I wanted to join up with those in Jalisco. My dead brother and I bought guns" (p. 267). The cause of the *cristeros* was supported by those in favor of the Church. As the author states:

> In those days there arose a new political calamity: the relationship between Church and State had become strained. There were special favors given and the two parties in power were ready to fight and this offered the advantage of distracting the people from the one point that needed to be hidden: the redistribution of land. . . . The newspapers spoke of 'Christian faith' and the 'rights of the revolution.'

> Between the Catholic supporters of Porfirio and the atheist revolutionaries the grave of agrarian reform was prepared [p. 153–54].

Thus, if the Moncada family's plan had worked, Isabel and her brothers would have become the heroes of the *cristeros*. Isabel would then perhaps have had to confront a different kind of alternative: to remain single because no one could take the place of Nicolás, or to marry someone from her own social group like Tomás Segovia and thus follow the example of her Aunt Matilde:

> In her youth, Matilde was happy and tumultuous, she was not like her brother Martín. Her years of married life, the silence and loneliness of the house, all combined to make her a pleasing and agreeable old woman. She lost her ability to deal with people and her timidity, almost adolescent in nature, caused her to blush and to laugh each time she found herself in the presence of strangers. 'Now, only I know the paths of my house' (p. 52).

As this future never happens, we must return to the time when escape was the only hope for the Moncada siblings. Escape from conformity is the plan that presents itself to Nicolás and Isabel when they try to solve their problem; it is easy for them to feel persecuted by the system, as represented by the military. It is ironic that the master plan fails simply because of the Montufar servant's betrayal. It also shows that their escape plan, like those in the theater, has little consistency. Too many people were compromised, too much noise, music, dancing and too many costumes had been arranged to permit a safe escape. The complications are obvious. Isabel remains faithful to her dramatic role when she follows General Rosas, because she is a rebellious and inexperienced girl who has read too many novels. Nevertheless, Isabel follows Rosas not only for her brother's sake, but also because she is—as the novel points out several times—an "outsider"; her actions have never followed the social conventions of her parents and friends. Even in the part Hurtado writes for her in their "play" she is the non-conformist, the stranger.

The author wishes to show that two women, Julia and Isabel, are victims of the system. Both represent forms of escape by women from group and sexual domination and both noncomformists, each in her own way. The myth-like ending explains the collective wishes to save or to punish these women.

The idealized woman Julia represents beauty and love. The narrator, who is in reality the entire town of Ixtepec, describes her thus:

> Beautiful Julia, the General's beloved, wrapped in an aura of fragrant roses, her loose hair tangled in her golden earrings. . . . Since that afternnon I saw her get off the military train I thought she was dangerous. There had never been a woman like her in Ixtepec before. Her habits, her way of speaking, of walking, of looking at men, everything was different with Julia [p. 39].

What most captures the imagination of the town is that Julia is unattainable. It is true that her body is fragile and can be used, beaten, even destroyed by a thoughtless lover, but she remains faithful to her true love, to her dream. Thus, the General, "a solitary warrior confronting the besieged city" realizes that his only alternative is to kill her because he will never possess her completely, since at least in her thoughts she belongs to Hurtado. When Julia dies, the collective imagination resurrects her; the luminous ghosts of Julia and Hurtado escape on horseback and triumph over all the limitations of the prisons and death ordained by man.

Isabel represents nonconformity. Nicolás, her brother, is the projection of her rebellion, of her need for escape, of her impetuosity. She is a prisoner because of her sex; her brothers go and work in another city but she must stay behind and marry someone from the town. However, these are her parents' plans; she is only waiting for something to happen which will break her out of her immobility—like the game she plays:

> 'Marble statues, one, two, three. . . .' This phrase from a children's game, melodious and repetitive, sounded like the church bells to her. She and her brothers remained motionless when they repeated the phrase, as if someone who knew the secret would pass by, touch them and thus break the spell. Now no one would come and awaken her; her

> brothers, too were motionless forever. Marble statues, one, two, three . . . ! [p. 292].

This spell is her life of expectation up to the decisive moment which will change the course of her life. It is significant that Rosas plays an important role in the lives of Isabel and Nicolás. He is the "someone" who is to touch them. But in the world of memory, Rosas has no room for Isabel in the same way that in Isabel's world there is only room for her brother. Nicolás thinks, before he dies, "Only my sister lives outside of my memory, day and night she is caught up by my hand" (p. 283). Thus, it is as impossible for Isabel to enjoy sex with Rosas as it is for Julia; both are, in a way, prisoners of their own bodies which can be enjoyed but not possessed. The author also tries to suggest a parallel between the two women as they try to save their beloved. The only difference between the two women is that everyone understands Julia because she is the traditional lover who is loyal even to death, whereas Isabel is misunderstood by everyone, even her parents, because each one views her according to their own weaknesses. To the officers she is a willing "gift," to the concubines of these officers she has gone astray, to her mother she is "bad," to the town she is a traitor and to everyone she is a female who follows her instincts. No one sees the generous nature or the valor of Isabel when she breaks with convention without any explanation or self-justification. In her last moments "the name of Rosas was scarcely familiar to her," while her obsession—that she has been tricked by him who promised to save Nicolás—persists: "He killed Nicolás, he tricked me. . . . Rosas tricked me" (p. 293). Gregoria is incapable of understanding Isabel because she, like the old servant who is an expert in love potions, can only see human beings in one dimension and thus stereotypes her as one of Rosa's lovers:

> Guilty: after much looking, Gregoria found her, on the ground and turned to stone, and terrified, Gregoria crossed herself. Something told her that little Isabel had not wished to save herself: she was very taken by General Francisco Rosas [p. 294].

The predictions of the villagers when Isabel and Nicolás were children—"This will not turn out well" or "Isabel, for whom do you dance? You look crazy!" (p. 12)—are fulfilled. In the eyes of many, Isabel has committed many crazy deeds but in her eyes everything is normal. Isabel finds her path to freedom in her apparent "perdition." She is condemned by public opinion, but in her own soul she knows that she has risked her body, her security, her reputation as well as that of her family, all for her only true love, her brother.

The literal title of the book, *Memories of the Future*, indicates that it will deal with both memory and time. Thus when the narrator says, "Memory contains all time and order is unforeseen" (p. 12), both Julia and Isabel become one, even as have Hurtado and Nicolás. Only General Rosas remains:

> He felt disgrace and thought angrily of Nicolás, who was looking at his defeat with dead eyes. The Moncada family showed him a world of friendship and when he confidently entered this world, everything was taken from him and once again he was left alone, alone with the emptiness of his days. They had fooled him and he had played fairly. 'I will never again pardon anyone,' he said painfully and he remembered the false promises of Isabel and the haughty face of her brother. But something had broken inside of him and he felt that in the future all of his great revelries would involve only alcohol [p. 289].

LUISA JOSEFINA HERNANDEZ

Luisa Josefina Hernández was born in Mexico City in 1928.[1] In 1955 she obtained a master's degree in dramatic arts.[2] She has received scholarships and has studied at the Columbia University in the United States and in Europe.[3] In 1964 she traveled to Cuba.[4] Her initial efforts were dramatic works which from the beginning were presented with great success.[5] She is a very prolific writer and has many novels to her credit. Among them are *El lugar donde crece la hierba* (1959), *La plaza de Puerto Santo* (1961), *Los palacios desiertos* (1963), *La cólera secreta* (1964), *La noche exquisita* (1965), *La primera batalla* (1965), *El valle que elegimos* (1965), and *La memoria de Amadís* (1967).[6]

La cólera secreta[7] has as its protagonist Ana, a beautiful, distinguished and intelligent woman of 28, who works as a translator in an office. She has been married for eight years to Eduardo Robira, an architect. Ana is very unhappy in her marriage and has relations first with Armando Suárez, and later with Miguel do la Cueva, both of whom work in the same office. Miguel is fortyish and unmarried, but he had had a great love for a girl named Miriam when he was a student in the United States. Armando, after Ana breaks off their affair, decides to direct his amorous attentions to Julia, another office employee, whom he later marries. Ana becomes gravely ill and Miguel realizes that he cannot live without her. Eduardo Robira is finally convinced that the best thing to do is to divorce Ana. The novel ends when Ana begins to recuperate and make plans for her divorce and marriage to Miguel.

Family

There are no details concerning the families of Ana or Eduardo. We know, however, that Miguel comes from a provincial family from Guadalajara. The family ambience is quite conventional, the women see marriage as the culmination of their plans. When Miguel decides not to marry the ideal girl of whom his family approves, he says:

> In my house there was a great turmoil and many comments. They thought that like a good child of God I would marry Natalia and take her with me to Mexico City, where she would be unhappy as long as she could not locate a maid, and happy for always when she found one, where she would cry when I showed up late for dinner and laugh should I show up early, where she would howl while giving birth to my children, yet also howl if she did not have any, where she would annoy me to death with her ordinary conversation and I, her, with mine which has little of the ordinary [p. 122–123].

He adds that Natalia married another and did all those things "which she had hoped to share with me."

In contrast to Natalia, a girl from the provinces, both Ana and Julia, being city girls, continue working after marriage and do not have children. Armando tells Julia after they are married:

> Do not act as if I were in love with you. I will never have a son by you and I want you to continue working to support yourself. I'll give you money for the household expenses, but not for your expenses. That you will take out of your own pay [p. 110].

In the case of Ana, she explains the absence of children in her marriage:

> Your friends lamented that we were missing having children. I ceased to share in the feeling from the moment I realized the scaffolding of unhappiness in which I was trapped. . . . As for you, Eduardo, since the first months of our marriage when you were accustomed to asking me if I felt any symptoms of pregnancy, upon always receiving negative replies, you did not continue busying yourself with the matter. But I have seen how you cringe from the noise

> that children make, how you are not amused by their cuteness, how you detest the disorder they make. One day you said, 'I don't like children.' Since then, now more than ever, I am happy for not having given you any [p. 99–100].

Social Class

The Office of Translations is a little microcosm in which live two types of the middle class: the professional upper middle class to which belong Ana and Miguel, both of whom have traveled abroad and who speak more than one language, and the class of office employees or lower middle class represented by Armando, Julia, and Martha, the old secretary. Miguel de la Cueva is the boss and has the title of doctor of international law with post-graduate studies in New York. At the beginning of his career he worked in Guadalajara near his family, but at the first opportunity he went to the capital where he could be able to live the life-style of the Hispano-American executive. He lives in an apartment, keeps a maid, has lovers and even buys an automobile to transport Ana who lives at a distance.

In contrast to Miguel, Armando is a young man who earns relatively little but gives the appearance of dressing well because he is so given to neatness, even though he owns but one suit. With great sacrifice he saves enough to be able to buy furniture when he marries. He is very aware of the social differences between himself and Ana and later confides to Miguel:

> If Ana had been single or happy, she never would have noticed me. Thanks to her unhappiness I was able to approach her. I know it is bad to feel this way, but it is true. If she had been divorced, she would not have feigned to look at me, and if she had gotten divorced after knowing me, she would not have married me. Doesn't she realize that I am grateful for her unhappiness? [p. 174].

The same difference that exists between Miguel and Armando exists between Ana and Julia. The narrator of the novel is Miguel who, of course, exalts Ana and looks with condescension on Julia who, even though young and pretty, does not have the "refined tastes" and "class" of Ana. This is manifested in small details. As does Eduardo Robira, Ana and Miguel have cultural tastes for the theatre, the opera, and foreign movies. The only things that interest Julia are the amusements for the masses: nationally produced movies, cheap books and magazines. Ana maintained such discretion in her relations with her lovers that Miguel never found out that the "other" man was Armando. As for Julia, her relations with Armando are the conventional ones of a girl who is not sophisticated. She kisses her boyfriend in front of people who criticise her, she displays excessive admiration for objects she sees such as furniture and clothes, and towards the end she even has sexual relations with her sweetheart Armando in her brother's car. Miguel says that Julia after marrying "acquired, I don't know from where, a good taste" for clothes. Ana, however, has always seemed "neat and exquisite" to him (p. 111). The inferiority complex of a man like Armando when he is with Ana becomes a superiority complex when he is with his equal, Julia. Of Ana he says:

> I do not have proper social behavior, nor do I know how to dress, nor how to carry myself at times, although I want to do things well. And she is one of those women who are very elegant at everything . . . [p. 129].

In order to show Ana that he has good taste, Armando spends his savings of four years on furniture that he buys for Julia while shouting at her:

> All right Julia, now you have everything you wanted, a house, a husband, some furniture, and pretty clothes. Are you satisfied? Because you'll never obtain more as long as you live [p. 109].

But it is not to be thought that Miguel is liberal when it comes to differences of social class. He can be very refined and diligent with Ana when it comes to taking her flowers, getting her a taxi, and putting on the airs of a man of the world, but when he has to deal with women he considers beneath his social level he displays the brutality of a vulgar man and the cruelty of a villain. During the first months of the affair between Miguel and Ana, he also has relations with a divorcée named Lolita. On one occasion the two women find themselves in the same room through pure coincidence and Miguel has to decide quickly between the "elegant Ana, with her newly styled hair and her beautiful black coat," and Lolita "the beast" with "her accursed dress which surely she had designed specially for those occasions" (to slip out of quickly and easily). He takes the following actions towards Lolita:

> I cuffed her to her feet, pushed her towards the door, threw her coat and purse in her face and closed the door, leaving her standing in the middle of the hallway. At once I ran towards the street [pp. 76–77].

Of course Ana, offended and horrified, has disappeared by now in the avenue. Miguel, like the conventional man, upon seeing that the scandal in his building has leaked out "to an avid and obviously satisfied public," thinks of nothing but saving his own name: "As a last resort, I'll change apartments" (p. 77).

Eduardo Robira, Ana's husband, is a well-to-do architect with sophisticated manners. He constantly travels to the United States and is more prominent than the others as far as his social and economic position are concerned.

Sexuality

Nothing is known of the life of Ana before her marriage to Eduardo Robira at the age of 20. She admits that they were very much in love, which indicates that it was love match, even though they possibly did not know each other very well, given that Ana appears completely surprised by Eduardo's conduct. She interprets his attitude as one of "superiority," which puts her in the position of hiding her true feelings and giving the outward appearance of indifference so that he will not make fun of her. Considering that the problems between them are not economic, social or cultural, given that both belong to the same social level, have traveled, and are relatively free of the prejudices of the middle class, we find ourselves with a case of interaction on the communicative level. The more submissive she is, the more arrogant is he. The more emotional she is, the more logical is he. When she appears more direct he appears more evasive. Consequently both live together in a marriage which appears to be happy to all their friends, because he does not have any of the common defects of the Hispano-American male: that is to say he is faithful, does not drink and is financially responsible. He has instead "other defects" which Miguel compares with "those of him and with those of the other man" in the life of Ana—Armando Suaréz:

> Suaréz wasn't better than Robira and I refuse to think him better than I. Not even when referring to his defects. Robira was immature, I was obstinate and cruel. Robira was childish and helpless, I was egotistical. Perhaps the sum of our weaknesses would add up to the character of Suárez and yet he possessed that 'something': the secret adequateness, the sporadic illumination which knows nothing but hallucination and surrender [p. 161].

Ana does not act with much maturity towards Eduardo, who sophisticatedly is able to make fun of "love" as she feels it. To protect herself, she converts herself into what she calls "a hypocrite" and "a prostitute":

> Hypocrite because I never told him what I was thinking but rather a type of general commentary devoid of any emotional color. . . . After one year of marriage to him, I had become converted externally into a human entity in which only the most ordinary parts functioned.
>
> Prostitute because our sexual relations were governed by two motives: first, his will, never mine; the other, the desire to not call his attention and make myself the recipient of some reproach or criticism. I became submissive and disgraceful; neither did I have any possibilities of expressing myself and I could not even conceive that there would remain to me the option of going along with him. We were in two opposite situations and in order to live together, I had to contradict myself.
>
> I say prostitute because when I went to bed with him with no wish to compromise, only because it occurred to him and I didn't dare to refuse him, I felt that it would be the same with him as with any other, that there was no difference between that and what goes on in a brothel [p. 97].

Ana analyzes her marriage in perspective and she begins to realize her own motivations:

> Four years passed in this state of things; each one of us worked for himself, thought and felt for himself, and my continual surprise was that Eduardo considered himself very happy. At times in some meeting or other I could instinctively feel the pride with which Eduardo would introduce me as though he were a perfect husband with a perfect wife, and I suffered because within that vivid appearance there was only decay. A lonely woman, silenced, the worst, the most immoral of women, the most vain: because in that silence of mine, in that frightening image that that implied, the acceptance of a normality imposed by another, there was an immense arrogance. That arrogance that is born of the terror of criticism, of being made fun of, of the momentary loss of dignity. During four years I lived my indignity completely with the most bitter of humiliations. That Ana who hid and disguised herself, that one, that one was the one who suffered, while in public, in her office, in her own house and bed, there grew an artificial and deformed being: that whore who submitted for the price of not being molested or injured, for the price of being considered perfect by a man full of imperfections [p. 98].

In this novel the protagonist does not resign herself to an artificially maintained marriage and attempts to search for love on her own account and at her own risk. She finds that Armando, a few years younger than she, seems to be a romantic escape from her housewifely anxiety. At the beginning, she acts like an adolescent and the two live a simple period of seeing each other on the sly, going to local cinemas or to the zoo. One night when she and Eduardo are together in the living room there is an anonymous telephone call from Armando's mother, and Eduardo returns laughing to say:

> You great hypocrite, crippled woman, weak-willed, nonexistent being, scum. How are you, miserable thing, capable of having a lover? From that moment I saw everything differently, as though I had put on glasses of a different color . . . [p. 116].

Ana's first reaction is a desire for revenge, but for three days she is incapable of expressing herself. Afterwards, it is Eduardo himself who urges her to recount all the details without attempting at any time to get her to break up with Armando. But he will not grant her a divorce because, after all was said and done, she was "ridiculous, melodramatic, deluded" almost at the level of a mental defective incapable of making wise decisions. He continues taking the position of superiority and, even though she becomes hysterical, he goes off to the movies leaving her alone in her despondency. It is true that Ana breaks up with Armando afterwards, but not because Eduardo interferes, Ana realizes that Armando is a mere boy who does not understand her either. When she rents an apartment so that the two can meet he accepts it naturally enough, even though they go there very seldom to see one another. He also accepts that she handles all the bills and that she pays her own expenses when they go out. She begins to realize that now it is she who is always showing proof of love and that it is Armando who always appears evasive, condescending at times, but who always acts as if it would be the same to him to have or not to have her near him. The day that Ana surprises him looking at Julia in the office she breaks down because she is not able to stand this new role:

> I already was the one who put up with scorn, the one who paid, the one who didn't ask for anything, the one who bought the clothes, the one who laid down on the floor when the other got drunk. Now, not yet an old woman, nor ugly, nor vile, I had to become the lover who looks the other way before unfaithfulness, because she knows that she needs to preserve a little warmth in her body and some hope in her soul. That very night I left him for good [p. 137].

What is most pathetic is that Ana prophesied what would later occur: "You will fall in love with another and marry her and forget me" (p. 137). With the exception of the last part of the sentence, it happens that Armando and Julia do marry and Ana is there like a secret witness to the courtship which goes on in the office, since they all work together. Ana, who never gave a thought to killing herself for Eduardo, considers suicide over Armando, but only for a short time.

On the third step of her disillusionment Ana goes to a party and for all practical purposes it is she who, since Miguel asks her to dance, takes him by the hand, and afterwards in the intimacy of his apartment asks him: "Will you go to bed with me?" "Yes, of course, if you want to" (p. 15), he answers, his masculinity offended because the roles have become reversed and she has become the aggressive element of the conquest. Moreover, from the beginning the conditions of future encounters are established when Miguel asks her cautiously:

> 'Are you sure that this won't cause any difficulties . . . ? I mean, at home, with . . . .'
>
> 'No. And what about you?'
>
> 'I don't have any obligations towards anyone.'—I [Miguel] decided to take advantage of the opportunity to make the accursed declaration which had always occurred to me—'I don't like obligations.
>
> 'Nor do I. That is to say, I am not in a condition to make others be obliged.'
>
> This was the absolute truth, but he had never heard such a thing from any woman, even if she were married with fifteen children [p. 18].

There are various levels on which to interpret the attitude of Ana. The most obvious is that she is looking for someone to make her happy regardless of the future. On a second level, she has lost faith in a "special" love, and one seems as good as another to her. Another appears later, given her own explanation: "I wanted to prostitute myself"—a sort of voluntary giving of her body, almost as if separating it from the rest of her did not matter.

It is not possible to understand Ana without understanding what the narrator, Miguel, tells us about the relations between them which last for almost a year without "the dates becoming more frequent, with the exception of the occasions in which I invited her to go somewhere; to the opera, the theatre, the movies at times" (p. 31). Even more important is that Ana appears to be completely indifferent to what he does with his time when they are not together. Whether he has other women or not is something that is not her "business," since after the experience with Armando, Ana seems to have lost her possessive and passionate feelings—even to the point that her intimate relations seem to be mechanical. As Miguel describes it:

> Ana was passive, docile, calm, totally satisfied most of the time; but she did not seem to share in the pleasure which she gave, nor did she seem to be present even as a spectator, which was the worst of all. The threat was that while this was humiliating, nobody in my place would have spurned her, because in spite of anything that can be said about it, in this case it was much more agreeable to receive than to give [p. 16].

We must not forget that Ana also has divisions in her emotional life which are in conflict, and that it requires tremendous composure for her to control herself when she is confronted with her husband Eduardo in their house, or with her ex-lover and his sweetheart in the office, since Armando and Julia are constantly making one sort of emotional scene or another in front of everybody. While Ana is trying perhaps to forget Armando, she doubtlessly continues suffering, since on more than one occasion she becomes pale, or squeezes her fists until the fingernails draw blood, or she suddenly becomes ill and must leave the office. During all of this time she has never told Miguel the name of her former lover and Miguel has no reason to associate her sudden attacks of illness with their immediate surroundings. The secret illness is an ulcer that springs from an equally secret emotion. Ana repeats her defensive mechanism by demonstrating external control—which is what everyone sees—but is being consumed by a corrosive anger. As it is Miguel who throughout the novel gives us the development of her illness, we have to assume that Ana has to continue doing this intimate violence to herself, given that even Eduardo does not realize what is going on inside her and continues making his "husbandly" demands as if it were his natural right. She says:

> At once I felt myself being watched, I turned my head and saw him looking at me through half-closed eyelids, with a mean smile on his lips. Instinctively I became horrified:

> 'What do you want?" I said.
>
> 'I want you to stop pretending to be busy and go to bed with me.'
>
> The honorable woman in me became frightened and finally howled in indignation. He had caught me off guard and didn't give me time to adopt the quiet submission of a whore nor the passive indignation of the raped [p. 124].

The sexuality of Ana is obstructed by certain scruples which, even though she appears to apply them only to her husband, transcend the conjugal sphere. Ana basically is one of those who, if she is the one who wills it, the morality or immorality of an act does not matter. She never felt guilty either with Armando or with Miguel because in a certain way it was she who initiated both relationships: "I was dreaming of a happy marriage, of an engagement, of an affair, of trips, of friends, of everything which was daily denied me. I was dreaming of affection, of whatever kind of affection" (p. 99).

Then what is the true cause of her illness? Ana senses that she is not affirming her will with any of her "chosen ones" because even though she appears to be free, she is not. Eduardo has his own logical reasons for impeding the divorce and for holding her by force:

> I know for sure that she has never pardoned my refusal to grant her the divorce and maybe even now she doesn't understand that I did it to protect her and because I love her. Ana wishes to die. Do you imagine that I don't realize that she wants to die? . . . Because she thinks that that is the best way to get away from me, to show me that she hasn't forgiven me. And I prefer to see her die in this falsehood and not in the deception of another falsehood, one which would have done her even graver damage [p. 146].

On the other hand Ana has experienced rape in the sense that, being older than Armando, she has not been able to be in control of the situation, as she confides to her new lover:

> Miguel, the love of a woman for a man younger than she is a very destructive thing for both. . . . It is horrible, horrible.

> She, for her part, comes to do things—excessive. Because she feels that he, in the long run, will have to abandon her for lack of interest, or because of social conventions, or because he grows to hate her. But the fundamental reason is youth. The woman senses this and begins to give things to the man she loves, to sacrifice all, to humiliate herself... and he becomes corrupt. Young men are corrupted very easily and they become unscrupulous, demanding, insensitive, and the women finally allow them to go even though it may cost their life. Do you see? A love like that costs a woman her life... and a man his moral integrity. That combination is fatal.... It is the worst that can occur for both [p. 45].

Ana also understands that her relationship with Miguel is quite artificial during their first year of dating. That "deafness masquerading as love, as happiness and perfection, even when we both knew that it was not" (p. 44), Miguel says analytically. Ana has to feel that even though between them there are no conflicts, neither are there expectations. In that instance the true realities are kept from emerging. The two of them behave with impeccable etiquette in the office, given that Ana does not change in the least the routine she followed before becoming the lover of the "boss," don Miguel de la Cueva. He also adopts through imitation the same formality—so much in contrast to the familiarity that exists between Julia and Armando, which he views with the scepticism of the mature man. The masks begin to fall away only when Ana becomes so gravely ill that she is no longer able to pretend. The illness lasts nearly one year and it is only then when Miguel and Ana face each other without masks.

It is necessary to mention that Miguel de la Cueva has certain disruptive elements in his personality which in a certain way cause him to identify with Ana. Like her, he has in his past—when he was a student in the United States—a great love. She was Miriam, who was a married woman quite a bit older than he. She had been the wife of a professor with young children and left her husband to go live with Miguel while her divorce was in process. Miriam loved him very much and worked and sacrificed for him in every way. He repaid her by leaving all at once without even so much as a goodbye. When he returned to Guadalajara he finally realized what he had done, not only did he report of his villainy but also could not console himself for having lost such a great love. Miguel realized that such a relationship requires that which Ana had also experienced with Armando: exclusive and absolute attention. But Miguel, who has learned to resign himself to love affairs of little consequence during the past twenty years of his life, knows also that it is possible to continue living like a survivor of a shipwreck in which he has lost all that which he valued the most. Because of that, even though Miguel is cynical and has been around, he realizes that his relationship with Ana is important and what he feels for her is a pressure that dams up his purely physical needs. He says that his anxiety-filled emptiness of before has been replaced by her beneficial presence in the office and in his life. During her illness he begins to recover for himself that which he thought he had lost during so many years of exploitive masculinity: his human dignity. Unlike Eduardo Robira who had not been resigned to losing Ana, he now wants to win her and "fall in love."

From Ana's point of view, she picked Miguel one month after breaking up with Armando because he is a mature man at least 11 years older than she, and because, as she later confesses to Miguel:

> I was falling into an abyss and I grabbed hold of you, rather than some other, because I knew you and felt I understood you, perhaps mistakenly. I knew that you had enough fear of the amorous life and its obligations to not attempt to receive me and give yourself up and at the same time you seemed to be lonely enough to accept me even though it might be momentary and I would be able to locate myself in the world, find some reality in the world for me, even though partial, even though fleeting, even though artificial [p. 186].

Before, Miguel had required "the expensive prostitutes," but now he begins again to vindicate himself in his own eyes because he starts to give over to Ana that "dimension of his life" he had always held in reserve. The communication increases between the two during the year of illness; she tells him:

> For the first time someone was telling me by his conduct, by his attitudes and by his little everyday considerations: you and I are man and woman, we are equals, we form part

> of a species, we are cells in an effervescent body that is eternal [p. 188].

If Ana had wanted before to die, there now began to arise in her an intense struggle to live, but the basic change which takes place in her is that she becomes "different" instead of "indifferent." It is the emotion of at last being able to share her life with somebody without masks, without suspicions, without defenses, that causes her to overcome her illness.

In the novel, the couple represented by Armando and Julia provides a series of perspectives to help understand why a woman of Hispano-American tradition, but of the new generation, is able to resort to infidelity. Perhaps the novelist only explains a certain set of causes, but she deduces certain generalizations by means of the commentaries that Miguel makes about the situation. Miguel feels that between him and Armando there is a parallel: both have suffered the consequences of having abandoned "cowardly and infamously the only good thing" of their lives (Miguel, Miriam and Armando, Ana). Armando continued in a chain of mistakes because in order to punish Ana he entered into a love affair with Julia without really loving her. He then married Julia, a girl who did not perceive the truth, and later made her unhappy by revealing to her that it was all a whim. In order to console herself she sets out to look for another man, a lover. As the author notes: "That is what women do when they they are fed up with the treatment they receive from their husbands and particularly when they are left alone all day and all night" (p. 171). Miguel is much more direct when he talks with Armando and advises him:

> . . . You are encouraging adultery with your attitude. . . . You forget that women change into hypocritical and nervous animals, wanting to hide yet exhibit themselves at the same time, beings who live on a thread of anguish; rejecting sometimes, at other times becoming possessed by a series of small and large depravities which can overcome them at any moment, depravities which are strangely born of their scruples. In some it is shame, in others it is fear, in others pride; but there they remain—half prostituted, half degraded, with a doctrine of deceit and unhappiness, over-

> whelmed by the impossibility of loving openly, with freedom, with honor [p. 173].

It should be noted that delusion is a form of escape from a love that is lacking. If they love another passionately it is in a "negative and morbid form" in order to alleviate their suffering, to fill the emptiness and sordidness of their marriage.

Message

If one carefully observes the time sequence of the novel, it can be seen that psychological change takes place in the characters when they are confronted with similar situations, but with personal decisions which are going to affect them in a not too distant future. Let us begin with Miguel when he is 24 years old and falls in love with an older woman, Miriam. At the present time Armando has also been impressed and fascinated by Ana. Likewise the Julia of the present is the Ana of eight years before, when she married Eduardo. The trap into which they have fallen according to Miguel, with the exception of Julia, is that "we rejected the small and ordinary pleasures. We set off in search of great loves, we suffered great repentance, we plotted great treacheries" (p. 177).

At the same time all of them have the ability to "choose." Freedom of choice in each situation is what gives them a flexibility to change until they determine not only a life-style but also the somatic reactions of their inner self. The title of the novel, *La cólera secreta* ("the secret fury") indicates that Ana becomes ill when her external behavior, which is incapable of reflecting her emotions, becomes alienated.

Perhaps the author wishes to add her perspective of the "divorce," inasmuch as one of the motives for Ana's becoming ill is that she is not able to find an open escape from her prison. The conclusion of the novel shows that Eduardo Robira finally accepts the facts and gives Ana the divorce. He handles himself with perfect sophistication. There is no trace of violence when husband and lover (Miguel) sit down together to drink coffee and to discuss Eduardo's trip to New York, his last conversations with Ana, and his acceptance that Miguel be the next husband in line. Unlike them, Julia and Armando have a colossal fight in which she behaves like a tigress when he asks for divorce. She gives it to him but not without first having openly demonstrated her hostility. Armando leaves scratched and bleeding. It should not be interpreted that Julia has gotten angry because it was he who asked for the divorce, but rather because she is a woman who, fed up with so much abuse, needs at the end to discharge her violence in a physical manner. She says "Yes I want a divorce, naturally" (p. 182).

By showing us Eduardo, the author also wants to emphasize the lack of communication that exists between him and Ana. The two were in love when they married and little by little they have become emotionally distant even though their marriage does not appear to be a bad one. It is not simply a lack of dialogue, since the two are both very verbose, it is fear which infiltrated between them—Ana's for her vulnerability and Eduardo's of having to confront himself alone. Ana tells him at the end, "You have never said a good word that has not been born of fear, nor have you made a sincere act which has not been born in hate" (p. 190).

The problem of misunderstandings in communication is established. Adultery, which in this case is circumstantial, is not being dealt with. The real misunderstanding arises from the characters' pretending to be persons they are not. Ana from Eduardo, Miguel from Miriam, Armando from Julia—all three hid the most vital feelings which connected then with that person. In the case of Ana it has been that she is haughty because in reality she is very insecure. Her criticism and ridicule of Eduardo have caused her to pretend and to never attempt to establish a dialogue with him. When Miguel was young and with Miriam he felt that by giving so much of herself to him, she was plundering him emotionally, she was absorbing him to the point that he needed to escape, but he never dared to discuss it with her, not even when he left, so that she might have been able to understand the reasons. In the case of Armando, he has chosen a relatively simple and lovestruck girl in order to make her the instrument of his revenge against Ana, who broke off with him because she began to see his true character. Armando wants to show Ana that there is a young and pretty girl who is ready to believe whatever he wants her to, and he premeditatedly courts and wins Julia. All of them have had to pass through a series of painful confrontations to at last discover what they really need and who they really are. This is not a "love story" as one Mexican critic superficially judged it, even though love is the force that causes the personality changes. The author insists on experience and perhaps the blind repetition of mistakes to find—by accident or by sudden illumination—the solution and rectification of the situation.

One asks upon reading the novel what elements are there that the characters hope to find in love. The author makes a clear distinction between the characters before they have experienced love and after. Even though all the characters need physical tenderness, that alone is not enough. The main character, Ana, is obsessed by her "prostitution" as a married woman (which appears to be a common note in novels by other women writers). The woman has to feel that she is not divided, that when she gives herself to a man she does so with both body and soul, that an element of free will enters into consideration. She does not want to do it because she is obligated, because of matrimonial conventions, or because her husband says it is her "wifely duty." She has to express her femininity in a complete acceptance of the act. The author goes even further by presenting to us two married women, Miriam and Ana, who, dissatisfied with their matrimonial situation, set off in search of a lover who can satisfy them. The only mystery of the novel is why Eduardo keeps Ana. They have no children, and Eduardo is a handsome, rich and intelligent man capable of finding another woman who loves him and who need not be kept around by force. The explanation according to Eduardo is that his desire to establish communication with Ana shines through his "obscenely expressed desire" of the sex act. Moreover, he blames himself for "his inability to employ the superficially expressive forms of love" and he also feels that he is unable to allow her to go with Armando because he is "an insignificant fellow with little human worth." On the other hand, from Ana's point of view he has become used to playing sadistically with her and she has become a victim. Ana explains:

> In relation to him I am like one of those animals which are fooled and tricked in order to perform experiments on them: you ring a bell and give them something to eat for three days, the fourth day you ring the bell and give them nothing, the sixth day you ring the bell and the animal is tormented because it doesn't know what to do, on the seventh the animal doesn't pay any attention to the bell. That is

> me. Eduardo has experimented too much and such is the result [p. 119].

This expresses the fact that Eduardo, say what he will, does not give the divorce to Ana because he likes to play with her on a sophisticated level and intellectually anticipate her reactions. This "proof of intelligence" on his part satisfies him because he is not particularly secure in his masculinity, but causes her constant frustrations. Ana is not innocent either, and she admits that "like a good trickster, I shaped a natural and hidden death, which would not require responsibilities and which would exempt the three of us from all blame" (p. 139). The escape and the interiorization of the guilt is her illness. The author emphasizes that

> One could find oneself in the middle of various emotional levels and, while not understanding consciously, arrive at a feeling that they depended on the same phenomenon. The marriage of Suarez, the unhappiness of Julia, the illness of Ana, they were one thing. Life is not simple and isolated in its events, but rather complicated and interrelated [p. 140].

In this way love is not reduced to a simple formula of "boy meets girl," because there is an interior progression which determines what each one begins to appreciate and value in love. Neither Ana nor Miguel expects to fall in love when they meet, thus the author proves her thesis that life is complicated and interrelated. At the same time, the reason love triumphs over illness and death is that it causes the rebirth of hope in two beings who had made tragic mistakes before in love. It is Ana who, from the feminine point of view, expresses that for the first time she is learning to give value to the "simple action of taking a hand in my hands for the simple reason that that hand belongs to another person equal to me, the two of them equal before the universe" (p. 187). An original message of the author is that the new Hispano-American woman, especially the intelligent, educated and modern one, feels that it is not so easy to fool herself with the same justifications that her grandmother had. Family, class and religion will not impede her from analyzing herself and looking for new alternatives to her problems. For her, the relations between the sexes can no longer be based only on the dominance of the male. The protagonist, after having passed through her romantic crisis with Armando, realizes that he allows himself to be treated like a child, and that there is no equality between them. With Miguel, on the other hand, there is established between them a relationship of adults who accept each other, know each other, and communicate not only on the sexual level but also as two human beings.

ELENA PONIATOWSKA

Elena Poniatowska was born in France and came to Mexico when she was only ten years old. Her father was a Polish nobleman.[1] She became a journalist by interviewing important people.[2] Her works *Meles y Teleo, Palabras cruzadas* and *Todo empezó en domingo* are all journalistic testimonies.[3] Her novel *Hasta no verte, Jesús mío* is a documentary and was written thusly:

> Three times a week Elena went to Jesusa's house. . . [and] there she recorded and recorded and recorded their long talks, full of the wiles of that Mexican woman an *Adelita* and who today washes and irons clothing in the old way with irons heated by charcoal. . . . Her stories, typed by Elena time and time again, constitute a first-hand confession of how a common woman was able to have such a fertile yet unknown life.[4]

The protagonist of *Hasta no verte, Jesús mío*[5] is Jesusa, whose life from the age of five until her old age is told in the first person. She was born in Tehuantepec, in southern Mexico. At age five her mother died and, together with her father Felipe Polancares—a vagabond and a skirt-chaser—and her brother Emiliano, she travels from place to place where her father works at whatever he can find. Even for one so young, she rebels against her father's women. Only her "stepmother" Evarista is exempt from her scorn. These were the years of the revolution, and when her father and brother join the revolutionary troops, Jesusa follows them into battle. Pedro Aguilar, a captain, marries her almost by force and she then follows him. When he dies, she wants to return to Tehuantepec but on her way, near the capital, she is robbed of all she has and is forced to remain in Mexico City the rest of her life. Her work and her many amusements take up most of her time. By accident she comes across La

Obra, a spiritualist movement. Little by little she is converted to their beliefs when she experiences strange manifestations. Her life is always full of complications because she constantly helps those less fortunate than she. In her old age, she works as a laundress. She is very sick and believes she is beginning to understand her destiny and the reason for her existence.

Family

Her life begins in Tehuantepec, where her family has moved from Oaxaca, and thus she has no family other than her father and brother. She is very much attached to her brother Emiliano. When her mother dies, her father brings another woman home a week later. This is when she begins to rebel and to make life miserable for these women. Only her "stepmother" Evarista earns her respect because she is the only one who teaches Jesusa to work with discipline: "I loved her because she taught me . . . She did it for my own good" she says of the punishment she received.

> My stepmother never wanted me to call her 'mother,' I always called her Señora Evarista. I do not deny that she was a mother to me, because if she had not taught me, what would I be today? But I knew I had another mother and there was never any 'mother-daughter' relationship between us [p. 282]

Evarista's family is predominantly matriarchal; her grandmother is a jailer and Evarista is a rich landowner. But Jesusa's father is a vagabond and thus they move to another town. The child goes to live with her godmother "who is white and rich and who exploited me like a servant without pay". Later Jesusa goes to work for various families, among them Frenchmen and North Americans. She then learns that her brother Emiliano has died. Her father now takes her with him because "he had already lost a son, he did not want to lose me" (p. 63). The revolutionaries arrive in Acapulco with all their families and Jesusa loves the atmosphere with its adventures and fights. The *Adelitas*, or camp followers, also do some exploring and act as revolutionary spies. Jesusa fights with her father's women, especially "La Guayavita," whom she accuses of being her father's concubine. Jesusa relates:

> My father was a man and of course he was in love. He always had women, and I always beat them because they were abusive, gluttonous drunkards, wasting my father's money . . . [p. 68].

But Jesusa will not allow even her father to strike her when she rebels because he forbids her to see some boys who speak Zapotec. She takes refuge in General Blanco's house for eight months. Meanwhile a young captain who has been following her around wishes to marry her. As he has never spoken to her, Jesusa says no, but the General decides to have the marriage "for the good of the girl," since her father does not approve of a civil rather than a religious marriage and the General fears something worse will happen to this child of 15 (Captain Aguilar is 17).

By 1913 Jesusa's father has died and the revolution turns toward San Luis Potosí, Merfa, and Texas. Pedro is a strange boy and, raised by his grandmother and nursed by a nanny goat, he does not know how to communicate with Jesusa. Nevertheless he affirms his rights as a husband and uses her sexually. He locks her up and brutally beats her when he gets the urge. She compares him with her father who, although he had many defects, at least had a certain cordiality, and she arrives at the conclusion that Pedro had married her on a whim because she would not have anything to do with him; he wants to dominate her, to teach her a lesson. At last she rebels. Afterwards Pedro dies in battle and Jesusa, who has taken charge of her husband's troops, asks to be sent home. She is now a widow at 17 and free from every tie with either society or family. What can she do? She works at whatever she can and spends her wages in amusing herself: parties with her girlfriends, getting drunk, dances, and love affairs that do not lead to marriage. She is a great friend to all and by pure chance she makes contact with a group of spiritualists as well as with homosexuals and prostitutes. She has no limits; once, when she was very sick and thought she was going to die, she gave away all her belongings. Later she goes to work in a hospital for prostitutes and realizes the consequences prostitution brings to these poor, abandoned women. She still loves adventure and is always ready to join the troops who are off to fight the *cristeros.* She loves her independence, since neither man nor child ties her down. At the same time, in jest, she begins to hypnotize her friends in her room. She is surprised by unforeseen apparitions, proof of a supernatural world she has never suspected existed. Out of curiosity she visits some of the spiritual meetings. There her late father gives her a message:

> 'Don't be afraid, my dear, come over here,' my father said. 'I want to talk to you and give you some advice that I could not give you while I lived on earth. Please don't make me suffer. Become more moderate in character because we are in chains thanks to you. Leave behind all these words. Don't fight with people on the street because as soon as you do, they put us in chains. Don't be foolish, behave yourself. Use good sense [p. 164].

She begins to realize that she is not alone. From the other world spirits come to tell her things she does not wish to hear and she begins to see things that others cannot. To test her invisible companions she uses her wits, but they become more and more real and she begins to change her bad habits: alcoholism, fighting and a carefree attitude. Perhaps one characteristic that has always been positive is her generosity towards those more unfortunate than she, and her sense of justice that will not allow the weak to suffer brutal, forceful abuses. When she begins to realize that nothing is coincidental, she states:

> Things are predestined for a certain period, because none of my relatives knew of La Obra. No one. No one found out. No one had his eyes opened and all bumped into each other and everything was 'we'll see.' And among my relatives, only I was the mobile one, the mover, the one who had been everywhere. My father never saw what I saw. I have followed every road because it was written that I was to wander. I know many countrysides. My father did not. He only traveled a little and then he fell in battle. My husband swore he would not leave me alive on earth but God would not permit it. That is why I say that these things are already written and that God has planned them [p. 315].

Social Class

For Jesusa the color of one's skin is important and she makes distinctions even among her own family, even though all are "Indians." She says that she and Emiliano are more "white" than the others and that there must be some French blood in them. Even among the Indians she makes distinctions based on education, which is most important for her. She says of her stepmother:

> My stepmother was another kind of person. She had studied. Her mother, Fortunata, was as ignorant as my father, an Indian who spoke only Zapotec and Spanish, but in spite of everything, Fortunata sent her to school. She was wise. But I had no choice, my father left again [p. 52].

Thus she alludes to her own lack of education and her animosity toward the nuns because her father insisted that she go to a school run by nuns, where they taught her only how to pray, never to read. Later she tried to learn but never could do so because no one bothered to teach an adult woman. Jesusa also had a certain pride from having come from Oaxaca. When she returns and her relatives treat her with mistrust, because they believe she is seeking an inheritance, she haughtily takes leave of them without saying goodbye. Jesusa's identity has nothing to do with either the Indians or the mestizos. Even in her nationality she is separated. Here is her explanation that she could not even call herself a Mexican:

> After all, I have no country. I am like the Hungarians: from nowhere. I don't feel like a Mexican and I don't recognize my Mexican heritage. Here there is nothing more than private interests and personal convenience. If I had some money and possessions I would be Mexican. But I am worse than garbage, I am nothing. I am garbage that dogs look at and then continue on their way. The wind comes along and blows everything away. . . . I am garbage because I cannot be anything else. I have never been good for anything. My whole life I have been the same microbe you see. . . . [W]hen I was left alone, my intentions were to return to my homeland. I would have had a better life in Salina Cruz or in Tehuantepec and I would have seen my

stepmother, but the years went by and I was never able to save enough for the transportation [p. 218].

As to social classes, she feels the Mexicans and Spanish are the most avaricious. With her job as a maid in several homes, she saw people as they really were and drew her own opinions. Other foreigners—North Americans, Chinese, French—come out better:

> It is not that these foreigners don't give orders, it's that they do so differently; they are less despotic and don't meddle in your life. 'Did you go to Church?' 'Go to pray.' 'What time did you come home last night?' 'Don't talk to strange men. . . ." [p. 245].

She remembers three foreigners who wanted to marry her. One was Chinese and owned a store in Santa Cruz when she was a teenager. She said no and he married another girl. Another was a North American who became interested in her when the troops were stationed at the border. Another North American who worked in a bank in the capital came every Sunday to the restaurant where she worked to take her and some girlfriends for a ride; she was afraid that he would later treat her as an inferior person. The only man she ever really wanted to marry was a taxi-driver, a friend who treated her with great respect, but their class differences separated them:

> Antonio did not marry me because we were not from the same class. He was more 'decent,' more educated than I. How? His family, his brothers and sisters already had a girl ready for him from a better class. She did not work. And they knew that I was a factory worker, a dancer, a wanderer, and all this did not please them. I was what I was and that was all there was to it. I like to dance and take walks and so did he; and besides, his brothers knew we frequently drank together. They wanted a lady. A lady, please! Well, that is the way it was [p. 205].

Doctors, politicians, scholars, all came under Jesusa's critical eye. She distinguished between the soldiers of "yesterday" and those of "today." Yesterday's soldiers earned their positions by their valor, like Pedro, her husband, who was named captain for confiscating the cattle of the ranch on which he worked. The soldiers of today, on the other hand, do not know how to fight. As for ecclesiastics—"All the priests eat well, have women and are as fat as barn mice" (p. 209). This is why she later joins up with the troops who are off to fight the *cristeros*. It is revealing when one realizes that Jesusa's father must have been very religious, since he was the one who insisted on her going to a school run by nuns and was opposed to her civil marriage to Pedro. Nor does she respect the uniform for itself alone, since on several occasions she becomes involved in brawls with police and soldiers when she sees them abusing others.

Without being a proletarian she is very happy working in the factories until the labor unions come and begin to take some of what she earns. She has many managerial positions and even becomes completely in charge of the businesses of others, such as a restaurant and a barber shop. However, she fails in her own enterprises because she is too compassionate. People borrow money and do not pay her back or they take advantage of her, like some children who rob her after she takes them into her home when they have been abandoned.

It is for the farmers that she has the most respect because they have always offered her their hospitality although, "we both were completely destitute and dying of hunger" (p. 242). Thus she always helps those more unfortunate, like Dona Reginita or Perico's mother, both of whom she supports as if they were of her own family. Jesusa feels the poor help each other more because they know what hunger and suffering really are, while the rich and middle classes never feel compassion.

Sexuality

Jesusa grew up in a hot climate, a hammock was her bed and her father slept in the same room, so she knew when he left home to go see his lady friends. She realizes that her father loved her, even if he was not "full of loving gestures, kisses etc." (p. 21). Her aggressiveness is a result of the jealousy she feels towards her father's women. Her desire to fight with the other children is to prove that she can control a situation. She says about herself: "I was bitchy, very evil" (p. 23). This aspect of her character is accentuated when she travels with the revolutionary troops because she dresses as a man: "I wanted to do men's things, to get into fights, to go to cockfights, to sing and play the guitar when time permitted" (p. 70). Her husband was interested in her not because she was attractive but because she was wild, tough and haughty, and they never exchanged words until he asked her to marry him. Immediately after the wedding, he locked her in her room for two weeks with this admonition: "Here you will remain until you become more humble" (p. 84). She endured hunger and beatings without a whimper because of her pride until one day when she decided to stand up to him: she took out two pistols, gave one to him and said, "Here, we will kill each other. Take out your gun" (p. 99). Pedro backed down and from that day on, she fought to the end because she would not allow herself to be beaten. Likewise, she would not allow Pedro's camp girls to make fun of her and she even beat them, not because they meant anything to her, but because "it made me angry that people talked about me" (p. 106). She even went without eating at times to show her displeasure to Pedro:

> I am strong, really I am. This is my way of doing things. My body is used to starving. I can stand up to it. My anger sustains me. All my life I have been bad tempered, easily angered. If I did not eat, I thought: 'Good, I wasn't hungry anyway.' And with the effort I made, my hunger left [p. 109].

She learned to drink for one reason—to show men that she could drink better than they and could win their bets. Years later, after she had given up the vice, she once again got drunk to prove she could still do it.

> When I said 'I no longer drink' I stopped drinking. I have a strong will, which is more than the truth! Once I decide I am never going to do something, I never do it. I have been this stubborn ever since I was a child [p. 254].

Even though she rebels against the double standard from her earliest childhood games, she realizes that the man, for being "macho," is compulsively attracted to women, or at least this is what she sees in her father. Later she finds that Pedro is the same. In the years they are married he convinces her that it is so. Moreover, the two of them do not have any privacy and she wears pants all the time (her husband will not allow her to take her clothes off because there are other men all around), and so much of their sex life takes place fully clothed. This confirms the idea that sex is the only thing about a woman that is of interest to a man. Many times she rebels at the way in which men treat their women: "They say we are whores; but aren't the men then the same?" (p. 78). Her language is very crude but descriptive. Neither does she like to see women chasing after men and reacts violently:

> I was not jealous of my husband. How could I be jealous if I was never interested? I was only angry that others talked about it. I had to do something to get him back because I am not made of wood. I really gave him his own in the end, I didn't want to be the one he came home to only when his girlfriends were tired. Why should I go around trying to find out about Pedro? What do I care about those whores? [p. 107]

Several times she admits that she does not know what love in a marriage is because Pedro never spoke of it to her nor she to him. She also comments that she does not know how Pedro learned to read, for he liked love stories that she could not understand at the time. She is offended when men talk to each other about women in ugly ways and is also angry that Mexican women are so subservient and never rebel or fight back lest they lose their husbands. Jesusa comments:

> They let themselves be beaten. The men shout and beat the women. Not for me. As for them, foolish girls, the men do everything to them.
>
> 'Get up, let's go, come on.'
>
> They have already bought the slave, in order to boss them about as the men see fit. . ." [p. 154].

She tries to maintain a camaraderie with the men and they treat her as a friend, but she does not want either sex or marriage:

> Since I suffered so much with Pedro, I said to myself, 'I would be better off alone.' They say that the ox by himself

> licks himself well and why not the cow? How could I guess whether or not things would go well for me if I married a foreigner? If a man is bad, it makes little difference if he is Mexican or a foreigner. They all beat the same. They all give it to you. They are like the male lion and we the female. When he wants the lioness, he licks her, rubs against her, seeks her out, everything. As soon as he has her in his grasp, he swats her. That is the way men are . . . that is why I have never been interested in marriage. It is better to suffer hardships than to put up with a husband. Alone. I don't need men nor do I like them and in fact they get in my way even when they are not around. I wish they were never born! And this neighborhood is full of brats who scream so much that I feel like strangling them [p. 173].

At 19, when she first met Antonio Pérez, she was greatly attracted to him: "We loved each other like brother and sister, that is, with great esteem, we loved each other and we were prudent, very prudent in our dealings" (p. 158). When her friends tell her that "this is not loving," she realizes that perhaps she is different from the rest. But if we analyze her sexuality we can see that Jesusa is conforming to that image of love she has for her brother, one of kindness and protection for Emiliano who was a good boy and who never abused her or her father in word or deed. Jesusa is likewise not a lesbian and she is even intolerant towards those who are:

> It is not legal. With things that are legal I agree, but *this* is something else again. If they really want sex, why don't they take up with a man? According to history, that is the way it is to be and if a man and a woman together is bad, then a man with a man or a woman with a woman is nothing more than disgraceful [p. 261].

Jesusa is an ignorant woman who affirms her independence in a world of "macho" males. In some ways, she has been able to isolate the "masculine" and this is not what she sees in daily life:

> Men are always abusive. As if that is what it means to be a man! That is a sickness of Mexican males: to think they are great cowboys because they mount us. And they make a grave error because we are not all tame mares. Of course,

> many of them are used to being able to say any nonsense anything to the girls, and these silly girls laugh at these jokes and then go off with them [p. 178].

Jesusa also realizes that the poor women work hard, but that the men take their meager savings and waste them in drinking. She herself realizes this when she adopts Perico; after he becomes a man he comes back to live with her because he can have free room and board which she provides by her hard work as a washerwoman. She says that there is no way she can say, "My son will look out for me" (p. 314), because he is lazy and prefers that she be the one to do the work. Jesusa's major weakness is her motherly instinct which is best illustrated in the case of Perico. She never had children and has raised Perico from a child, even to sacrificing her last dime in order to give him an education:

> He has to learn something in his lifetime, I don't want him to end up like me. I hit him a good one and sent him off to school. I forced him. Do you understand? I did not want him to be a porter, I wanted him to teach him something useful. I bought his books, notebooks, everything. Now you don't have to buy the books, but when Perico went to public school you did [p. 286].

She is also pragmatic about what ought to be taught and learned, and once she demanded "What I am really interested in is that you teach me to read and write and count" (p. 201).

It is possible that Jesusa is sterile, because she never mentions abortions, children or pregnancies. Her maternal instincts are so strong that once, during her revolutionary days, she took in a coyote. When the General kills it, she continues to dream, "I missed it greatly, I needed it" (p. 117). She continues to take in stray animals and children because, as she says, "He to whom God does not give children, the devil gives nephews" (p. 312).

A common way of life among the poor is to live together in order to save on rent. This communal type of living offers possibilities for the weak to depend on those stronger. As Jesusa is always the one with the strongest protective instincts, she always ends up in charge—often of entire families, as in the case of Perico or

Reginita. She does not mind working hard for others but she does have certain stipulations. With Reginita, the condition is that her daughters do not bring any men into the house when Reginita is there. With Perico, she demands that he behave himself and not act like the other boys in the neighborhood and she is very strict. She wants him to be a "respectful man" because she still believes that she can make him the kind of man she wants all men to be. Unfortunately Perico is not an exception to the rule, and she soon learns that each person must receive his own spiritual calling if any change is to occur. It is not easy to be different when one lives in an atmosphere where people take advantage of others and where there is no loyalty. Those that are together today, tomorrow will take separate paths because poverty does not permit permanent ties, not even between those protected and those who protect. As she states with great disillusionment:

> I do not believe people can be good, really I don't. Only Jesus Christ, and I never met him. And my father, but I never knew if he loved me or not. But in this life, who do you expect to be good? [p. 316].

How then does Jesusa find in the spiritualist work of La Obra the answers she needs and her purpose in life? First, there is hypnotism, which she is able to do with ease. Then she becomes a "medium," again easily. At first she resists believing, but when spirits begin to appear to her she no longer doubts. She stops drinking and begins to attend these spiritualist sessions. There, others discover she has healing powers and that she brings with her the presence of a "superior being" who protects her and listens to her petitions to heal others. As a point of information, Jesusa has suffered in the past from catatonic fits that have occurred from time to time until she was twenty. Her faith develops slowly and her surrender only comes when she herself experiences the supernatural phenomena, and then the presence of her protector helps her to understand that this earthly reality is only a small portion of a much larger reality. She interprets the spiritualist lessons her own way:

> We pay for what we do in this life. What one owes, one pays here, in the other world we do not have to pay because we are returned here to earth to pay for our wrongdoing [p. 296].

She even begins to see herself in other reincarnations and has visions and dreams that are very symbolic. Jesusa learns that she must change her personality greatly because she is able to analyze herself with great objectivity: "I was a stupid animal, a very stubborn mare" (p. 161). Thus her spiritual manifestations surprise her:

> 'Oh, Lord, I am not worthy of these great treasures of yours because a woman as evil as I ought not to see such marvels.'
>
> But they are continually before me and I continue, astonished, to see them until I implore:
>
> 'No, Lord, let me sleep because if you don't I will awaken bewildered by all your matchless wonders' [p. 299].

She describes her "trances" as something physical, as if something causes her to lose her strength and she feels the pricking of pins all over her body. But even in her trances she experiences great things. Later she leaves the congregation of La Obra but she continues in the faith. She leaves because she feels they have become too much involved in business, but nevertheless she continues to influence them.

In Jesusa's sexual life, one constant is the appearance of a spirit which she calls, due to his physical characteristics, "Light of the East." When she comes out of her trance, she says to her sisters in La Obra:

> He speaks very nicely, very prettily; he said hello and that I should not forget him; he watches over me because the Lord has given him the great responsibility of taking care of my flesh [p. 11].

She is sure that he loves her and if we can speculate somewhat into Jesusa's sexuality, we can see that he is the only male who has never awakened that sense of resentment and that agressiveness which men in general produce in her. It is interesting that she begins to associate sexual experiences with the suffering of each individual. She tells the story of her friend Sebastiana, who suffered a great deal physically because she had a dead child in her womb. She concludes—following her visions and interpretations—that Sebastiana suffers because she left "rotting children" in the wombs of other women when in another reincarnation she was a man. As penance, Sebastiana begins to take care of other people's children, those that "came out sickly and were never loved nor cared for." And perhaps Jesusa herself comes to some conclusions about her own sterility.

The mature Jesusa learns that suffering in life is important in order to purify the human being of all its defects and impurities. She explains:

> How can we cleanse ourselves? Through pain and suffering. We think He makes mistakes but he doesn't; it is we who make the mistakes because we don't hear, we don't listen, we refuse to recognize the true path, because if a majority of the people were to find the true, pure path of God there would be no men who abuse women nor would there be any women who would permit it. At night when I am alone, I begin to think and I say, 'Oh, Lord, give me strength, I am not asking for more strength to bear the sufferings you send to me.' And now that I am old and take medicine, I begin to think: 'Medicine is worthless because the real joke is not to take it and then truly feel His purification.'
>
> In this reincarnation God has not held me as he would a silver cup. . . . God said: 'You must suffer alone. You have to suffer in order to learn what it is to love God in the land of the Indian.' Although I am very ignorant, I, by myself, with what is revealed to me, am beginning to clear up my past [p. 12].

She searches and becomes aware that her life has meaning. She confesses:

> Mentally I dig deep, so much so that my head hurts as if within I had this entire world of calamities. Oh no! If I began to dig, I might find out that I am going crazy! But these are things that we must find out because we bring them with us when we are born and if we look at them

> when we should, they become clearer. There are many 'eyes' in the brain, it is like a starry sky. Thus we have to close those eyes of our bodies, very tightly, and then even if night comes, even if it is not daylight, we will be able to see the past. These things I say although I don't have the gift of tongues, but I have crossed many precipices. This is why I can reflect: 'Only God can know all I have suffered since my mother died and all that remains for me is to suffer' [p. 13].

We must go back to the early years of Jesusa when she lived near the sea. She swam every day and kept her clothing very clean. She took good care of herself until the days of the Revolution, but afterwards went through a period of corporal and spiritual contamination. She used to help her husband Pedro load the machine gun: "I don't know if I killed anyone." Later, her life in the capital is very chaotic and she says, "I have been very wild, a drunk, and a fighter. I did everything. I cannot say I have been a good person" (p. 13). This crazy youthfulness gives way to old age somewhat darkened by illness, but if she does not work, she does not eat. Work that has never frightened her now becomes a means of facing up to her strong will. She says,

> I am all broken inside, I am old, old, old, everything is old, nothing but old age everywhere. If Jesus Christ complained because he could not stand the pain, how much more right do I have, I who am little more than garbage [p. 307].

She knows she is going to die but she wants to do so in the open air, looking at the sky so that the vultures can eat her and then she will fly away in their guts "wherever the wind takes us" (p. 316).

Message

In a documentary novel it is necessary to emphasize a particular purpose. The novelist went to great pains to make recordings. She put much time and patience into each episode and then into the whole composition because she recognized that Jesusa offered a life so interesting that it would be hard to neglect. A very poor woman rarely writes her memoirs because she does not have the confidence, time, support or education. This does not mean, however, that this same woman does not have an extraordinary command of the language which would show the many variations of her spirit and her emotions. Such is Jesusa's case; the richness of her expression is such that we could say that she has a cinematographic language. While each reader may find interest in different facets of Jesusa's character, it is the attitude of a woman face-to-face with a male-dominated society that interests me here. In her evolution towards a transcendent reality Jesusa offers us the biography of a rebel, a non-conformist. If Margaret Mead were to have studied her, she would have come to the conclusion that Jesusa is more intelligent, more alive and full of resources than most of the rest of the women around her. Many episodes prove it. To prove it we have only to observe her curiosity, her character as a vagabond among her father's women, and later on her declaration of independence. Since she is very young she begins to show certain characteristics that she believes will help her overcome male dominance. Later, the Revolution is the perfect atmosphere in which to give free rein to her aggressive inclinations. The open challenge she offers to her husband when he beats her is one point in the affirmation of her equality. From that time on she will never allow any man, no matter how strong or important he may be, to abuse or mistreat her or any of those in her care and keeping. Of course as she explains, when she fights she does use "some" help—a beam, a pole or surprise. But Jesusa is not merely a fighter, she has a clear sense of justice and she soon becomes the spokeswoman who shows others that they can live alone, and need be neither exploited nor mistreated. Jesusa believes in work and as she has always been poor she does not hesitate to change jobs, to move without accounting to anyone. When she is widowed she refuses to marry again because she realizes that she can no longer pretend nor adapt to the tyranny of a husband. Also, she believes that if other women would be more courageous, the situation would be better for all. Of course she can never convince other women that she is right because no Mexican woman wants to end up as she does: alone, without children and a little fanatical about her parapsychological ideas.

Jesusa is capable of love, she is a kind and generous woman. Only once has she wished to marry—and that was to Antonio Pérez, the only male who ever treated her with respect, friendship and companionship. He is under the social pressures of his own family even though they are from the lower classes. Jesusa realizes that marriage is a trap for the woman who is poor. The case of Epifania, a friend of hers, clearly shows the middle-class woman's mentality. Jesusa relates:

> Epifania tells me, 'I am very grateful José married me but you see how he mistreats me, he gives me a hard time. . . ."
>
> 'But you are crazy, if he gives you such a hard time, you are getting in even deeper with marriage.'
>
> 'No, in order to visit my parents I had to get married.'
>
> 'Even if my parents had told me I was lost, I would never have married José.'
>
> She lowered her head. I believe that from so many blows, assured of so many kicks, the poor, unfortunate Epifania came here to La Joyita to die [p. 270].

Jesusa does not feel any identification with her Indian heritage; neither is she bound by family prejudices. Where did she get such unusual ideas? She is not the typical female stereotype because, without knowing it, she assimilated ideas from here and there. From her stepmother and her mother in turn, she gained her desire for education and self-sufficiency. From the foreigners she met she probably gained a realization of the diversity of behavior possible and learned that evidently these "macho" Mexicans are not the ones who are right. And having fought shoulder to shoulder with other soldiers gives her confidence. She frequently repeats, "I am not afraid. . . ."

Another aspect of Jesusa that is different from the other women of her group is that she is free to choose the style of life and beliefs that suit her rather than having to follow the Catholic teachings of her country. When she joins La Obra she belongs to a religious minority, since the idea of reincarnation is foreign to the doctrine of the Catholic Church. Because she is anticlerical it is easier for her to assimilate new ideas which help her to understand social injustices, misery, pain and the destiny of mankind. Since she cannot read nor write, she has only her intuition and inductive reasoning to help her find solutions to the philosophic concepts that bother her. When her supernatural powers manifest themselves she voluntarily experiments in the occult and other esoteric areas. Her sense of independence allows her to work for herself but she begins to accept the karmic laws of cause and effect. Her force of will causes her to reform and not to continue incurring debts that will have to be paid in another life. When she acquires a "conscience," she learns to be responsible for her weaknesses—as a person with a bad temper who often fights. Her concept of motherhood becomes much more altruistic and she never hopes for gratitude nor recognition. She never changes her opinion of this world, a world which she considers a showcase of egotism and evil, but at the same time she learns of a new relationship between her and a superior force. "Only God and I" (p. 316), she says at the end of her life. A metaphor of her life is repeated: the Indian girl who stands in the sea and the waves turn her white and then, full of foam, she is transformed into an old woman who accepts the problems of life with integrity because they purify and cleanse her. She has many moments of mystical and transcendental experiences:

> I have had many visions that I do not deserve, revelations that sweeten the air as if incense were burning. At times I smell orange blossoms, at other times fruits and other aromatic herbs and a rain of very delicate violet light falls in the room. But the visions go by like motion picture film. Even with my eyes open in an instant they are here and gone [p. 298].

Jesusa is a living testimony of the changes that can occur in a woman in spite of her poverty, ignorance and humble origins. In reality Jesusa partakes of none of these; she is a woman in search of an identity that goes beyond the barriers of class distinctions. She is neither Indian, Mexican, lower class, *Adelita*, soldier, or laundress, these are only facets of her life. She is above all a woman who attains her human and spiritual dignity through her own efforts.

Conclusions

CONCLUSIONS

In making my conclusions, I shall speak of the *family* from the three aspects of feminine education, of marriage seen as a goal, and of interpersonal affective relationships. With regard to *social class,* I shall concentrate on socio-familial, economic, racial, and religious factors. I shall treat *sexuality* from the perspective of the submission to the myth of feminine inferiority and the dynamics of the evolution of the rebellion against this myth.

Education varies among ethnic groups. In the traditional Hispanic family, it is most common for the daughter to be treated as was her mother or grandmother. This means that the family will try to keep her ignorant of sexual matters—e.g., the physiology of the sex act, venereal diseases, contraception, and so forth. When a girl from the middle or upper classes learns about some of these things, she does so clandestinely and from friends or maids who often have an absurd conception of reality. To the various notions of impurity, sin, and illegality are added a religious education, which teaches that the flesh leads to evil. Later during her married life, she will feel certain inhibitions and prejudices that will be difficult to pinpoint. Since the masculine system demands that women be pure and innocent, she must hide her thoughts and desires. When her wedding night arrives, it is quite common for her to experience "the little death" as does Nucha in *Los pazos de Ulloa.*

According to their economic position, the family may or may not have plans for the formal education of its daughters. These plans vary according to place, period and social class. In the nineteenth century, women's education was very brief and consisted of religion and of domestic skills, as best described by Fernán Caballero and Mercedes Cabello de Carbonera. But in the twentieth century many of the middle- and upper-class families have high aspirations for their daughters. For the upper class, it is important that their daughters be educated, that they should have some knowledge of languages, music, the arts, and of some sports so that they might come of age to marry with a certain elegance and style. Many women from the middle class in Spain and Latin America have professions and attend the university. If they have intellectual motivation, they can count on the family for support. Many meet their future husbands at the university and abandon their studies when they marry. The great majority of the women novelists belong to this professional class of women, except that they have persisted in their plans and have been able to realize their ideals through literature.

According to some families, every woman should aspire to be married. This idea is the major factor in the education of women that sets them apart from their brothers. While the domestic chores are the birthright of the women, in some homes the books are still the exclusive privilege of the men, as notes the young feminine protagonist of *Balún Canán.* The physical appearance of the woman is of importance because a woman who is very beautiful may help the family to ascend the social ladder. A good marriage automatically gives the family more hope for social prestige. But Silvina Bullrich shows most vividly that marriage guarantees nothing to the women, whether they are beautiful or not. If they are not prepared to support themselves with a profession or other means, when the marriage breaks up they remain at the mercy of a hostile husband. The fathers hand over their authority to the husbands once their daughters marry and no longer feel responsible for what happens after the girls have left home. As attested to by the female protagonists of María Luisa Bombal, Beatriz Guido and Teresa de la Parra, there is a certain ambivalence in these girls of marrying age—they realize that marriage means a change of atmosphere, a change of authority, and for some, a change of "owner." While these changes may be attractive for some, many women are hesitant. Ana María, in *La amortajada,* prefers the freedom of her parents' home to the sexual submission of a newlywed. Since many of the girls are treated as children at home, they have developed defense mechanisms to protect their "interior space." The married woman is expected to be a woman when the previous day she was only a "child." Marta Brunet shows us in *María Nadie* a protagonist who, even following an abortion, insists on playing with children in the woods. The most appropriate metaphor to describe this transition is the "fall of the angel." The Latin American girl, as she leaves the wedding ceremony, must confront all of the responsibilities of a married woman.

Especially in the provincial and out-of-the-way places, interpersonal relationships generally take place within the immediate circle of the extended family. Women only know those men who come to their homes or who live near them: brothers, cousins, uncles, fathers, friends of the family. In many novels, such as *Sab, Clemencia, Los pazos de Ulloa, La madre naturaleza, Los recuerdos del porvenir, Viento del norte,* and *Fín de fiesta,* we can see that love can even develop between immediate members of the same family. Since the majority of the primary and secondary schools still separate the boys from the girls, the girls do not have much opportunity to deal with members of the opposite sex. Moreover, the family tries to maintain vigilance over the women and only close friends have access to the house. Elena Garro shows us the social atmosphere of a Mexican town in *Los recuerdos del porvenir,* and Beatriz Guido shows us the development of the social life of some young college students as they become adults in the capital in *Fín de fiesta.* Jesusa belongs to the lower class and shows another area of society. The closeness of family ties explains the unity that exists between her and Emiliano. Jesusa even creates her masculine hero on the basis of her kind and patient brother.

With respect to social class, there are many factors that help the family determine the future of the daughter. With matrimony as the most accepted goal, the family tries hard to see that the daughter marries in the best possible manner. The saying "to each his own" well explains the desire of the middle and upper classes to preserve the system. In the past it was common, as shown by María de Zayas, Emilia Pardo Bazán and Concha Espina, for the parents to force their daughters to accept marriages that best suited the family. The dowry was a determining factor in the type of marriage a daughter might obtain. A woman with a large dowry never lacked for marriage proposals, even if it were only for the money, while the woman without a dowry stood little chance of marrying within her class. Parents who could not afford a large dowry because they had too many girls of marrying age began to use the exchange principle—a young and beautiful daughter for an old and rich husband. This system was perfectly logical to the society of the nineteenth century. Pardo Bazán shows us another type of exchange, one that is still practiced today: a pure and virtuous woman instead of a more attractive one with a "past." The rich heir of *Los pazos de Ulloa* chooses the most "religious" of his many cousins because she offers the best guarantee for his honor. In a male-dominated society, the man wants to be very sure that no other man will be able to threaten his domain. Elena Soriano shows us that the demands for respectability in an older, more corrupt man are greater than those of the young man who follows his amorous impulses. Many authors, such as Soriano, Elena Quiroga, and Concha Alós, show us cases of mature men who are in love with girls young enough to be their daughters, and in many of these cases the woman accepts his proposal for monetary reasons. Several novels, such as *Blanca Sol* and *Las hogueras*, have ambitious protagonists who wish to show off and to spend money and so they marry for economic interest without loving the man in question. Rosario Castellanos describes for us the situation of poor women who become like merchandise, to be exchanged, and for whom marriage is the only hope to climb the social ladder. And it is these protagonists of Castellanos and Alós who find that once they have reached their goals, life is empty and they need something else. For the wife in *Balún Canán*, the birth of a male child allows her, although vicariously, to enjoy the masculine privileges which have been denied to her, even as a wife. Sibila, who does not want to have children, decides to act as the men do, and she accentuates the aggressive and autonomous elements in her male-female relationships.

The racial factor is also important in these novels. Gertrudiz Gómez de Avellaneda shows the aspirations of the mulatto slave Sab to love his owner unconditionally. In *Aves sin nido,* Manuel courts Marcela, daughter of some Indians (although we later learn that this is not entirely true), and his humility is explained by the fact that he knows he is the illegitimate son of a priest. In *Hasta no verte, Jesús mío,* Jesusa finds opposition from the family of a man she wants to marry because she is an unlearned Indian. Matilde, in *Balún Canán*, is ashamed for having given herself to her cousin because he is illegitimate and a mestizo. The presence of European immigrants brings another source of conflict to the ruined aristocracy: now their daughters marry men from the lower social classes who have money. Such is the case of the poor young girl from a good family who marries a rich Italian in *Blanca Sol.* The opposite, however, does not occur. The rich young Italian, son of immigrants, in *María Nadie,* does not marry the poor girl of humble circumstances; she is good enough to be his lover but not his wife. Elena Garro describes other differences in the Mexican provinces. Although some of the officers' lovers come from the white aristocracy, since they are living as mistresses they have come down the social scale. Luisa Josefina Hernández shows us that the offices in the capital are a microcosm of the social and racial prejudices of the people. The men are tolerant of the white, sophisticated, liberated women from the middle and upper classes but are unmoving when it concerns the women of humble circumstances—especially those who are divorced—who are trying to free themselves. Silvina Bullrich and Carmen Laforet have demonstrated the existence of a great variety of invisible barriers between men and women that have arisen because of origins and social standings. The saying "love conquers all" is not proven in these novels—quite the contrary. A direct example is one that appears in *Viento del norte,* where the hostility between maid and master is carried into the bedroom, showing that even in marriage, social prejudices have their influence.

Religious choices appear at different levels. Sometimes women sacrifice their beliefs for love. The divergence between Catholic and Protestant is presented in *Sab.* Here, the protagonist, Carlota, marries the man she loves regardless of his denomination. In *Clemencia,* the female protagonist decides not to marry a Protestant because of the great differences in their ways of thinking and feeling. In *Medea 55*, a girl from a conservative Catholic family marries in a civil ceremony a man who is agnostic and a leftist. Ironically, 17 years later, he divorces her in order to marry a young girl in a Catholic ceremony and start in this fashion a very conservative and "respectable" life. Wars and revolutions bring along extremes of devotion to the Church among women. A good example appears in *Los recuerdos del porvenir* where ladies and prostitutes are united in defense of the priests in the cause of the *cristeros.* Perhaps an exception is Jesusa in *Hasta no verte, Jesús mío.* Following the example of the revolutionary soldiers she adopts a very strong anti-clerical attitude.

There are a lot of personal conflicts in the families that owe to the lack of consistency of beliefs among their members. While religious mothers will teach their daughters to believe in God, incredulous fathers will affirm their ideas and scorn the ways of thinking of the women. Also, different racial backgrounds add to the differences in the family. White children, in *Balún Canán*, are raised by Indian servants with a very definite view of the universe. At the same time the same children are being educated in religious schools that affirm different ideas. Choices appear sometimes. In *Balún Canán*, Francisca adopts the beliefs of the Indians.

There are also different levels of morality according to the social class of women. In *Ifigenia*, the protagonist bear the pressures of her social class and has to go through all the preliminaries of a wedding ceremony. Her servant, Melchora, will tell her that by being black and poor she is free to love whom and when she pleases. Jesusa, in *Hasta no verte, Jesús mío*, shows in great detail the situation of the poor, workingclass women: they have many children and are frequently abandoned by irresponsible men who leave behind illegitimate offspring.

In many novels we see women who learn very early in their lives that there are two sets of rules and that they must obey the system. However, women are constantly aware of the inequality of treatment between themselves and their brothers in the family. Later on, the double standard also applies to the courtship period and to the marriage. Most of the protagonists would like to rebel and change the system but they can't. Only orphans such as the protagonists of *La madre naturaleza* or *La amortajada* run free without supervision. In most of the cases the system enforces the rules and women have no choice but wait until they reach adulthood. Still, we see in many novels, like in *Ifigenia* a rigid system of indoctrination and vigilance. The authority of the parents is then delegated into the husbands. By then women start questioning the double standard and very often they try to keep their husbands for themselves. When they realize that men don't tolerate their expectations, the crisis arrives. Women again have to learn that they live in a masculine system and that they have to obey.

One interesting characteristic which may be observed in many of these novels is the ignorance of women concerning their own sexuality. When women become aware, around adolescence, of the changes in their own bodies, they try to ignore their sexual desires. Still, there is a great deal of curiosity for all that which is prohibited. An outlet for their supressed desires is literature. Women read about romantic lovers and they imagine beautiful scenes. They transfer all the qualities of those romantic men to *the one* they select either in reality or in their imagination. Very often women really don't have a chance to get to know their future husbands. Opportunities for intimacy are limited. Men and women put on their best behavior during their courtship. Since women don't really want to risk their virginity they really have to wait, hoping for the best. The protagonist of *La playa de los locos* defends her virginity, yet it takes her 20 years to finally explain her reasons for saying "no." What seems to be very real is that men expect their brides to be pure. Virginity forces the majority of the women from the middle and upper classes to wait patiently for their wedding night, when their husbands will reveal what they want to find out. Perhaps it is the educational system, with its many restrictions, which causes the women to develop a concept of love that looks on sex as something dirty, thus they have a great deal of trouble maintaining sexual relationships even if they are in love. In *La sobreviviente* the protagonist is always questioning the differences between love and sex. Also in *Su vida y yo* we see the analysis of the approaches toward love and sex on the part of men and women. For many protagonists sex without love is the equivalent of prostitution even in marriage.

In Spanish and Latin American system, the woman, from the time she is born, has a fixed place in the family. She is considered, because she is a woman, to be vulnerable, delicate, subject to all types of danger, but especially to the dangers of men who will try to bring about her fall. Family protection, therefore, creates a series of methods that have no other function than to maintain the girls always in sight. It is not accidental that the only protagonists from the middle and upper classes who lose their virginity in their adolescence are the orphans of *La amortajada* and *La madre naturaleza*. Moral indoctrination is very strong and from early youth the women are admonished to be pure, obedient, submissive and monogamous. On the other hand, the men enjoy a great deal of freedom from earliest youth. Thus, when they marry, there is no reason to change. Conflicts naturally arise when the husband is unfaithful. The wife demands his faithfulness based on her own loyalty. She has not only her love for him but also the "legitimacy" of her marriage and her children. Among the resources that many of the protagonists use to force their husbands to be faithful are jealous confrontations, hostility, retaliation and even sexual indifference. In the moments of crisis the protagonists are also forced to confront their own individuality. They come to realize that the husband is neither their owner nor their possession. In spite of the tears, suffering and daily torture that they endure, these women begin at this moment to free themselves from the social convention. The desire to remain at the side of the husband is traditional for the Hispanic woman, but there is a clear reason for it: she has been taught all of her life that marriage is destined to work and when her husband is unfaithful, she feels lost and without any real reason to exist. Yet, at the same time, this may be the first opportunity in her life to be honest with herself. Each of the protagonists chooses according to her mental state. If she is a very religious woman, she can take refuge in the Church. If she is very motherly, her refuge is in her children. If she is intelligent but with little desire to take action, such as the wife in *Su vida y yo*, she may come only to understand the power of the male which is perpetuated by a system that maintains social and economic inequality between the sexes. In exceptional cases, like the protagonist of *La sobreviviente*, she will become aware of her social responsibility, of a vital purpose that goes beyond sexual goals. Perhaps the greatest revelation for all women comes from the protagonist of *La amortajada*: she herself has created a passion for her husband in order to fill a life without purpose; when he ceases to love her, she is empty. This is the moment of truth for her and for all women who believe in the ideal of everlasting love. In those novels where we find strong women, such as *Diario de una maestra* and *Las hogueras*, we can also observe an identity crisis in that they try vainly to find the ideal man and reject many for being too common. When they become convinced that their "chosen" ones are like all the rest, they must confront their own reality, the sad and lonely reality of those women who, due to their independence are marked by society as "spinsters."

Physical and psychological abuse is one of the most degrading aspects of a male-dominated society. Garro, Poniatowska, and other novelists have shown that the woman has no family or social protection when her husband abuses her. In *Los recuerdos del porvenir*, Julia is beaten and finally killed by the tyrannical general who forces her to be his concubine. She, through a process which could be called a "psychic unfolding," is capable of withstanding an intolerable situation for a long period of time, but the fact remains that the man continues to believe that he owns her even to the point of killing her. In *Hasta no verte, Jesús mío,* Jesusa shows us the sadistic side of the men of the lower classes of Mexico and then affirms her own rebellion. She not only challenges her husband to a duel, but she beats other men who are mistreating their women. This is perhaps the first document of female self-defense which shows a change in the stereotyped pattern of women as victims. The lack of social protection leaves the majority of the women at the mercy of their husbands. In *La cólera secreta* we find a case of psychological abuse. The author proves that the only solution is divorce, but here we are dealing with more sophisticated people from the upper classes. In the majority of cases, divorce does not appear as a solution, either because in many countries it does not exist, or because it is extremely difficult for women from the upper classes to support themselves and their children. The other solution is to leave him, and in *María Nadie,* after being beaten to the point of aborting her child, the protagonist leaves and goes elsewhere to begin a new life without dependence on any man.

Obviously, in the very process of writing these novels the authors have shown their awareness of the feminine cause. Their crusade extends to all women who have felt the injustices of the double standard. This system creates the major difficulties between the sexes. What is worse, hypocrisy makes open communication impossible. The men continue to support their masculine superiority, while the women are obliged to dig deep into the souls to find the necessary power to make an honest and valiant testimony of their personal crisis. These authors have placed great emphasis on novelistic honesty because they know that some male readers might realize that they too are victims of the system. According to these novelists, sooner or later the man becomes insensitive, egotistical and sensual to the extent of losing his greatest potentials for love and growth. On the other hand, the protagonists of these novels, after living in an oppressive system, are finally able through their own suffering to break the vicious cycle. They discover within themselves the power of their own individuality and often they find a *raison d'être* without hypocrisy or deceit. They also discover that the myths of beauty and youth have been used by men to manipulate them. The men, too, grow old and lose their attractiveness without gaining anything—be it wisdom, kindness, or compassion for other human beings. Each novel is a personal testimony of a dynamic individual who has been able to obtain freedom from stereotyped norms. María de Zayas is the only author who shows a collective force for liberation. Women are alone because a great many of them are still hampered by ignorance, economic dependence and social pressures—all of which mold them into traditional roles. Each of these novels is a valiant testimony of feminine awareness, of women's dreams and frustrations, of their struggles, and above all, of their hopes for a better world.

Chapter Notes

Bibliography and *Index*

CHAPTER NOTES

INTRODUCTION

1. Celia de Zapata in "One Hundred Years of Women Writers in Latin America" does a preliminary analysis of the "critical discrimination against women writers." See *The Latin American Literary Review* III, 6 (Spring 1975), 9.

2. Agustín de Amezua y Mayo, *Formación y elementos de la novela cortesana* (Madrid: n.p., 1929).

3. Agustín de Amezúa y Mayo in the "Prologue" to *Novelas completas de María de Zayas* (Madrid: Biblioteca Selecta de Clásicos Españoles, 1948), vol. IX, p. 5.

4. Mary Wollstonecraft published *A Vindication of the Rights of Women* in 1792.

5. Fernán Caballero wrote a letter to Juan Eugenio Hartzenbusch. It appears in *Cecilia Bohl de Faber y Juan Eugenio Hartzenbusch,* edited by Theodor Heinerman (Madrid: Espasa Calpe, 1944), p. 97.

6. *Ibid.*, p. 38.

7. Carmen Bravo Villasante, *Vida y obra de Emilia Pardo Bazán* (Madrid: Revista de Occidente, 1962), p. 97.

8. "Carta de Marcelino Menéndez de Pelayo a Juan Valera" is quoted by Mercedes Bravo Villasante en *Vida y obra de Emilia Pardo Bazán*, pp. 134–35.

9. Juan Cano quotes the author in "La mujer en la novela de Concha Espina," *Hispania* (1939), 51–60.

10. Concha Espina, *Esclavitud y libertad* (Valladolid: Edición Reconquista, 1938).

11. José Ortega y Gasset, *La rebelión de las masas* (Madrid: Espasa Calpe, 1966), p. 123.

12. Hipólito Escolar and José García Mazas interviewed Carmen Laforet. The interview appears in *Primera antología de autores españoles* (Philadelphia: Chilton Books, 1965), p. 192.

13. Juan Luis Alborg, *Hora actual de la novela española* (Madrid: Taurus, 1958), p. 199.

14. Elena Soriano, *Espejismos* (Madrid: Calleja, 1955), p. 132.

15. Elena Soriano in "Coloquio de mesa redonda," *Urogallo* (Madrid) VI (1975), 31.

16. Dolores Medio, *Nosotros, los Rivero* (Barcelona: Ediciones Destino, 1970), p. 185.

17. Gemma Roberts, *Temas existenciales en la novela española de postguerra* (Madrid: Editorial Gredos, 1973), p. 43.

18. Concha Alós, *Rey de gatos* (Barcelona: Barral Editores, 1972), p. 136.

19. Alberto Ghiraldo quotes her in *Diario de amor de Gertrudiz Gómez de Avellaneda* (Madrid: Ediciones Aguilar, 1928), pp. 14–15.

20. Alberto Tauro, *Literatura peruana* (Lima: Imprenta Leoncio Prado, 1969), p. 157.

21. Manuel González Prada in "Esclavas de la Iglesia" in *Horas de Lucha* (Buenos Aires: Editorial Americale, 1946), pp. 62–68 analyzes the women's condition in Peru.

22. Clorinda Matto de Turner, *Herencia* (Lima: Matto Hermanos, 1895), pp. 49–50.

23. Mercedes Cabello de Carbonera in her "Prologue" to *Blanca Sol* (Lima: Imprenta Carlos Prince, 1889), p. iv.

24. Teresa de la Parra, *Tres conferencias inéditas*, edited by Arturo Uslar Pietri (Caracas: Ediciones Garrido, 1961), p. 24.

25. *Ibid.*, p. 22.

26. Margaret Campbell, "The Vaporous World of María Luisa Bombal," *Hispania* 44 (1961), 415–419.

27. Silvina Bullrich, *Teléfono ocupado* (Buenos Aires: Ediciones Emece, 1971).

28. Silvina Bullrich, *Mañana digo basta*, 3d ed. (Buenos Aires: Editorial Sudamericana, 1969), p. 13.

29. Martha Restuccia's letter to Lucía Fox, Montevideo, May 25, 1977.

30. Clara Silva, *El alma y los perros,* 2d ed. (Montevideo: Colección Carabela, 1962), pp. 111–12.

31. Martha Allen, "Dos estilos de novela, Marta Brunet and María Luisa Bombal," *Revista Iberoamericana* 18, 35 (1952–53), 88.

32. Emmanuel Carballo in his interview of Rosario Castellanos, which appears in *Diecinueve protagonistas de la literatura mexicana del siglo XX* (Mexico City: Empresas Editoriales, 1965), p. 420.

33. *Ibid.*, p. 416.

34. Elena Garro, *La semana de colores* (Mexico City: Universidad Veracruzana, 1964), p. 20.

35. Quoted by John K. Knowles in "The Labyrinth of Form" in *Dramatists in Revolt*, edited by Leon F. Lyday and George W. Woodyard (Austin: University of Texas Press, 1976), p. 137.

36. *Ibid.*, p. 137.

37. Sylvia Jean Brann, "El teatro y las novelas de Luisa Josefina Hernández," doctoral dissertation at the University of Illinois, 1969, p. 312.

38. María Luisa Mendoza, *Oiga usted* (Mexico City: Editorial Samo, 1973), p. 90.

MARIA DE ZAYAS

1. Manuel Serrano y Sanz, *Apuntes para una biblioteca de autoras españolas* (Madrid: n.p., 1903), vol. II, pp. 583–586.

2. Quoted by Edwin Place in "Maria de Zayas, an Outstanding Woman Short-Story Writer of Seventeenth Century Spain," *University of Colorado Studies* XIII, (1923), 26–30.

3. María de Zayas, *Novelas amorosas y ejemplares* (Madrid: Aldus, 1948). In this edition there is a long introduction written by Agustín de Amezua.

4. María de Zayas, *Desengaños amorosos* (Madrid: Aldus, 1950). Page references for quotations in the text are to this edition.

5. Sor Juana Inés de la Cruz, *Obras completas de Sor Juana Inés de la Cruz,* edited by Alfonso Mendez Plancarte (Mexico City: Fondo de Cultura Económica, 1951). Sor Juana Inés de la Cruz is a Mexican poet who lived in Colonial times (1748–1695).

6. Helmut Hatzfeld, in *Estudios literarios sobre mística española* (Madrid: Editorial Gredos, 1968), devotes several chapters to women in Spain and their religious convictions.

FERNAN CABALLERO

1. Quoted by Theodor Heinerman in *Cecilia Bohl de Faber y Juan Eugenio Hartzenbusch* (Madrid: Espasa Calpe, 1944), p. 27.

2. Alfred Morel Fatio's "Fernán Caballero d'après sa correspondance avec Antoine de Latour" appears in the *Bulletin Hispanique* III (1901), 270.

3. Theodor Heinerman in *Cecilia Bohl*. . . offers many German sources for the biographical study of Fernán Caballero. His bibliography appears on pp. 259–262.

4. In the book by Theodor Heinerman appear many letters from the author to Hartzenbusch explaining the reasons for hiding herself and using a pen name; see pp. 167–170.

5. See José María Asencio's prologue to *La familia de Alvareda* (Madrid: Rivadeneira, 1893).

6. Fernán Caballero, *Clemencia* (Madrid: Casa Editorial Hijos de Guijarro, 1902). Page references for quotations in the text are to this edition.

EMILIA PARDO BAZAN

1. Robert Osborne, *Emilia Pardo Bazán, su vida y obras* (Mexico City: Ediciones Andrea, 1964). Osborne mentions the major influences in her education.

2. Quoted by Carmen Bravo Villasante in *Vida y obra de Emilia Pardo Bazán* (Madrid: Revista de Occidente, 1962), p. 91.

3. Carmen Bravo Villasante, *Vida y obra de Emilia Pardo Bazán*, pp. 99–109.

4. Nelly Clemessy, *Emilia Pardo Bazán* (Paris: Centro de Recherches Hispaniques, 1973). In Chapter IV the author develops the theme "La femme espagnole, realité et ideal," pp. 496–513.

5. Emilia Pardo Bazán, *Obras completas* (Madrid: Aguilar, 1957), vol. I, p. 510.

6. *Ibid.*, p. 309.

7. *Ibid.*, p. 648.

8. *Ibid.*, vol. II, p. 429.

9. *Ibid.*, vol. II, p. 519.

10. It appeared in articles published in *La España Moderna,* May, 1890.

11. *Ibid.*, May, 1890.

12. Ronald Hilton, "Emilia Pardo Bazán et le mouvement politique en Espagne," *Bulletin Hispanique* LIV (1952), pp. 153–164.

13. *Vida y obra de Emilia Pardo Bazán*, p. 161.

14. *Ibid.*, p. 287.

15. Emilia Pardo Bazán, *Los pazos de Ulloa.* It appears in *Obras completas* (Madrid: Aguilar, 1957), I. Page references for quotations in the text are to this edition.

16. Emilia Pardo Bazán, *La madre naturaleza*; in *Obras completas*, I.; references are to this edition.

17. Emilia Pardo Bazán, *Un viaje de novios* (Barcelona: Editorial Labor, 1971). In the Prefacio, pp. 57–62, the author clarifies her ideas about the novel.

18. Irving H. Barlett and C. Glenn Cambor, in "The History and Psychology of the Southern Women," quote Thomas Wilson Page on p. 9. See *Women Studies* I, 1 (1974).

19. See Donald Fowler in *The Catholic Naturalism of Pardo Bazán* (Chapel Hill: University of Carolina Press, 1957), pp. 3] -41.

CONCHA ESPINA

1. Josefina de la Maza, *Vida de mi madre Concha Espina* (Alcoy: Editorial Marfil, 1957).

2. S. L. Millard Rosenberg, "Concha Espina," *Hispania* (1927), pp. 321–329.

3. Frances Douglas, "Recent Works by Concha Espina," *Hispania* VI (1923), 185–187.

4. Frances Douglas, "Concha Espina: A New Star Ascendant," *Hispania* VII (1924), 11–120.

5. Concha Espina, *Esclavitud y libertad* (Valladolid: Ediciones Reconquista, 1938).

6. Concha Espina, *Obras completas* (Madrid: Ediciones Fax, 1955). Page references for quotations in the text are to this edition.

7. Juan Cano, "La mujer en la novela de Concha Espina," *Hispania* XXII (1939), 51–60. Concha Espina continued writing until 1953, the date of her *Una novela de amor*.

CARMEN LAFORET

1. Carmen Laforet, *Mis páginas mejores* (Madrid: Editorial Gredos, 1956). Read the "Introduction" by the author, pp. 7–11.

2. Graciela Illanes Adaro, *La novelística de Carmen Laforet* (Madrid: Editorial Gredos, 1971), pp. 9–21.

3. Federico Carlos Saínz de Robles, in *La novela española en el siglo XX* (Madrid: Pegaso, 1957), explains the reasons for her quick recognition, pp. 263–264.

4. Hipólito Escolar y José García Mazas, *Primera antología sonora de autores españoles contemporáneos* (Philadelphia: Chilton Books, 1965), pp. 187–189.

5. Manuel García-Viñó, *La novela española de post-guerra* (Madrid: Publicaciones Españolas, 1971), affirms that *Nada, La isla y los demonios* and *La mujer nueva* represent an autobiography. On the other hand, *La insolación* is the result of Laforet's observation of other people's realities (p. 13). José Domingo, a critic, considers *La isla y los demonios* a failure, in *La novela española del siglo XX* (Madrid: Colección Labor, 1973), p. 51.

6. Carmen Laforet, *La llamada* (Barcelona: Ediciones Destino, 1952) is a collection of short novelettes, such as "Un noviazgo," "El piano" and "El último verano."

7. Carmen Laforet, *La mujer nueva* (Barcelona: Ediciones Destino, 1955). Criticism about this novel can be found in García-Viñó, *La novela española actual* pp. 71–82. Also on Graciela Illanes' *La novelística de Carmen Laforet*, pp. 107–123.

8. Carmen Laforet, *La insolación* (Barcelona: Editorial Planeta, 1963). Carmen Laforet in an interview (*Primera antología sonora. . .*) announces her next trilogy to be *Tres pasos fuera del tiempo*, which contains *La insolación, Al volver a la esquina* and *Jaque mate*, pp. 192–193.

9. Carmen Laforet, *Novelas*, 4th ed. (Barcelona: Editorial Planeta, 1965), vol. I. *Nada* appears on pp. 23–260. Page references for quotations in the text are to this edition.

ELENA QUIROGA

1. Arturo Rioseco, "Tres novelistas españolas de hoy," *Revista Hispánica Moderna* (New York) 31 (1965), 418–424. See also Ronald Schwartz, *Spain's New Wave Novelists* (Metuchen, N.J.: Scarecrow Press, 1976), pp. 66–73.

2. See Antonio Iglesias Laguna, *Treinta años de novela española* (Madrid: Prensa Española, 1970). The critic says also that from her first novel Quiroga shows her lyric, deep temperament, p. 270.

3. Elena Quiroga, *La sangre* (Barcelona: Ediciones Destino, 1953). Many critics consider *La sangre* her best novel, among them Manuel García-Viñó.

4. Elena Quiroga, *Algo pasa en la calle* (Barcelona: Ediciones Destino, 1954). Schwartz in *Spain's New Wave of Novelists* says: this novel "is particularly interesting to us because the author attempts to provide her readers with a different notion of reality" (p. 67).

5. Federico Carlos Saínz de Robles in *La novela española en el siglo XX* thinks that this novel is very confusing and that the author "falls into Faulkner's trap" (p. 21).

6. García-Viñó in *La novela española de post-guerra* says that the last of Quiroga's novels show her obsession with narrative techniques (p. 21).

7. Elena Quiroga, *Viento del norte* (Barcelona: Ediciones Destino, 1951). She won a Nadal Prize with this novel and many critics consider it to be her best novel.

ELENA SORIANO

1. Federico Carlos Saínz de Robles, *La novela española en el siglo XX* (Madrid: Pegaso, 1921), p. 264.

2. Elena Soriano, *Caza menor* (Madrid: La Nave, 1951).

3. Antonio Iglesias Laguna, *Treinta años de la novela española* (Madrid: Editorial Prensa Española, 1970) considers this trilogy a model "para Preceptiva literaria," (p. 272). Read also José Domingo's review of the trilogy in *La novela española del siglo XX*.

4. Elena Soriano, *La playa de los locos* (Madrid: Calleja, 1955). Page references for quotations in the text are to this edition.

5. Elena Soriano, *Espejismos* (Madrid: Calleja, 1955). References are to this edition.

6. Elena Soriano, *Medea 55* (Madrid: Calleja, 1955). References are to this edition.

7. Elena Soriano is editor of *El Urogallo,* a quarterly magazine published in Madrid. She devoted the whole edition of 1975 to the International Year of Women. See No. 31–32, Año VI, March–April 1975.

DOLORES MEDIO

1. Janet Winecoff, "Fictionalized Autobiography in the Novels of Dolores Medio," *Kentucky Foreign Language Quarterly* 13 (1966), pp. 170–178.

2. Antonio Iglesias Laguna, in *Treinta años de la novela española actual*, says that we can see personal cases in her novel of the Civil War in Spain (p. 81). Also in order to understand the philosophical frame of the novel *Diario de una maestra* one can read Gemma Roberts' *Temas existenciales de la novela española de postguerra* (Madrid: Editorial Gredos, 1973).

3. Federico Carlos Saínz de Robles, in *El espíritu y la letra* (Madrid: Aguilar, 1966), analyzes the National Novel Prizes won by women since 1939 (p. 223). The same critic in *La novela española en el siglo XX* (Madrid: Pegaso, 1957) declares that *Nosotros, los Rivero* is "the most authentic Spanish novel that has won the Premio Nadal" (p. 262).

4. Dolores Medio, *Funcionario público* (Barcelona: Ediciones Destino, 1956.

5. Dolores Medio, *El pez sigue flotando* (Barcelona: Ediciones Destino, 1959).

6. Delores Medio, *El diario de una maestra* (Barcelona: Ediciones Destino, 1960). Page references for quotations in the text are to this edition.

7. Dolores Medio, *Los que vamos de pie* (Barcelona: Ediciones Destino, 1961).

8. Dolores Medio, *Bibiana* (Madrid: E. Bullon, 1963). See Ronald Schwartz, *Spain's New Wave Novelists* (Metuchen, N.J.: Scarecrow Press, 1976), p. 310.

CONCHA ALOS

1. Concha Alós, *Rey de gatos* (Barcelona: Barral Editores, 1972).

2. Concha Alós, *Los enanos* (Barcelona: Plaza y Janes Editores, 1962). She won the Planeta prize for this novel, entailing publication by Ediciones Planeta, but had to renounce it because of a commitment to Plaza y Janes.

3. She is not only prolific but also attained "great prominence in the late sixties," says Schwartz in *Spain's New Wave Novelists*, p. 311.

4. Concha Alós, *Los cien pájaros* (Barcelona: Ediciones G.P., 1967).

5. Concha Alós, *Las hogueras*, 1st ed. (Barcelona: Ediciones Planeta, 1964).

6. Concha Alós, *El caballo rojo* (Barcelona: Ediciones Planeta, 1966); Planeta prize.

7. Concha Alós, *La madama* (Barcelona: Ediciones Planeta, 1969); Planeta prize.

8. Alós' short story "Armor" appeared, translated by Doris Rolfe, in *Aphra: The Feminist Literary Magazine* V, 1 (Winter 1973–74), 2–8.

9. Concha Alós, *Las hogueras*, 18th ed. (Barcelona: Ediciones Planeta, 1974). Page references for quotations in the text are to this edition.

GERTRUDIZ GOMEZ DE AVELLANEDA

1. Gertrudiz Gómez de Avellaneda, *Diario de amor*, edited by Alberto Ghiraldo, (Madrid: Aguilar, 1958), p. 56.

2. Mercedes Ballesteros, *Vida de la Avellaneda* (Madrid: S. Aguirre, 1949).

3. Carmen Bravo Villasante, *Una vida romántica de la Avellaneda* (Barcelona: Editorial Rojas, 1967).

4. Max Henriquez Ureña, *Panorama histórico de la literatura cubana* (New York: Las Américas, 1963), vol. I.

5. Edwin Bucher Williams, "*The Life and Dramatic Works of Gertrudiz Gómez de Avellaneda*," doctoral dissertation at the University of Pennsylvania, 1924. It was published in a series in *Romantic Languages and Literatures* (Philadelphia), no. 11 (1924).

6. Avellaneda wrote *Sab* between 1836 and 1838. Helena Percas Ponsetti, in "Sobre la Avellaneda y su novela *Sab*," offers detailed information in *Revista Iberoamericana* 28, 54 (1962), 347–371.

7. Edith Kelly, "Bibliografía de la Avellaneda," *Revista Bimestral Cubana* 35 (1935), 107–39 and 261–95.

8. Edith Kelly, "La Avellaneda's *Sab* and the Political Situation in Cuba," *The Americas* (Washington), I (1945), 303–16.

9. Gertrudiz Gómez de Avellaneda, *Sab* (La Habana: Imprenta de la Biblioteca Nacional, 1914). Page references for quotations in the text are to this edition.

10. *Diario de amor.*

CLORINDA MATTO DE TURNER

1. Matto de Turner wrote many *Tradiciones cuzqueñas* following Ricardo Palma's historical approach.

2. Clorinda Matto de Turner, *Aves sin nido* (Lima: 1889). See John Miller's article, "Clorinda Matto de Turner and Mercedes Cabello de Carbonera: Societal Criticism and Morality," *Latin American Women Writers Yesterday and Today* (Pittsburgh: Carnegie Mellon University, 1975). Page references for quotations in the text are to *Aves sin nido* (Lima: Ediciones Peisa, 1973).

3. Quoted by Francisco Carrillo in *Clorinda Matto de Turner y su indigenismo literario* (Lima: Ediciones de la Biblioteca Universitaria, 1967), p. 16.

4. Matto de Turner wrote *Indole* (Lima: Imprenta Bacigalupi, 1891) trying to recapitulate a real scandal that took place in Cuzco. For details read Mario Castro Arenas in *La novela peruana y la revolución social* (Lima: José Godard, n.d.) p. 108.

5. Clorinda Matto de Turner, *Boreales, miniaturas y porcelanas* (Buenos Aires: Juan Alsina, 1902), pp. 312–313.

6. Clorinda Matto de Turner, *Herencia* (Lima: Imprenta Masias, 1895). First she titled the book *Cruz de Agata*, but she changed it to *Herencia* later on. In the prologue to *Herencia* she establishes the fact that she wanted to write a novel that would reform social mores (p. vi).

7. Matto de Turner was exiled after President Avelino Cáceres, the liberal incumbent, was defeated by Nicolás de Pierola, the ultraconservative leader.

8. Clorinda Matto de Turner, *Viaje de Recreo* (Valencia: F. Sampere, 1910). This novel was published posthumously.

9. Manuel González Prada, *Horas de lucha* (Buenos Aires: Editorial Americale, 1946), p. 62.

MERCEDES CABELLO DE CARBONERA

1. See Jorge Basadre, *Historia de la República del Perú* (Lima: Editorial Cultura Antártida, 1949), vol. II, p. 288.

2. Cabello de Carbonera in the Prologue to *Blanca Sol* (Lima: Imprenta Carlos Prince, 1889) establishes her purpose for writing her novels (p. iv).

3. Mercedes Cabello de Carbonera, *Sacrificio y recompensa* (Lima: Editorial Torres Aguirre, 1887).

4. Mercedes Cabello de Carbonera, *Las consecuencias* (Lima: Editorial Torres Aguirre, 1880).

5. Mercedes Cabello de Carbonera, *El conspirador* (Lima: Imprenta "La Voce d'Italia," 1892).

6. Mercedes Cabello de Carbonera, *Blanca Sol* appeared in the first edition in 1888 (Lima: Imprenta Torres Aguirre). References for quotations in the text are to the second edition: *Blanca Sol* (Lima: Imprenta Carlos Prince, 1889).

7. Cabello de Carbonera's *La novela moderna* won first prize in the "Concurso Hispanoamericano in Buenos Aires" in 1892. In this long essay she endorses the "novela social." *La novela moderna* was republished in Lima (Hora del Hombre, 1948).

8. Luis Petriconi and Juan Copello, *Estudios sobre la independencia económica del Perú* (Lima: Imprenta Nacional, 1874), p. 99.

9. José Carlos Mariátegui, *Siete ensayos de interpretación de la realidad peruana* (Lima: Empresa Editora Amauta, 1964), p. 17.

10. Carlos Lisson, quoted by Ernesto Yepez del Castillo, *El Perú 1820–1920* (Lima: Instituto de Estudios Peruanos, 1972), p. 129.

TERESA DE LA PARRA

1. Fernando Paz Castillo, "El sentido de intimidad en Teresa de la Parra," *Revista Nacional de Cultura* 10, 72 (1949), 7–14.

2. Lucía Fox, *Ensayos hispanoamericanos* (Caracas: García e hijo, 1966), pp. 43–49.

3. Ramón Díaz Sánchez, *Teresa de la Parra: Claves para una interpretación* (Caracas: n.p., 1954). Read Nelida Torres' doctoral dissertation, "A Critical Appraisal of Teresa de la Parra," University of California, 1970.

4. Jose Antonio Galao, "Hispanoamérica a través de sus novelas: *Ifigenia* o el hechizo de Europa," *Cuadernos hispanoamericanos* 150 (1962), 373–378.

5. Victor Fuentemayor Ruiz, "La dimensión amorosa de la escritura," *Revista de la Literatura Hispanoamericana* (Universidad de Zulia) I (1971), 23–46.

6. Teresa de la Parra, *Tres conferencias inéditas* edited by Arturo Uslar Pietri (Caracas: Ediciones Garrido, 1961), p. 150.

7. Teresa de la Parra, *Ifigenia* (Caracas: Las Novedades, 1945). Page references for quotations in the text are to this edition.

8. Ramón Díaz Sánchez, *Venezuela independiente* (Caracas: Fundación Mendoza, 1962), p. 545.

MARIA LUISA BOMBAL

1. María Luisa Bombal, *La última niebla*, 2d ed. (Santiago de Chile: Editorial Nascimiento, 1941).

2. María Luisa Bombal, *La amortajada,* 2d ed. (Santiago: Editorial Nascimiento, 1941).

3. It appears in *Time Magazine*, XLIX (April 14, 1947).

4. María Luisa Bombal, *House of Mist* (New York: Farrar Straus, 1947).

5. Margaret Campbell, "The Vaporous World of María Luisa Bombal," *Hispania* 44 (1961), 415.

6. María Luisa Bombal, *The Shrouded Woman* (New York: Farrar Straus, 1948). Page references for quotations in the text are to this edition.

7. M. Ian Adams, in *Three Authors of Alienation* (Austin: University of Texas Press, 1975), mentions that she was working on another novel, *El Canciller,* which had originally written in English in 1953. In the recent book *Obras completas de María de Luisa Bombal* (Clear Creek: The Ameri-

can Hispanist, 1978), under the heading "Los Dramas Inéditos" appears The Foreign Minister. See advertisements in *Hispania* 68, (March 1978), xvii.

SILVINA BULLRICH

1. She is the most prolific writer in Argentina. However, her name doesn't appear in many critical works. It is possible that many scholars consider her to be a so-called "popular" writer. Nevertheless, she has gained her place in the Argentinian letters. Corina Mathieu in the essay "Argentine Women in the Novels of Silvina Bullrich" says: "The totality of her literary production reveals an abated interest in analyzing the innermost feeling of women in love. She has done so over and over, but always within a specific frame of reference, i.e., Argentine society." The essay appears in *Latin American Women Writers Yesterday and Today* (Pittsburgh: Carnegie Mellon, 1975), p. 68.

2. She has also written about social struggles. She said: "I cannot help standing as my country's judge while at the same time rebelling against it. It is a love relationship." Silvina Bullrich, *Entre mis veinte y treinta años* (Buenos Aires: Emece, 1970), p. 620.

3. Silvina Bullrich, *Mañana digo basta* (Buenos Aires: Sudamericana, 1966).

4. Silvina Bullrich, *Tres novelas,* 1st ed. (Buenos Aires: Sudamericana, 1966). Page references for quotations in the text are to this edition. This book also contains *Mientras los demas viven* and *Un momento muy largo.*

5. For a recent study of the country read Tomas Roberto Fillol's *Social Factors in Economic Development; The Argentine Case* (Cambridge, Mass.: The M.I.T. Press, 1961).

CLARA SILVA

1. Ileana Renfrew wrote a letter to Lucía Fox in which she states: "justamente Clara Silva acaba de morir el 23 de setiembre, siguiendo en muy poco tiempo a su esposo Alberto Zum Felde"; December, 1978.

2. Carmen Conde, *Once grandes poetisas américo-hispanas* (Madrid: Ediciones Cultura Hispánica, 1967), considers that Clara Silva, Delmira Agustini and Juana de Ibarbourou are the three greatest Uruguayan women poets (p. 335).

3. Clara Silva, *La sobreviviente* (Montevideo: Ediciones Tauro, 1966). Page references for quotations in the text are to this edition.

4. Clara Silva, *El alma y los perros* (Montevideo: Alfa, 1962). Marta Restuccia in a letter to Lucía Fox establishes the fact that Clara Silva had read Kierkegaard and believed that existential anguish was very essential to the poet. Letter written on May 25, 1977, in Montevideo.

5. Clara Silva made several declarations to the newspapers in Montevideo. Some of these clippings were sent to me by Marta Restuccia; there is no date. Clara Silva declared: "Nunca estoy satisfecha con lo que hago. Nunca creo que llegué a lo me proponía hacer. Cuando me releo, me pregunto, ¿cómo pude hacer eso? porque me creo incapaz ahora de hacer lo mismo otra vez. Me sentiría incapaz de hacer *La Sobreviviente* o *Habitación testigo* otra vez."

6. Conde, *Once grandes . . .* , p. 372.

7. *Ibid.*, pp. 365–366.

8. Newspapers clippings sent by Martha Restuccia to Lucía Fox in a letter dated May 25, 1977.

9. It is revealing since she was married to a famous critic, Zum Felde, author of *Indice crítico de la literatura hispanoamericana* (Mexico City, Equarania, 1959). There is a big section dedicated to Clara Silva in this book.

MARTA BRUNET

1. Hernán Díaz Arrieta, *Panorama de la literatura chilena del siglo XX* (Santiago: Editorial Nascimiento, 1931), pp. 147–48. The same critic has written about her in *Historia personal de la literatura chilena* (Santiago: Editorial Zig-Zag, 1954).

2. Marta Brunet, "Obras completas (Santiago de Chile: Editorial Zig-Zag, 1963). The prologue is written by Hernan Díaz Arrieta who often wrote under the pen name "Alone."

3. Marta Brunet, *Humo hacia el Sur* (Buenos Aires: Editorial Losada, 1946). It reprints the short novel *María Rosa, flor del Quillén* published in 1927.

4. César Rosales, "*Humo hacia el Sur,*" *Revista Sur* 138 (1946), 94–104.

5. Victor Valenzuela, "Marta Brunet y María Nadie," *La Nueva Democracia* XXXVII, 2 (1958). The same critic has written "Marta Brunet" in *Revista Hispánica Moderna* XXIV, 2 (1958), 225.

6. Marta Brunet, *Amasijo* (Santiago: Editorial Zig-Zag, 1966). For further study of this novel and others there is a doctoral dissertation by Roger Peel, "The Narrative Prose of Marta Brunet," Yale University, 1966.

7. Marta Brunet, *María Nadie* (Santiago: Editorial Zig-Zag, 1957). Page references for quotations in the text are to this edition.

ROSARIO CASTELLANOS

1. Walter M. Langford, *The Mexican Novel Comes of Age* (Notre Dame, Ind.: University of Notre Dame Press, 1971), p. 183.

2. Rhoda Dybvig, *Rosario Castellanos, biografía y novelística* (Mexico City: Andrea, 1965).

3. Evon Z. Vogt, *Los Zinacantecos: un grupo Maya del siglo XX* (Mexico City: Septentas, 1969).

4. See Langford, *The Mexican Novel . . .* , pp. 181–83.

5. Emmanuel Carballo, in *Diecinueve protagonistas de la literatura mexicana del siglo XX* (Mexico City: Empresas editoriales, 1965), interviews Rosario Castellanos, pp. 412–424.

6. Castellanos' *El eterno femenino* (Mexico City: Fondo de Cultura Económica, 1975) and *El mar y sus pescaditos* (Mexico City: Secretaría de E.P., 1975) were published after her tragic death in Israel.

7. Carballo, *Diecinueve protagonistas*, p. 414.

8. José Emilio Pacheco, editor of Rosario Castellano's *El uso de la palabra* (Mexico City: Excelsior, 1974), introduces her numerous articles.

9. Carlos González Peña, *History of Mexican Literature*, 3d ed. (Dallas: Southern Methodist University Press, 1968), pp. 438–439.

10. Rosario Castellanos, *Balún Canán* (Mexico: Fondo de Cultura Económica, 1957). Page references for quotations in the text are to this edition.

11. Rosario Castellanos, "La novela mexicana contemporánea y su valor testimonial," *Hispania* 47 (1964), 223,230.

12. Octavio Paz, *The Labyrinth of Solitude* (New York: Grove Press, 1961), pp. 29–46.

BEATRIZ GUIDO

1. Christine Mary Gibson, "Cinematic Techniques in the Prose Fiction of Beatriz Guido," doctoral dissertation, Michigan State University, 1974. Biographical material can be found in the second chapter "Beatriz Guido, the Writer, the Scenarist."

2. Diane Salomón Birkemoe, "Contemporary Women Novelists of Argentina," doctoral dissertation, University of Illinois, 1968.

3. Carlos Viola Soto, "La casa del ángel," *Sur* 235 (July–August 1955), 95–96.

4. David Lagmanovich, "La narrativa argentina de 1960 a 1970," *La nueva narrativa hispanoamericana* II, 1 (January 1972), 99–117.

5. Isis Tuel, "Style and Structure in the Works of Beatriz Guido," master's thesis, University of Oklahoma, 1969.

6. Alejandro Hidalgo, "Beatriz Guido: *Escándalos y soledades,* o la anti-novela política," *Atlántida* LII, 12 (October 1970), 8–9.

7. Oscar Hermes Villordo, "La mano en la trampa," *Sur* 275 (March–April 1962), 109–110.

8. Norma Dumas, "Beatriz Guido y Torres Nilsson frente a frente," *Platea* II (July 7, 1961), 15–17. There are many good articles that relate novel and movies and take Guido in consideration; Mireya Bottone has written a book *La literatura argentina y el cine* (Rosario: Universidad Nacional del Litoral, 1964).

9. Beatriz Guido, *Fín de fiesta* (Buenos Aires: Editorial Losada, 1964). Page references for quotations in the text are to this edition.

ELENA GARRO

1. Carlos González Peña, *History of the Mexican Literature,* 3d ed. (Dallas: Southern Methodist University Press, 1968), p. 455.

2. Garro was a member of a group called Poesía en Voz Alta that read and put on plays. Plays written for this group were later collected in the

volume *Hogar sólido y otras piezas en un acto* (Mexico: Universidad Veracruzana, 1958). The play that made her famous, "La señora en su balcón," has been republished and appears in *Teatro hispanoamericano contemporáneo* (Madrid: Aguilar, 1970).

3. José Miguel Oviedo, in "Notas a una deprimente lectura del teatro hispanoamericano," affirms that Garro achieves "una muy lograda versión latinoamericana del teatro del absurdo"—in *Revista Iberoamericana* 76–77 (Julio–Diciembre 1971), 758.

4. See Manuel Durán's "El Premio Villaurrutia y la novela mexicana contemporánea," *La Torre* XIII (1965), 237.

5. Gabriela Mora, "A Thematic Exploration of the Works of Elena Garro," in *Latin American Women Writers Yesterday and Today* (Pittsburgh: Carnegie Mellon, 1975).

6. Elena Garro, *Los recuerdos del porvenir* (Mexico City: Joaquín Mortiz, 1963). Page references for quotations in the text are to this edition. This novel has been translated into English with the title *Recollections of Things to Come* (Austin: University of Texas Press, 1969).

7. Alicia de Bonfils, *La literatura cristera* (Mexico City: Instituto Nacional de Antropología e Historia, 1970).

LUISA JOSEFINA HERNANDEZ

1. Carlos González Peña, *History of Mexican Literature*, 3d ed. (Dallas: Southern Methodist University Press, 1968), p. 458.

2. Walter M. Langford, *The Mexican Novel Comes of Age* (Notre Dame, Ind.: University of Notre Dame Press, 1971), pp. 188–91.

3. Silvia Jean Brann, "El teatro y las novelas de Luisa Josefina Hernández," doctoral dissertation at the University of Illinois, 1971, pp. 188–191.

4. In Hernández' novel *Nostalgia de Troya* the protagonist evokes Cuba.

5. See Francesca Colecchia and Julio Matas, *Selected Latin American One-Act Plays* (Pittsburgh: University of Pittsburgh Press, 1973), pp. 125–140.

6. Gloria Feiman Waldman, "Three Female Playwrights Explore Contemporary Latin American Reality: Myrna Casas, Griselda Gambaro and Luisa Josefina Hernández," in *Latin American Women Writers* (Pittsburgh: Carnegie Mellon, 1975), pp. 74–84. There is a very good article about her plays in Leon Lyday and George W. Woodyard's *Dramatists in Revolt* (Austin: University of Texas Press, 1976).

7. Luisa Josefina Hernández, *La cólera secreta* (Xalapa: Universidad Veracruzana, 1964). Page references for quotations in the text are to this edition.

ELENA PONIATOWSKA

1. There is a biography in María Luisa Mendoza's *Oiga usted* (Mexico City: Ediciones Soma, 1973), pp. 86–88.

2. Beth Miller, "Interview with Elena Poniatowska," *Latin American Literary Review* IV (Fall-Winter 1975), pp. 72–78. In that interview Poniatowska mentions her other work, *Los cuentos de Lilus Kikus.*

3. Elena Poniatowska's *Todo empezó en Domingo* and *La noche de Tlatelolco* had been published to some acclaim: *La noche . . .* has been translated by Helen Lane with the title *Massacre in Mexico* (New York: Viking Press, 1971).

4. In *Oiga usted*, p. 90. Also Charles Tatum has written about Poniatowska; see *Latin American Women Writers* (Pittsburgh: Carnegie Mellon, 1975), pp. 49–58.

5. Elena Poniatowska, *Hasta no verte, Jesús mío* (Mexico City: Ediciones Era, 1973). Page references to quotations in the text are to this edition.

BIBLIOGRAPHY

MARIA DE ZAYAS

Alborg, Juan Luis. *Historia de la literatura española.* Madrid: Editorial Gredos, 1972.

Goyri de Menéndez Pidal, Maria. *La difunta pleiteada, estudio de literatura comparada.* Madrid: 1909.

Morby, Edwin, "The Difunta Pleiteada Theme in María de Zayas." *Hispanic Review* XVI (1948), 238–242.

Pfandl, Ludwig. *Historia de la literatura nacional española en la Edad de oro.* Barcelona, 1933, pp. 369–370.

Place, Edwin. "María de Zayas, An Outstanding Woman Short-Story Writer of the Seventeenth Century Spain." *University of Colorado Studies* XIII, 1 (1923), 26–30.

Praag, J. A. van. "Sobre las novelas de María de Zayas." *Clavileño* XV (1952).

Senabre, Ricardo. "La fuente de una novela de doña María de Zayas." *Revista de Filología Española* XLVI (1963) 163–172.

Serrano Poncela, Segundo. "Casamientos engañosos (Doña María de Zayas, Scarron y un proceso de creación literaria)." *Bulletin Hispanique* LXIV (1962), 248–259.

———. *Apuntes para un estudio de escritoras españolas desde el año 1401 al 1833.* 2 vols. Madrid, 1903–1905.

Sylvania, Lena. *Doña María de Zayas y Sotomayor.* New York: AMS Press, 1966.

Ticknor, George. Vol. III, *Histoire de la littérature espagnole*. Paris, 1864–72.

Zayas, María de. *Novelas amorosas y ejemplares*. Madrid: Aldus, 1948.

———. *Desengaños amorosos*. Madrid: Aldus, 1950.

———. *Nouvelles de Dona María de Zayas*. Paris: La Boutique de G. Quinot, MDLXXX.

———. *Novelas de doña María de Zayas*, selected by Emilia Pardo Bazán. Madrid: Biblioteca de la Mujer, 1892. Vol. III.

FERNAN CABALLERO

Asencio, José María. *Fernán Caballero y la novela contemporánea*. Madrid: Rivadeneyra, 1893.

Barja, Cesar. *Libros y autores modernos*. New York, 1924.

Becher, Hubert, *Personalidades españolas, Doña Francisca de Larrea Bohl de Faber*. Biblioteca Menéndez y Pelayo, 1931 and 1932.

Blanco, García F. *La literatura española en el siglo XIX*. Madrid, 1891–94.

Caballero, Fernán [also Bohl de Faber, Cecilia]. *Obras completas*. 17 vols., 1893–1914.

———. *Clemencia*. Madrid, 1892.

———. *Elía*. Madrid, 1857.

———. *La familia de Alvareda*. Madrid, 1856.

———. *La gaviota*. Madrid, El Heraldo, 1849.

Cotareo y Mori, Emilio. *Estudios de historia literaria de España*. Madrid, 1901.

Coloma, Luis. *Recuerdos de Fernán Caballero*. Bilbao, n.d.

Fitzmaurice-Kelly, James. *A New History of Spanish Literature*. Oxford, 1926.

Gomez de Baquero. *Novelas y novelistas*. Madrid, 1918.

———. *El renacimiento de la novela en el siglo XIX*. Madrid, 1924.

———. *De Gallardo a Unamuno*. Madrid, 1926.

Gonzalez Blanco, A. *Historia de la novela en España desde el romanticismo hasta nuestros días*. Madrid, 1909.

Heinerman, Theodor. *Cecilia Bohl de Faber y Juan Eugenio Hartzenbusch*. Madrid: Espasa, 1944.

Herrero, Gabriel. *Fernán Caballero: Nuevo planteamiento*. Madrid: Gredos, 1963.

Hesper, T.E.L. "The Genesis of *La familia Alvareda*," *Hispanic Review* II (1934).

———. "Francisca de Larrea, A Spanish Feminist of the Early Century." *Hispania* XXII (1930).

Hurtado, Juan, and González Palencia Angel. *Historia de la literatura española*. Madrid, 1925.

Madariaga, Salvador de. *The Genius of Spain*. Oxford, 1923.

Menéndez y Pelayo, Marcelino. *Estudios de crítica literaria*. Madrid, 1893–1908.

Montesinos, Jose. *Introducción a una historia de la novela*. Madrid: Editorial Castalia, 1966.

———. *Fernán Caballero: Ensayo de justificación*. Mexico City: El Colegio de 1961.

Morel Fatio, Alfred. "Fernán Caballero d'après sa correspondance avec Antoine de Latour." *Bulletin Hispanique* III (1901).

———. *Etudes sur L'Espagne*. Paris, 1888–1925.

Palma, Angélica. *Fernán Caballero: La novela novelable*. Bilbao, 1931.

Pitollet, C. "Les Premiers Essais littéraires de Fernán Caballero." *Bulletin Hispanique* IX (1907), X (1908).

———. "A propos de Fernán Caballero." *Bulletin Hispanique* XXXIII (1931).

———. "Deux Mots encore sur Fernán Caballero." *Bulletin Hispanique* XXXIV (1932).

Valencia, Diego de. *Cartas*. Madrid, 1919.

EMILIA PARDO BAZAN

Alas, Leopoldo [Clarín]. "Prólogo," in Pardo Bazán's *La cuestión palpitante*. Madrid: Imprenta Central, 1883.

Barja, Cesar. *Emilia Pardo Bazán*. Madrid: Editorial Molino, 1925.

———. *Libros y autores modernos*. Los Angeles: Las Américas, 1933.

Biles, Mary. "Pardo Bazan's Two Styles." *Hispania* (1965), 456–462.

Bravo Villasante, Carmen. "El patriotismo de dona Emilia Pardo Bazán." *Cuadernos hispanoamericanos* XLIX (Feb. 1962).

———. *Vida y obra de Emilia Pardo Bazán*. Madrid: Revista de Occidente, 1962.

Brown, Donald Fowler. *The Catholic Naturalism of Pardo Bazán*. Chapel Hill: University of North Carolina Press, 1957.

———. "Two Naturalists' Versions of Genesis: Zola and Pardo Bazán," *Modern Languages Notes* (Baltimore), June 1937, 243–248.

Chandler, Arthur. "The Role of Literary Tradition in the Novelistic Trajectory of Emilia Pardo Bazán." *Dissertation Abstracts* XVI, Doctoral dissertation, Ohio State University, 1950.

Clemessy, Nelly. *Emilia Pardo Bazán* Paris: Centro de Recherches Hispaniques, 1973.

Davis, Clifford. "The 'coletilla' to Pardo Bazán's *Cuestión palpitante*." *Hispanic Review* (Philadelphia) XXIV (1956), 50–64.

———. "The Critical Reception to Naturalism in Spain before *La cuestión palpitante*." *Hispanic Review* (Philadelphia) XXII (1954), 97–108.

Fowler, Donald. "The Influence of Émile Zola on the Novelistic and Critical Works of Emilia Pardo Bazán." Doctoral dissertation, University of Illinois, 1935.

González Lopez, Emilio. *Emilia Pardo Bazán, novelista de Galicia.* New York: Institute of Galicia, 1944.

Hilton, Ronald. "Emilia Pardo Bazán et le mouvement féministe en Espagne." *Bulletin Hispanique* (Bordeaux) LIV (1952), 153–164.

———. "Pardo Bazán and Literary Polemics about Feminism." *The Romantic Review* XLIV (1953), 80–99.

———. "Pardo Bazán and the Spanish Problem." *Modern Language Quarterly* (Washington) XIII (1952), 292–298.

———. "Pardo Bazán's Analysis of the Social Structure of Spain." *Bulletin of Hispanic Studies* (Liverpool) XIX (1952), 1–15.

Nilken, Margarita. *Las escritoras españolas.* Barcelona: Editorial Labor, 1930.

Osborne, Robert. *Emilia Pardo Bazán, su vida y sus obras.* Mexico: Ediciones Andrea, 1964.

———. "Emilia Pardo Bazán y la novela rusa," *Revista Hispánica Moderna* (New York) XX (1954), 273–281.

Pardo Bazán, Emilia. *La cuestión palpitante.* Madrid: Imprenta Central, 1883.

———. *Obras completas.* Madrid: Aguilar, 1957. 2 vols.

Pattison, Walter B. *El naturalismo español.* Madrid: Editorial Gredos, 1965).

Perez, Minik. *Novelistas españoles de los siglos XIX y XX.* Madrid: Editorial Gresos, 1965.

Senob, Alice. "Pardo Bazán and Naturalism." Doctoral dissertation, University of Arizona, 1933.

Valera, Juan. *Obras de crítica literaria.* Madrid: Aguilar, 1949.

Zulueta, Emilia de. *Historica de la crítica española contemporánea.* Madrid: Editorial Gredos, 1966.

CONCHA ESPINA

Alemany, José "Voces de Maragatería y de otra procedencia." *Boletín de la la Academia Española* III 1915; ———, ———, 1916.

Alvarez Palacios, Hernando. *Novela y cultura española de post-guerra.* Madrid: Edicusa, 1975.

Cano, Juan. "La mujer en la novela de Concha Espina." XXII, 1939, 51–60.

Cansinos-Assens, Rafael. *La nueva literatura.* Madrid: Renacimiento, 1917.

———. *Las literaturas del Norte. Concha Espina.* Madrid, 1929.

Cejador y Frauca, Julio. *Historia de la lengua y literatura castellana.* Madrid: Tipografía de Archivos, Bibliotecas y Museos, 1919–1922. Vol. 10–14.

Douglas, Frances. "Recent Works by Concha Espina." *Hispania* VI (1923), 185–187.

———. "Concha Espina: A New Star Ascendant," *Hispania* VII (1924), 111–20.

Espina, Concha. *Obras completas,* 2d ed. Madrid: Ediciones Fax, 1955. 2 vols.

———. *Agua de nieve.* Madrid: Renacimiento, 1912.

———. *El amor de las estrellas.* Madrid: Renacimiento, 1916.

———. *Altar mayor.* Madrid: Renacimiento, 1926.

———. *El cáliz rojo.* Madrid: Renacimiento, 1923.

———. *Despertar para morir.* Madrid: Renacimiento, 1910.

———. *Dulce nombre.* Madrid: Renacimiento, 1921.

———. *La esfinge maragata.* Madrid: Renacimiento, 1914.

———. *El metal de los muertos.* Madrid: Renacimiento, 1920.

———. *La niña de Luzmela.* Madrid: Renacimiento, 1909.

———. *Las niñas desaparecidas.* Madrid: Renacimiento, 1927.

———. *El príncipe del cantar.* Madrid: Renacimiento, 1929.

Fría Lagoni, Mauro. *Concha Espina y sus críticos.* Toulouse: Ed. Figarola Maurin, 1929.

Romera Navarro, Miguel. *El hispanismo en Norte America.* Madrid: Renacimiento, 1917.

———. *Historia de la literatura española,* Boston: Heath, 1928.

Rosenberg, Millard. "Concha Espina." *Hispania* (1927).

Serrano Poncela, Segundo. *La novela española contemporánea.* Madrid: La Torre, 1953.

CARMEN LAFORET

Alborg, Juan Luis. *Hora actual de la novela española.* Madrid: Taurus, 1962.

Allot, Miriam. *Los novelistas y la novela.* Barcelona: Seix Barral 1966.

Ayala, Francisco. "Testimonio de la nada." *Realidad* (Buenos Aires), 1947.

Buckley, Ramon. *Problemas formales en la novela española contemporánea.* Barcelona: Editorial Península, 1973.

Castilla del Pino, M. *Cuatro ensayos sobre la mujer.* Madrid: Alianza Editorial, 1971.

Corrales Egea, José. *La novela española actual.* Madrid: Editorial Cuadernos para el Dialogo, 1971.

El Saffar, Ruth. "Structural and Thematic Tactics of Suppression in Carmen Laforet's *Nada,*" *Symposium,* 28, 1954.

Eoff, Sherman. "*Nada* by Carmen Laforet," *Hispania* XXV (1952).

Escolar, Hipólito, and García Mazas, José. *Primera antología sonora de autores contemporáneos.* Philadelphia: Chilton Books, 1965.

Feal Deibe, Carlos. "*Nada*: La iniciación de una adolescente," *The Analysis of Hispanic Texts.* New York: The Bilingual Press, 1976.

Foster, William David. "Nada de Carmen Laforet: Ejemplo de neo-romance en la novela contemporánea," *Revista Hispánica Moderna* XXXII, 1-2 (Jan. 1966).

García-Viñó, Manuel. *La novela española de post-guerra.* Madrid: Publicaciones Españolas, 1971.

Hoppe, Else. *El hombre en la literatura de la mujer.* Madrid: Editorial Gredos, 1960.

Illanes Adaro, Graciela. *La novelística de Carmen Laforet.* Madrid: Editorial Gredos, 1971.

Laforet, Carmen. *Nada.* Barcelona, Ediciones Destino, 1944.

———. *La insolación.* Barcelona: Editorial Planeta, 1963.

———. *La isla y los demonios.* Barcelona: Ediciones Destino, 1952.

———. *La llamada.* Barcelona: Ediciones Destino, 1952.

———. *Mis páginas mejores.* Madrid: Ediciones Grepus, 1956.

———. *La mujer nueva.* Barcelona: Ediciones Destino, 1955.

———. *Novelas.* Barcelona: Editorial Planeta, 1965. Vol. I.

———. *Obras,* Vol. I. Barcelona, 1957.

Martínez Cachero, J. M. *La novela española entre 1939 y 1969.* Madrid: Editorial Castalia, 1973.

Meyer, Spacks, Patricia. "Taking Care: Some Women Novelists." *Novel* (Fall 1972).

Moya, Carlos. "Familia e ideología política," *Las ideologías en la España de hoy.* Madrid: Seminarios y Ediciones, 1972.

Ordoñez, Elizabeth. "*Nada*: Bourgeois Initiation," *The Analysis of Hispanic Texts: Current Trends in Methodology.* New York, 1976.

Paz Velásquez, Flavia. "Las imágenes de la mujer en la novela actual," *La verdad sobre la mujer,* edited by M. A. Pascual. Madrid: Iter Ediciones, 1970.

Prjevalinsky Ferrer, Olga. "Las novelístas españolas de hoy," *Cuadernos Americanos* XX, 5 (1961).

Sobejano, Gonzalo. *Novela española de nuestro tiempo.* Madrid: Editorial Prensa Española, 1970.

Ullman, Pierre. "The Moral Structure of Carmen Laforet's Novels," in *The Vision Obscured,* edited by Melvin J. Friedman. New York: Fordham University Press, 1970.

Villegas, Juan. "*Nada* de Carmen Laforet, o, la infantilización de la aventura legendaria," *La estructura mítica del heroe en la novela del siglo XX.* Barcelona: Editorial Planeta, 1973.

ELENA QUIROGA

Alborg, Juan Luis. *Historia de la literatura española.* Madrid: Editorial Gredos, 1966.

Corrales Egea, José. *La novela española actual.* Madrid: Edicusa, 1971.

Garcia-Viñó, Manuel. *La novela española del post-guerra.* Madrid: Publicaciones españolas, 1971.

Gilcasado, Pablo. *La novela social española.* Madrid: Editorial Seix Barral, 1968.

Hoppe, Else. *El hombre en la literatura de la mujer.* Madrid: Ed. Gredos, 1960.

Iglesias la Guna, Antonio. *Treinta años de novela española.* Madrid: Prensa Española, 1970.

Quiroga, Elena. *Viento del norte.* Barcelona: Editorial Destino, 1951.

———. *Algo pasa en la calle,* Editorial Destino, 1954.

———. *La enferma* Editorial Destino, 1955.

———. *La sangre,* Editorial Destino, 1953.

———. *Tristura,* Editorial Destino, 1961.

Ríoseco, Arturo. "Tres novelistas española de hoy." *Revista hispánica moderna,* 31, 1965.

Sáinz de Robles, Federico. *La novela española del siglo XX.* Madrid: Pegaso, 1921.

Schwartz, Ronald. *Spain's New Wave Novelists, 1950–1974.* Metuchen, N.J.: Scarecrow Press, 1976.

ELENA SORIANO

Alvarez Palacios, Fernando. *Novela y cultura española de post-guerra.* Madrid: Edicusa, 1975. (Interview with E.S.)

Domingo, José. *La novela del siglo XX.* Barcelona: Ed. Labor, 1973. 2 vols.

Iglesias Laguna, Antonio. *Treinta años de novela española.* Madrid: Ed. Prensa Española, 1970.

Marías, Julián, and Bleiberg, German. *Diccionario de literatura española.* Madrid: Revista de Occidente, 1964.

Saínz Robles, Federico. *La novela española del siglo XX.* Madrid: Pegaso, 1921.

Soriano, Elena. "La abuela loca." *Aglae.* October 14, 1952.

———. "Las bachas." *Indice de Artes y Letras.* Number 107. (no date), 1967.

———. *Caza menor.* Madrid: Ed. Calleja, 1951.

———. *Espejismos.* Madrid: Ed. Calleja, 1955.

———. *Medea 55.* Madrid: Ed. Calleja, 1955.

———. "Los novios viejos." *Teresa,* March 1954.

______. "El perfume." *Destino.* November 19, 1949.

______. *La playa de los locos.* Madrid: Ed. Calleja, 1955.

______. "El testigo falso." *El español,* 1952.

______. "Tres sueños." *Indice de Artes y Letras.* Number 207. (no date), 1966.

______. "Viajera de segunda." *Revista de literatura,* 1952.

______. "El viejo pipero." *Solidaridad nacional,* May 29, 1949.

DOLORES MEDIO

Domingo, Jose. *La novela del siglo XX.* Barcelona: Ed. Labor, 1973.

Gil Casado, Pablo. *La novela social española.* Barcelona: Seix Barral, 1968.

Iglesias Laguna, Antonio. *Treinta años de novela española.* Madrid: Ed. Prensa Española, 1970.

Medio, Dolores. *Andrés.* Oviedo: Editora Richard Grandio, 1967; Barcelona: Editora Picazo, 1973.

______. *El bachancho.* Madrid: Emesa, 1974.

______. *Bibiana.* Madrid: Bullon, 1963; Barcelona: Destino, 1967.

______. *Biografía de Isabel II de España.* Madrid: Rivadeneira, 1966.

______. *Biografía de Selma Lagerlof.* Madrid: Espesa, 1971.

______. *Compás de espera.* Barcelona: Editorial Plaza, 1954.

______. *Diario de una maestra.* Barcelona: Destino, 1961.

______. *El fabuloso imperio de Juan sin Tierra.* Barcelona: Plaza Janes, 1978.

______. *Farsa de verano.* Madrid: Espasa Calpe, 1974.

______. *Funcionario público.* Barcelona: Destino, 1956.

———. *Guía de Asturias.* Barcelona: Destino, 1970.

———. *Mañana.* Madrid: Editorial Cid, 1954.

———. *El milagro de la noche de Reyes.* Burgos: Editora S. Rodríguez, 1948.

———. *Niña.* Madrid Colección Aguilar, 1945.

———. *Nosotros, los Rivero.* Barcelona: Editorial Destino, 1953.

———. *La otra circunstancia.* Barcelona: Destino, 1972.

———. *El pez sigue flotando.* Barcelona: Destino, 1956.

———. *El señor García.* Madrid: Alfaguara, 1966.

Saínz Robles, Federico. *El espíritu y la letra.* Madrid: Aguilar, 1966.

———, *La novela española en el siglo XX.* Madrid: Pegasui, 1957.

Schwartz, Ronald. *Spain's New Wave Novelists, 1950–1974.* Metuchen, N.J.: Scarecrow Press, 1976.

Winecoff, Janet. "Fictionalized Autobiography in the Novels of Dolores Medio." *Kentucky Foreign Language Quarterly* 13 (1966).

CONCHA ALOS

Alós, Concha. "Armor." *Aphra, The Feminist Literary Magazine* V, 1 (Winter 1973).

———, *El caballo rojo.* Barcelona: Editorial Planeta, 1966.

———, *Los cien pájaros.* Barcelona: Editorial G. P., 1967.

———, *Las hogueras.* Barcelona: Editorial Planeta, 1964.

———, *La madama.* Barcelona: Editorial Planeta, 1969.

———. *Os habla Electra.* Barcelona: Plaza Janes, 1975.

———, *Rey de gatos.* Barcelona: Barral Editores, 1972.

Bosch, Rafael. *La novela española del síglo XX.* New York: Las Américas, 1971.

Domingo, José. *La novela española del siglo XX.* Madrid: Colección Labor, 1973.

Rodríguez, Fermin. "La mujer en la sociedad española en la novelística de Concha Alós." Doctoral dissertation, University of Arizona, 1973.

Schwartz, Ronald. *Spain's New Wave Novelists 1950–1974.* Metuchen, N.J.: Scarecrow Press, 1976.

GERTRUDIZ GOMEZ DE AVELLANEDA

Aguirre, Mirta. *Influencia de la mujer en Iberoamérica.* Havana, 1948.

Arrom, José Juan. *Historia de la literatura dramática cubana.* New Haven, Conn.: Yale University Press, 1944.

Avellaneda, Gertrudiz Gómez de. *Antología.* Buenos Aires: Espasa Calpe, 1945.

———, *La baronesa de Jous.* Habana: Imp. la Prensa, 1844.

———, *Diario de amor.* Madrid: Aguilar, 1928.

———, *Dolores.* Habana: La Marina, 1860.

———, *Dos mujeres.* Madrid: Gabinete Literario, 1842.

———, *Espatolino,* Novela original. Habana: Imp. la Prensa, 1844.

———, *Guatimozín.* Madrid: Imp. Espinosa, 1846.

———, *Leoncia.* Madrid: Tip. Arch. Biblioteca, 1917.

———, *La mano de Dios.* Matanzas: Imp. Gobierno, 1853.

———, *Obras de la Avellaneda.* La Habana: Imp. Biblioteca Nacional, 1914. 6 vols.

———, *El príncipe de Viana.* Madrid: Repulles, 1844.

———, *Sab*. Madrid: Imp. Barco, 1841.

Ballesteros, Mercedes. *Vida de la Avellaneda*. Madrid: Ed. Cultura Hispánica, 1949.

Bucher Williams, Edwin. "The Life and Dramatic Works of Gertrudiz Gómez de Avellaneda." Doctoral dissertation, University of Pennsylvania, 1924.

Bueno, Salvador. "El epistolario amoroso de la Avellaneda." *Revista Cubana* XXXI.

Carilla, Emilio. *El romanticismo en la América Hispánica*. Madrid: Ed. Gredos, 1967.

Carlos, Alberto, "Rene, Werter, y la nouvelle Eloise," *Revista Iberoamericana* 31, 60 (1965).

Castillo de González, Aurelia. *Biografía de Gertrudiz Gómez de Avellaneda*. Havana: Imprenta Soler, 1887.

Cotarelo y Morti, Emilio. *La Avellaneda y sus obras*. Madrid, 1930.

Estenger, Rafael. *Los amores de cubanos famosos*. Havana: Alfa, 1939.

Figarola Caneda, Domingo. *Cartas inéditas de la Avellaneda*. Havana: Impresiones Biblioteca Nacional, 1914.

Henriquez Ureña, Max. *Panorama histórico de la literatura cubana*. New York: Las Américas, 1963. Vol. I.

Kelly, Edith. "Bibliografía de la Avellaneda." *Revista bimestral cubana* 35 (1935).

———. "La Avellaneda's *Sab* and the Political Situation in Cuba," *Américas* (Washington) I (1945).

Martí, José. "Juicio sobre la Avellaneda," in Martí's *Obras completas*. Havana: Ed. Trópico, 1940.

Pardo Bazán, Emilia. "La cuestión académica," *España moderna*, Feb. 1889.

Peers, Allison. "Side Lights on Byronism in Spain," *Revue Hispanique* 50 (1920).

Percas, Helena. "Sobre la Avellaneda y su novela *Sab*," *Revista Iberoamericana* (Mexico) XXVIII, 54 (July 1962).

Piñeyro, Enrique. *Gertrudiz Gómez de Avellaneda*. Havana: Consejo Nacional de Cultura, 1964.

CLORINDA MATTO DE TURNER

Aldrich, Earl. *The Modern Short Story in Peru*. Madison: University of Wisconsin Press, 1966.

Caréstegui, Narciso. *El padre Horán*. Lima:Imp. El Comercio, 1948.

Carrillo, Francisco. *Clorinda Matto de Turner y su indigenismo literario*. Lima: Ediciones de la Biblioteca Universitaria, 1967.

Castro Arenas, Mario. "La nueva novela peruana." *Cuadernos Hispanoamericanos* 31 (1961).

Crouse, Ruth Compton. "Clorinda Matto de Turner: An Analysis of Her Role in Peruvian Literature." Doctoral dissertation, Florida State University, 1964.

DeMello, George. "The Writings of Clorinda Matto de Turner." Doctoral dissertation, University of Colorado, 1969.

García Calderón, Francisco. *El Perou contemporain*. Paris, 1907.

Gold, Peter. "Indianismo and Indigenismo," *Romance Notes*. 14, 1940.

González Prada, Manuel. *Horas de lucha*. Buenos Aires: Editorial Americale, 1946.

Goodrich, Diane R. "Peruvian Novels of the Nineteenth Century." Doctoral dissertation, Indiana, 1966.

Leavitt, Sturgis. *A Tentative Bibliography of Peruvian Literature*. Cambridge, England, 1932.

McIntosh, C. B. "*Aves sin nido* and the Beginning of Indianismo." Doctoral dissertation, University of Virginia, 1932.

Mariátegui, José Carlos. *Siete ensayos de interpretación de la realidad peruana*. Lima, Biblioteca Amanta, 1964.

Matto de Turner, Clorinda. *Aves sin nido.* Buenos Aires: La Jouane, 1889. Lima: Ediciones Peisa, 1973.

———. *Boreales, miniaturas y porcelanas.* Buenos Aires: Juan Alsina, 1902.

———. *Herencia.* Lima: Imprenta Masias, 1895.

———, *Indole.* Lima: Bacigalupi, 1891.

———, *Tradiciones cuzqueñas y leyendas.* Arequipa: Imprenta la Bolsa, 1884.

———. *Viaje de recreo.* Valencia: F. Sampere y Compania, 1910.

Mendiburu, Manuel de. *Apuntes históricos del Peru.* Lima, 1902.

———. *Diccionario histórico-biográfico del Peru 1874–1890.*

Miller, John. "Clorinda Matto de Turner and Mercedes Cabello de Carbonera: Societal Criticism and Morality," in *Latin American Women Writers Yesterday and Today.* Pittsburgh: Carnegie Mellon University, 1975.

Reed, Ischer. "Curso de la novela femenina del Perú." Tesis, Lima: San Marcos, 1942.

Reinaga, Fausto. *El indio y los escritores de America.* La Paz: Ed. Don Bosco, 1968.

Sánches, Luis Alberta. *América sin novelistas.* Santiago: Ercilla, 1940.

———. *Escritores representativos de America.* Madrid: Gredos, 1957.

———. *La literatura del Perú.* Buenos Aires: Imp. de la Universidad, 1943.

———. *Proceso y contenido de la novela hispanoamericana.* Madrid: Gredos, 1953.

Tamayo Vargas, Augusto. *Literatura peruana.* Lima: n. p., 1953.

Tauro, Alberto. "Presencia y definición del indigenismo literario," *Memoria del II congreso internacional de literatura iberoamericana* (Los Angeles), 1944.

Urrello, A. "Antecedentes del indigenismo," *Cuadernos Hispanoamericanos* 268 (1972).

Valcárcel, Luis. *Ruta cultural del Perú.* Mexico City: Fondo de Cultura Económica, 1945.

———. "El indio en nuestra literatura," *Cuadernos* (Paris) 19 (July 1956).

Yepez, Miranda, Alfredo. "La novela indigenista," *Revista universitaria*, Cuzco, 1948.

MERCEDES CABELLO DE CARBONERA

Alegría, Fernando. *Historia de la novela hispanoamericana.* Mexico City: Studium, 1966.

Basadre, Jorge. *Historia de la república del Perú.* Lima: Ed. Cultura Antártida, 1949.

———. *Perú, Problema y posibilidad.* Lima, 1931.

Cabello de Carbonera, Mercedes. *Blanca Sol.* Lima: Imprenta Lopez Aguirre, 1888.

———. *Las consecuencias.* Lima: Ed. Torres Aguirre, 1880.

———. *El conspirador.* Lima: Imprenta "La Voce d'Italia," 1892.

———. *La novela moderna.* Lima: Hora del Hombre, 1948.

———. *Sacrificio y Recompensa.* Lima: Ed. Torres Aguirre, 1887.

Carrillo, Roberto. *La novela indoamericana.* Mexico: Col. Letras, 1937.

Coester, Alfred. *Historia literaria de la America Española.* 1929.

Grossmann, Rudolf. *Historia y problemas de la literatura latinoamericana.* Madrid: Revista de Occidente, 1969.

Petricón, Luis, and Juan Copello. *Estudios sobre la independencia económica del Perú.* Lima: Imprenta Nacional, 1874.

René, Gabriel. *Biblioteca peruana.* Chile, 1896.

Tamayo Vargas, Augusto. *Perú en trance de novela.* Lima: Ed. Baluarte, 1940.

Yepez del Castillo, Ernesto. *El Perú 1820–1920.* Lima: I&nstituto de Estudios Peruanos, 1929.

TERESA DE LA PARRA

Angarita Arvelo, Rafael. *Historia crítica de la novela en Venezuela.* Berlín: A. P. Leipzig, 1938.

Díaz Sánchez, Ramon. *Venezuela independiente.* Caracas: Fundación Mendoza, 1962.

———. *Teresa de la Parra: Claves para una interpretación.* Caracas: n. p., 1954.

Diaz Seijas, Pedro. *Historia y antología de la literatura venezolana.* Caracas, 1953. 2 vols.

Fox, Lucía. *Ensayos hispanoaméricanos.* Caracas: García e Hijo, 1966.

Fuente Mayor Ruiz, Victor. "La dimensión amorosa de la escritura." *Revista de la literatura hispanoamericana* I (1971).

Galao, José Antonio. "Hispanoamerica a través de sus novelas: *Ifigenia* o el hechizo de Europa." *Cuadernos Hispanoamericanos* 150 (1962).

Parra, Teresa. *Ifigenia.* Caracas, 1924.

———. *Las memorias de Mamá Blanca.* Caracas, 1929.

———. *Tres conferencias inéditas.* Caracas: Ediciones Garrido, 1961.

Paz Castillo, Fernando. "El sentido de intimidad en Teresa de la Parra," *Revista Nacional de cultura* 10, 72 (1949).

Picón Salas, Mariano. *Literatura venezolana.* Caracas: Edime, 1965.

Prisco, Rafael di. *Narrativa venezolana.* Madrid: Editorial Alcanzor, 1971.

Ralcliff, Dillwyn. *Venezuela Prose Fiction.* New York: Instituto Hispánico, 1933.

Stolk, Gloria. *Teresa de la Parra.* Caracas: Editorial Arte, 1978.

Waxman, Samuel. *Bibliography of the Belles Lettres of Venezuela.* Cambridge, England, 1935.

MARIA LUISA BOMBAL

Adams, M. Ian. *Three Authors of Alienation: Bombal, Onetti, Carpentier.* Austin and London: University of Texas Press, 1975.

Allen, Marta E. "Dos estilos de novela: Marta Brunet y María Luisa Bombal." *Revista Iberoamericana* 35 (1952), 63–91.

Alonso, Amado. "Aparición de una novelista." Introduction to *La última niebla,* 3d ed., p. 7–34. Santiago de Chile: Nascimento, 1962.

Bombal, María Luisa. *La amortajada.* Buenos Aires: Ediciones Sur, 1938.

———. "Historia de María Griselda." *Sur* 142 (Aug. 1946), 41–63.

———. *House of Mist.* New York: Farrar Straus, 1948.

———. "Mar, cielo y tierra." *Saber Vivir* 1 (Aug. 1940), 34, 35.

———. *Obras completas de María Luisa Bombal.* Clear Creek: American Hispanist, 1978.

———. *The Shrouded Woman.* New York: Farrar Straus, 1948.

———. "Las trenzas." *Saber Vivir* 2 (Sept. 1940), 36–37.

———. *La última niebla,* 2d ed. Santiago, Chile: Editorial Nascimiento, 1941.

Borges, Jorge Luis. "*La Amortajada.*" *Sur* 47 (August 1938), 80–81.

Brown, Catherine Meredith. "Haunted Hacienda." *Saturday Review of Literature,* 3 May 1947, 22.

Campbell, Margaret V. "The Vaporous World of María Luisa Bombal." *Hispania* 44, 3 (Sept. 1961), 415–419.

"Chile-Escapist." *Time* XLIX (April 14, 1947).

Correa, Carlos René. "María Luisa Bombal." *Atenea* 199 (1942), 17–22.

Díaz Arrieta, Hernán. *Historia personal de la literatura chilena.* Santiago: Empresa Editora Zig-Zag, 1954.

Goic, Cedomil. *La novela chilena: Los mitos degradados.* Santiago: Editorial Universitaria, 1968.

———. "*La última niebla:* Consideraciones en torno a la estructura de la novela contemporánea." *Anales de la Universidad de Chile* 128 (1963), 59–83.

———. "María Luisa Bombal." *Antología del cuento chileno.* Santiago: Instituto de Literatura Chilena, 1963.

Montes, Hugo, and Orlando, Julio. *Historia de la literatura chilena.* Santiago: Editorial del Pacífico, 1955.

Santana, Francisco. *La nueva generación de prosistas chilenos: Ensayo, biografía y referencias críticas.* Santiago: Editorial Nascimiento, 1949.

Silva Castro, Raúl. *Panorama de la novela chilena.* Mexico City: Fondo de Cultura Económica, 1955.

———. *Panorama literario de Chile.* Santiago: Editorial Universitaria, 1961.

Torres-Rioseco, Arturo. "El estilo en las novelas de María Luisa Bombal." *Ensayos sobre literatura latinoamericana,* 2d series. Berkeley: University of California Press, 1958.

White, Carolyn. "Fairy Tales Are the Enemies of Illusion," Paper read at *NEMLA,* Albany, N.Y., 1978.

SILVINA BULLRICH

Anderson Imbert, Enrique. *Historia de la literatura hispanoamericana,* 5th ed. Mexico City: Fondo de Cultura, 1966.

Arrieta, Rafael Alberto. *Historia de la literatura argentina.* Buenos Aires: Ediciones Peuser, 1959. Vol IV.

Bullrich, Silvina. *Los burgueses.* Buenos Aires, 1963.

———. *La creciente.* Buenos Aires, 1967.

———. *Entre mis veinte y treinta años*, Buenos Aires, 1970.

———. *El hechicero*. Buenos Aires, 1961.

———. *Mañana digo basta*. Buenos Aires, 1968.

———. *Un momento muy largo*. Buenos Aires, 1961.

———. *Los salvadores de la patria*. Buenos Aires, 1965.

———. *Tres novelas*. Buenos Aires: Sudamericana, 1966.

Dellepiane, Angela. "La novela argentina desde 1950 a 1965." *Revista Iberoamericana* XXXIV (1968).

Ghiano, Juan Carlos. *La novela argentina contemporánea 1940–1960*. Buenos Aires: D. G. Relaciones Culturales, 1960.

Mathieu, Corina. "Argentine Women in the Novels of Silvina Bullrich," *Latin American Women Writers Yesterday and Today*. Pittsburgh: Carnegie Mellon, 1975.

Pinto, Juan. *Panorama de la literatura argentina contemporánea*. Buenos Aires: Mundi, 1941.

Schwartz, Kessel. *A New History of Spanish American Fiction*. Coral Gables, Fla.: University of Miami Press, 1972.

Yahni, Roberto. *70 años de narrative argentina: 1900–1970*. Madrid: Alianza Editorial, 1970.

CLARA SILVA

Bordoll, Domingo Luis. *Antología de la poesía uruguaya contemporánea*. Montevideo: Dept. de Publicaciones, 1966.

Conde, Carmen. *Once grandes poetisas américo-hispanas*. Madrid: Ed. de Cultura Hispanica, 1967.

Gilbert de Pereda, Isabel. "Clara Silva." *Escritura*, 7, 1969.

Paganini, Alberto. *Cien autores del Uruguay*. Montevideo: Centro Editorial de America Latina, 1969.

Rama, Angel. *La generación crítica (1939–1969).* Montevideo: Arca, 1972.

Renfrew, Ileana, Letter to Lucía Fox. Sept. 1978.

Restuccia, Marta. Letter to Lucía Fox. Montevideo, 1978.

Silva, Clara. *El alma y los perros.* Montevideo, 1960.

———. *Las bodas.* Montevideo, 1960.

———. *La cabellera oscura.* Montevideo, 1945.

———. *Los delirios.* Montevideo, 1954.

———. *Genio y figura de Delmira Agustini.* Buenos Aires: Editorial Universitaria de Buenos Aires, 1968.

———. *Habitación testigo.* Montevideo, 1967.

———. *Memoria de la nada.* Montevideo, 1958.

———. *Preludio indiano y otros poemas.* Montevideo, 1961.

———. *La sobreviviente.* Montevideo: Ediciones Tauro, 1966.

Villarino, Idea. "Clara Silva," *Marcha,* 778, 1958.

Zum Felde, Alberto. *Indice crítico de la literatura hispanoamericana.* Mexico: Guarania, 1959.

———. *La narrativa hispanoamericana.* Madrid: Aguilar, 1964.

———. *Proceso histórico del Uruguay.* Montevideo, 1969.

MARTA BRUNET

Brunet, Marta. *Aguas abajo.* Santiago de Chile: Ed. Cruz del Sur, 1943.

———. *Amasijo.* Santiago: Ed. Zig-Zag, 1962.

———. *Bestia dañina.* Santiago: Ed. Nascimiento, 1926.

———. *Bienvenido.* Santiago: Ed. Nascimiento, 1929.

———. *Humo hacia el sur*. Buenos Aires: Ed. Losada, 1946.

———. *La mampara*. Buenos Aires: Ed. Emece, 1946.

———. *María Nadie*. Santiago: Ed. Zig-Zag, 1957.

———. *María Rosa, flor de Quillén*. Santiago: La Novela Nueva, 1929.

———. *Montaña adentro*. Santiago: Ed. Nascimiento, 1923.

———. *Raiz del sueño*. Santiago: Zig-Zag, 1949.

Castillo, Homero. "Marta Brunet." *Revista Iberoamericana* XXIII, 45 (1958).

Chase, Kathleen. "Latin American Women Writers: Their Present Position," in *Books Abroad* XXXIII, 2 (1959).

Cruz, Pedro. *Estudios sobre literatura chilena*. Santiago: Ed. Nascimiento, 1940.

Díaz Arrieta, Hernán. *Historia personal de la literatura chilena*. Santiago: Ed. Zig-Zag, 1954.

———. *Panorama de la literatura chilena del siglo XX*. Santiago: Ed. Nascimiento, 1931. [Writing as "Alone."]

García Oldin, Fernando. *Doce escritores*. Santiago: Ed. Nascimiento, 1929.

Latorre, Mariano. *La literatura de Chile*. Buenos Aires: Facultad de Filosofía y Letras, 1941.

Merino Reyes, Luis. *Panorama de la literatura chilena*. Washington, D.C.: Unión Panamericana, 1961.

Mistral, Gabriela. "Sobre Marta Brunet," *Repertorio Americano* (San José de Costa Rica) XVII, 6 (1928).

Rodríguez Monegal, Emir. "Marta Brunet en su ficción y en la realidad," *Marcha* (Montevideo) (Jan. 1955).

Rosales, César. "Humo hacia el sur." *Sur* 138 (1946).

Sutton, Louis Marie. "Marta Brunet and *María Nadie.*" *Books Abroad* XXXIII, 4 (1959).

Valenzuela, Victor. "Marta Brunet y *María Nadie,*" *La Nueva Democracia* (New York) 2 (1950).

———. "Marta Brunet," *Revista Hispánica Moderna* XXIV, 2 (1958).

ROSARIO CASTELLANOS

Baptiste, Victor. "La obra poética de Rosario Castellanos." Doctoral dissertation, University of Illinois, 1966.

Brushwood, John. *Mexico in Its Novel: A Nation's Search for Identity.* Notre Dame, Ind.: University of Notre Dame Press, 1971.

Carballo, Emmanuel. *Diecinueve protagonistas de la literatura mexicana del siglo XX.* Mexico: Empresas Editoriales, 1965.

Castellanos, Rosario. *Album de familia.* Mexico City: Mortiz, 1971.

———. *Balún Canán.* Mexico City: Letras Mexicanas, 1957.

———. "Cartas a Elías Nandino," *Revista de Bellas Artes* 18 (1974).

———. *Ciudad real.* Xalapa: Ed. U. Veracruzana, 1960.

———. *Los convidados de agosto.* Mexico City: Eds. Era, 1964.

———. *El eterno femenino.* Mexico City: Fondo de Cultura Económica, 1975.

———. *Juicios sumarios.* Xalapa: Ed. U. Veracruzana, 1966.

———. *Lívida luz.* Mexico City: Unam, 1960.

———. *El mar y sus pescaditos.* Mexico City: Secretaria de E. P., 1975.

———. *Materia memorable.* Mexico City: Unam, 1969.

———. *Mujer que sabe Latín.* Mexico City: Sep Setentas, 1973.

———. "La novela mexicana contemporánea y su valor testimonial." *Hispania* 47 (1964).

———. *Oficio de tinieblas.* Mexico City: Joaquín Mortíz, 1962.

———. *El uso de la palabra.* Mexico City: Ed. Excelsior, 1974.

Dybvig, R. *Rosario Castellanos, biografía y novelística.* Mexico City, 1964.

González Peña, Carlos. *History of Mexican Literature.* Dallas: Southern Methodist University Press, 1968.

Hurtado, Alfredo. "*Balún Canán* de Rosario Castellanos," *Estaciones* 3 (1957).

Langford, Walter. *The Mexican Novel Comes of Age.* Notre Dame Ind. University of Notre Dame Press, 1971.

Leal, Luis. *Breve historia de la literatura hispanoamericana.* New York: Alfred Knopf, 1971.

Megged, Nalum. "Entre soledad y búsqueda de diálogo," *Los Universitarios* (Mexico City).

Millán, Carmen, "En torno a *Oficio de tinieblas,*" *Anuario de Letras* 3 (1963).

Passafart, Clara. *Los cambios y estructura de la narrativa mexicana.* Rosario, Mexico: Universidad Nacional del Litoral, 1968.

Paz, Octavio. *The Labyrinth of Solitude.* New York: Grove Press, 1961.

Schwartz, Kessel. *A New History of Spanish American Fiction.* Coral Gables, Fla.: University of Miami Press, 1971.

Sommers, Joseph. "Changing View of the Indian in Mexican Literature," *Hispania* 47 (1964).

———. "Rosario Castellanos: Nuevo enfoque del indio mexicano," *La palabra y el hombre* 8 (1964).

———. "Traven y Castellanos," *Hispania* 1 (1961).

Urrutía, Elena. "Los últimos libros en prosa de Rosario Castellanos," *Los Universitarios* (Mexico City) 1975.

Vogt, Evon. *Los Zinacantecos: Un grupo maya del siglo XX.* Mexico City: Sepsetentas, 1969.

BEATRIZ GUIDO

Barkham, John. "An Interview with Argentine Novelist." *The Sunday Post Tribune* (Indianapolis), July 31, 1966.

Birkemoe, Diane Solomon. "Contemporary Women Novelists of Argentina 1945–1967." Doctoral dissertation, University of Illinois, 1968.

Bottone, Mireya. *La literatura y el cine.* Rosario, Mexico: Universidad del Litoral, 1964.

Cambours Ocampo, Arturo. *El problema de las generaciones literarias.* Buenos Aires, 1963.

Dellepiane, Angela. "La novela argentina desde 1950 a 1965," *Revista Iberoamericana* XXXIV (1968).

Dumas, Norma. "Beatriz Guido y Torres Nilsson frente a frente," *Platea* II (July 7, 1961).

Gibson, Christine. "Cinematic Techniques in the Prose Fiction of Beatriz Guido." Doctoral dissertation, Michigan State University, 1974.

Guido, Beatriz. "La agonía del escritor frente al cine," in *Semana de la literatura y cine argentino.* Mendoza: Universidad Nacional de Cuyo, 1972.

———. *La caída.* Buenos Aires: Losada, 1956.

———. *La casa del ángel.* Buenos Aires: Emece, 1955.

———. *Escándalos y soledades.* Buenos Aires: Losada, 1970.

———. *Estar en el mundo.* Buenos Aires: Ateneo, 1950.

———. *Fín de fiesta.* Buenos Aires: Losada, 1958.

———. *El incendio y las vísperas.* Buenos Aires: Losada, 1961.

———. *Los insomnes.* Buenos Aires: Ediciones Corregidor, 1973.

______. *Los dos Albertos en la novela contemporánea: Camus, Moravia.* Rosario, Mexico: Ed. Confluencia, 1950.

______. *Una madre.* Buenos Aires: Emece, 1973.

______. *La mano en la trampa.* Buenos Aires: Losada, 1961.

______. *El ojo único de la ballena.* Buenos Aires: Ed. Merlin, 1971.

______. *Regreso a los hilos.* Buenos Aires: Ateneo, 1947.

______. "Un testimonio autobiográfico," *Atlantida* LII (Oct. 1970).

Hidalgo, Alejandro. "Beatriz Guido: *Escándalos y soledades,* o la anti-novela política." *Atlántida* 12 (Oct. 1970).

Lagmanovich, David. "La narrativa argentina de 1960 a 1970." *La nueva narrativa hispanoamericana* II, 1 (Jan. 1972).

Rodríguez Monegal, Emir. *El arte de narrar.* Caracas: Monte Avila, 1968.

Soto, Carlos. "*La casa del ángel.*" *Sur* 235 (July–Aug., 1955).

Tuel, Isis. "Style and Structure in the Works of Beatriz Guido." Doctoral dissertation, University of Oklahoma, 1969.

Villordo, Oscar. "*La mano en la trampa.*" *Sur* 275 (March–April 1962).

ELENA GARRO

Bonfils, Alicia de. *La literatura cristera.* Mexico: Instituto Nacional de Antropología e Historia, 1970.

Brushwood, John. *Mexico in Its Novel.* Austin: University of Texas Press, 1966.

Dauster, Frank. *Historia del teatro hispanoamericano.* Mexico City: Ediciones de Andrea, 1966.

______. "El teatro de Elena Garro: Evasión e ilusión." *Revista Iberoamericana* XXX, 57 (1964).

Durán, Manuel. "El premio Villa Urrutia y la novela mexicana contemporánea," *La Torre,* XIII, 1965.

Fox-Lockert. "The Meaning of Freedom in the Mexican Feminist Novel." Sixth Conference of Ethnic Studies, University of Wisconsin-LaCrosse, 1978.

Garro, Elena. *Andarse por las ramas.* Mexico City, 1957.

———. "La culpa es de los Taxcaltecas," in *Narrativa mexicana de hoy.* Madrid: Alianza Editorial, 1969.

———. *Hogar sólido y otras piezas en un acto.* Xalapa: Universidad Veracruzana, 1958.

———. *La mudanza.* 1959.

———. *Recollections of Things to Come.* Austin: University of Texas Press, 1969.

———. *Los recuerdos del porvenir.* Mexico City: Ed. Joaquín Mortíz, 1963.

———. *La semana de colores.* Xalapa: Universidad Veracruzana, 1964.

———. "La señora en su balcón." *Teatro hispanoamericano contemporáneo.* Madrid, 1970.

———. "Testimonios sobre Mariana." *Espejo* (Mexico City) 4 (1967).

González Peña, Carlos. *History of Mexican Literature.* Dallas: Southern Methodist University Press, 1968.

Jodorowski, Alejandro. "Hacia un teatro nacional." *Espejo* (Mexico City) 4 (1967).

Langford, Walter. *The Mexican Novel Comes of Age.* Notre Dame, Ind.: University of Notre Dame Press, 1971.

Leal, Luis. *Breve historia de la literatura hispanoamericana.* New York: Alfred Knopf, 1971.

Mora, Juan Miguel. *Panorama del teatro en México.* Mexico City: Editora Latinoamericana, 1970.

Mora, Gabriela. "A Thematic Exploration of the Works of Elena Garro," in *Latin American Women Writers Yesterday and Today.* Pittsburgh: Carnegie-Mellon, 1975.

Oviedo, Jose Miguel. "Notas a una deprimente lectura del teatro hispanoamericano." *Revista Iberoamericana,* 1971.

Solórzano, Carlos. *Teatro latinoamericano en el siglo XX.* Mexico City: Pormaca, 1964.

LUISA JOSEFINA HERNANDEZ

Acosta, Leonardo. "Luisa Josefina Hernández, novelista." *Casa de las Américas* 7, 40 (1967).

Brann, Silvia Jean, "El teatro y las novelas de Luisa Josefina Hernández." Doctoral dissertation, University of Illinois, 1971.

Brushwood, John. *Mexico and Its Novel.* Austin: University of Texas Press, 1966.

Caraballido, Emilio. "Los huéspedes reales," *La palabra y el hombre* 8 (1958).

Colechia, Francesca, and Matas, Julio. *Selected Latin American One-Act Plays.* Pittsburg: University of Pittsburg, 1973.

Dallal, Alberto. "Reseña de *La cólera secreta.*" *Revista de Bellas Artes,* 1 (1965).

Dauster, Frank. *Historia del teatro hispanoamericano.* Mexico City: Ed. Andrea, 1966.

Donoso, José. "Reseña de *La cólera secreta.*" *La Cultura de México, 157, 16 (1965).*

Feiman Waldman, Gloria. "Three Female Playwrights Explore Contemporary Latin American Reality: Myrna Casas, Griselda Gambaro and Luisa Josefina Hernández," in *Latin American Women Writers.* Pittsburgh: Carnegie-Mellon, 1975.

Fox-Lockert, Lucía. "Luisa Josefina Hernández and Her Revolt." Paper presented at NEMLA Convention, University of New York at Albany, 1978.

González Peña, Carlos. *History of Mexican Literature.* Dallas: Southern Methodist University Press, 1968.

Hernández, Luisa Josefina. *Aguardiente de caña.* Mexico City, 1951.

———. "Arpas blancas, conejos dorados." *La palabra y el hombre* 28 (Oct.—Dec. 1963).

———. *La cólera secreta.* Xalapa: Universidad Veracruzana, 1964.

———. *Los frutos caídos.* 1957.

———. "Los frutos caídos," in *Teatro mexicano contemporáneo.* Madrid: Aguilar, 1962.

———. "Historia de un anillo." *La palabra y el hombre* 20 (Oct.—Dec. 1961).

———. *Los huéspedes reales.* Xalapa: Universidad Veracruzana, 1958.

———. *El lugar donde crece la hierba.* Mexico City, 1959.

———. *La memoria de Amadis.* Mexico City, 1967.

———. "The Mulatto Orgy," in *Voices of Change in the Spanish American Theater,* edited by William Oliver. Austin: University of Texas Press, 1971.

———. *La noche exquisita.* Xalapa: Universidad Veracruzana, 1965.

———. *Nostalgia de Troya.* Mexico City: Siglo XX, 1970.

———. *Los palacios desiertos.* Mexico City, 1963.

———. *La plaza de Puerto Santo.* Mexico City, 1961.

———. *La primera batalla.* 1965.

Knowles, John. "The Labyrinth of Form," in *Dramatists in Revolt.* Austin: University of Texas Press, 1976.

Langford, Walter. *The Mexican Novel Comes of Age.* Notre Dame: U. of Notre Dame Press, 1971.

Leal, Luis. *Breve historia de la literatura hispanoamericana.* New York: Alfred Knopf, 1971.

Lyday, Leon, and Woodyard, George. *A Bibliography of Latin American Theater Criticism 1940–1974.* Austin: Institute of Latin American Studies, 1976.

Miller, Beth. *Mujeres en la literatura.* Mexico City: Fleischer Editora, 1978.

Nomland, John. *Teatro mexicano contemporáneo.* Mexico: Instituto Nacional de Bellas Artes, 1967.

Schanzer, George. "The Mexican Stage in the Fall of 1971." *Latin American Theatre Review* 5 (1972).

Schwartz, Kessel. *Spanish American Fiction, II,* Coral Gables, Fla.: University of Miami Press, 1971.

Woodyard, George, and Leon Lyday. *Dramatists in Revolt.* Austin: University of Texas Press, 1976.

ELENA PONIATOWSKA

Fox-Lockert, Lucía. "The Magical Way of Self Transcendence in *Hasta no verte, Jesús mío.*" Paper read at the NEMLA, University of Pittsburgh, 1977.

______. "Novelística femenina," in *Memorias de la Asociación Internacional de Hispanistas.* Toronto, 1978.

Hinds, Harold. "Massacre in Mexico." *Latin American Review* IV, 9 (Fall 1976).

Mendoza, Maria Luisa. *Oiga usted.* Mexico: Ediciones Soma, 1973.

Miller, Beth. "Elena Poniatowska" in *Mujeres en la literatura.* Mexico City: Fleischer Editora, 1978.

Poniatowska, Elena. *Hasta no verte, Jesús mío.* Mexico City: Ediciones Era, 1973.

______. *Massacre in México.* New York: Viking Press, 1971.

______. *Palabras cruzadas.* Mexico City: Biblioteca Era, 1961.

Tatum, Charles. *Latin American Women Writers.* Pittsburgh: Carnegie-Mellon University, 1975.

Zapata, Celia de. "One Hundred Years of Women Writers in Latin America." *Latin American Review* III, 6 (Summer 1975).

INDEX

Adams, M. Ian 305, 330
Agonía 21
Alas, Leopoldo (Clarín) 315
Alborg, Juan Luis 21, 199, 318, 320
Album de familia 202
Alemany, José 317
Alexandria 121
Algo pasa en la calle 85
Allen, Martha (Marta) 295, 330
Allot, Miriam 318
El alma y los perros 17, 185
Alonso, Amado 330
Alós, Concha 10-11, 114-124
Alvarez Palacios, Fernando (Hernando) 317, 321
Amasijo 18, 95
Amezua y Mayo, Agustín de 293
La amortajada 166
Anderson Imbert, Enrique 331
El árbol 15
Arpas blancas, conejos dorados 21, 22
Arrieta, Rafael 331
Arrom, José Juan 324
El artista barquero 127
Asencio, José María 296, 313
El aura blanca 127
Aves sin nido 12, 137-138
Ayala, Francisco 318

Ballesteros, Mercedes 302
Baltazar 127
Balún Canán 282
Barja, Cesar 313, 315
Barlett, Irving 298
Basadre, Jorge 304
Bestia dañina 195
Bibiana 107
Biles, Mary 315
Blanca Sol 13, 147
Blanco García, F. 313
Las bodas 185
Bodas de Cristal 16, 175
La bolsa 137
Bombal, María Luisa 14-15, 166-173
Bonfils, Alicia de 310, 338
Bordoll, Domingo 332
Boreales, miniaturas y porcelanas 138
Bosch, Rafael 324
Bottone, Mireya 309
Brann, Silvia 295, 310
Bravo Villasante, Carmen 293
Brown, Donald 315
Brunet, Marta 18-19, 195-201
Buckley, Ramon 318
Bullrich, Silvina 15-17, 175-184
Los burgueses 176

El caballo rojo 114
Cabello de Carbonera, Mercedes 13, 147-155
Cáceres, Avelino 137, 303
Cambor, C. Glenn 298
Campbell, Margaret 295, 305
Cano, Juan 293, 298, 317
Carballo, Emmanuel 295, 308
La careta 85
Carrillo, Francisco 303
La casa del ángel 20, 216
Castellanos, Rosario 18-20, 202-215
Castilla del Pino, M. 318
Castro Arenas, Mario 303
Caza mayor 94
Cejador y Frauca, Julio 317
Chandler, Arthur 315
Chase, Kathleen 334
Los cien pájaros 114

Ciudad real 202
Clemencia 36–37
Clemessy, Nelly 297
Colecchia, Francesca 310
La cólera secreta 21, 214
Conde, Carmen 306, 307, 332
El conspirador 147
Los convidados de agosto 202
Copello, Juan 304
Corrales Egea, José 318, 320
Cruz, Sor Juana Inés de la 29, 296
La cuestión palpitante 4, 49, 64

La dama de Amboto 127
La dama joven 55
Davis, Clifford 315
Desengaños amorosos 2–3, 25
Despertar para morir 66
de Valencia, Diego *see* Valencia, Diego de
Diario de una maestra 9, 107
Díaz Arrieta, Hernán 307, 331, 334
Díaz Sánchez, Ramon 305
Domingo, José 300, 321, 324
Dos mujeres 127
Douglas, Frances 298, 317
Dumas, Norma 309
Durán, Manuel 310
Dybvig, Rhoda 308, 336

Egilona 127
En trance de novela 329
Los enanos 114
La enferma 85
Eoff, Sherman 319
Esclavitud y libertad 66
Escolar, Hipólito 192, 299, 319
Escribo tu nombre 85
La esfinge maragata 5, 66
La España de ayer y de hoy 52
Espejismo 7, 97
Espina, Concha 4–5, 66, 72
The Experimental Novel 49

La familia de Alvareda 37
Feal Deibe, Carlos 319
Fillol, Tomas Roberto 306
Fin de fiesta 20, 216
Fitzmaurice-Kelly, James 314
Foster, William David 319
Fowler, Donald 298, 316
Fox, Lucía 304, 306; *see also* Fox-Lockert, Lucía
Fox-Lockert, Lucía vii, 340, 342; *see also* Fox, Lucía
Fría Lagori, Mauro 318
Los frutos caídos 21
Fuentemayor Ruiz, Victor 305
Funcionario público 107

Galao, Jose Antonio 305
García Mazas, José 294, 299, 319
García-Viñó, Manuel 299, 300, 319, 320
Garro, Elena 20–21, 228–239
La Gaviota 37
Ghiano, Juan Carlos 332
Ghiraldo, Alberto 294, 302
Gibson, Christine Mary 309
Gilcasado, Pablo 320
Goic, Cedomil 331
Gómez de Avellaneda, Gertrudiz 11–12, 127–136
Gomez de Baquero, R. 314
Gonzalez Blanco, A. 314
González Lopez, Emilio 316
González Palencia, Angel 314
González Peña, Carlos 308, 309, 310, 340
González Prada, Manuel 145, 294
Goyri de Menéndez Pidal, Maria 312
Guatimozín 127
Guido, Beatriz 20, 216–227

La habitación testigo 185
Hartzenbusch, Juan 296
Hasta no verte, Jesús mío 22, 260
Hatzfeld, Helmut 296
Heinerman, Theodor 296, 314
Henriquez Ureña, Max 302
Herencia 12, 138
Hermes Villordo, Oscar 309
Hernández, Luisa Josefina 20–21, 241–259

Herrero, Gabriel 314
Hesper, T. E. L. 314
Hidalgo, Alejandro 309
Hilton, Ronald 297
Hinds, Harold 342
Un hogar sólido 228
Las hogueras 10, 114
Hoppe, Elsa 319
Horas de lucha 145
Humo hacia el Sur 18, 195
Hurtado, Juan 314

Ifigenia 14, 156
Iglesias Laguna, Antonio 299, 300, 301, 321
Illanes Adaro, Graciela 298, 319
Indole 137
La insolación 73
La isla y los demonios 73

Kelly, Edith 302
Knowles, John 295

El laberinto de la soledad 143
Laforet, Carmen 73–83
Lagmanovich, David 309
Lane, Helen 311
Langford, Walter 308, 310
Lisson, Carlos 304
La llamada 73
Los que vamos de pie 107
El lugar donde crece la hierba 21, 241

La madama 114
Madariaga, Salvador de 314
La madre naturaleza 4, 53
Magdala 145
La mampara 195
Mañana digo basta 15, 175
María Nadie 18, 195
María Rosa, Flor de Quillen 195
Marías, Julian 321
Mariátegui, José Carlos 150, 304
Martínez Cachero, J. M. 319
Matas, Julio 310
Mathieu, Corina 306
Matto de Turner, Clorinda 12–13, 137–144
Maza, Josefina de la 298
Mead, Margaret 275
Medea 7, 55, 101
Medio, Dolores 9–10, 107–113
Las memorias de Amadís 22, 241
Las memorias de mamá Blanca 14, 156
Memories of the Future 240
Mendoza, María Luisa 295, 342
Menéndez y Pelayo, Marcelino 314
Miller, Beth 311
Miller, John 303, 327
Montesinos, Jose 314
Mora, Gabriela 310
Morby, Edwin 312
Morel Fatio, Alfred 296
Moya, Carlos 319
La mujer nueva 6, 73
Munio Alfonso 129

Nada 5, 73
Nilken, Margarita 316
La niña de Luzmela 66
La noche exquisita 22, 241
North American Bible Society 145
Nosotros, los Rivero 9, 107
La novela moderna 155
Novelas amorosas y ejemplares 2, 25

Oficio de tinieblas 19, 202
El ojo único de la ballena 216
Ordoñez, Elizabeth 320
Ortega y Gasset 6, 123
Osborne, Robert 297, 316
Oviedo, José Miguel 310

Pacheco, José Emilio 308
Los palacios desiertos 21, 241
Palma, Angélica 314
Pardo Bazán, Emilia 4, 49–65, 92
Parra, Teresa de la 13–14, 156–165
Pattison, Walter 316
Paz, Octavio 143, 309
Paz Castillo, Fernando 304

Paz Velásquez, Flavia 320
Peel, Roger 308
Penelope 112
Penzotti, Francis 145
Percas Ponsetti, Helena 302
Perez Minik, I. 316
El Perú Ilustrado 145
Petriconi, Luis 304
El pez sigue flotando 107
Pierola, Nicolas de 145, 303
Pittollet, C. 315
La playa de los locos 7, 94
La plaza de Puerto Santo 21, 241
Poniatowska, Elena 22, 260–277
Prejevalinsky Ferrer, Olga 320
Preludio indiano 185
La primera batalla 21, 22, 241
El príncipe de Viana 127

Quiroga, Elena 6–7, 85–93

Raiz del sueño 195
La rebelión de las masas 6
Recaredo 127
Los recuerdos del porvenir 20, 228
Redondillas 29
Relaciones espirituales 34
Religiones politeístas de Asia 123
Renfrew, Ileana 306
Restuccia, Martha 16, 295, 307
Rey de gatos 10, 114
Rioseco, Arturo 299, 321
Roberts, Gemma 294
Rodríguez, Fermin 324
Rodríguez Monegal, Emir 338
Rolfe, Doris 302
Romera Navarro, Miguel 318
Rosales, César 307
Rosenberg, S. L. Millard 298, 318

Sab 11, 127
Sacrificio y recompensa 147
Saínz de Robles, Federico 299, 300, 301, 321
Salomón-Berkemoe, Diane 309
La sangre 85
Saul 127
Schwartz, Kessel 342
Schwartz, Ronald 301, 321, 324
Senabre, Ricardo 312
Senob, Alice 316
El señor de Bembimbre 69
Serrano Poncela, Segundo 312, 318
Serrano y Sanz, Manuel 295
The Shrouded Woman 166
Silva, Clara 16–18, 185–194
Sobejano, Gonzalo 320
La sobreviviente 18, 185
La soledad sonora 85
Soriano, Elena 78–79, 94–106
Stolk, Gloria 330
Sylvania, Lena 312

Tatum, Charles 311
Tauro, Alberto 294
Teléfono ocupado 15, 175
Ticknor, George 313
Torres, Nelida 305
Tradiciones cuzquenas 137
La Tribuna 50
Tristura 85
Tuel, Isis 309

Ullman, Pierre 320
La última niebla 15, 166
Urogallo 8

Valencia, Diego de 315
Valenzuela, Victor 308
Valera, Juan 317
Viaje de novios 62
Viaje de recreo 138, 146
Viento del Norte 7, 85
Villegas, Juan 320
A Vindication of Rights of Women 293
Viola Soto, Carlos 309
Vogt, Evon 308

Waldman, Gloria Feiman 311
Waxman, Samuel 330
White, Carolyn 331

Williams, Edwin Bucher 302
Wilson Page, Thomas 62, 63
Winecoff, Janet 301
Wollstonecraft, Mary 3, 293
Woodyard, George 342

Yahni, Roberto 332
Yepez del Castillo, Ernesto 304

Zapata, Celia de 293, 342
Zulueta, Emilia de 317
Zum Felde, Alberto 16, 306, 307